Between a Rock and a Hard Place

THE AT-RISK STUDENT IN THE OPEN-DOOR COLLEGE

By John E. Roueche
and Suanne D. Roueche

Published by the Community College Press, a division of the
American Association of Community Colleges
One Dupont Circle, NW
Suite 410
Washington, DC 20036
(202) 728-0200

ISBN 0-87117-259-3

This book is dedicated to our friend and colleague

Edmund J. Gleazer, Jr.

President Emeritus
American Association of Community Colleges

who, 25 years ago, challenged community colleges to make good on the promise of the open door. He understood then that true opportunity for students meant much more than access to college.

TABLE OF CONTENTS

The challenge that AACC President Emeritus Ed Gleazer first made to community colleges in the 1960s—"making good on the implied promise of the open door"—has become even more awesome in the 1990s. Community colleges continue the struggle to reduce barriers to higher education, to meet students where they are, and to develop a curriculum to meet expanding personal, economic, and societal needs. The struggle has been complicated further by reduced budgets; colleges are required to do more with less and, sadly, are forced to turn away potential students because facilities and equipment are inadequate to meet the demands. In a statement that mirrors the current capacity problems that colleges and universities are experiencing nationally, Don Phelps, chancellor of the Los Angeles Community College District, reported in 1992 (in his remarks to the NISOD International Conference on Teaching Excellence) that his district, presently serving more than 110,000 students each semester, has been forced to turn away literally thousands and thousands of potential students. All schools, colleges, and universities across the nation are failing at unconscionable levels to effectively meet the needs of the students that they enroll. And, to add another twist to the situation, we are being confronted with increasing numbers of students—those who we choose to call at-risk—that we simply are not teaching effectively.

The problem will not go away—the at-risk student is becoming the new majority. These students are not limited to a particular locale; as Tessa Tagle, provost of the Medical Center Campus of Miami-Dade Community College, observed: "Diversity and pluralism are here to stay—and they migrate. What is happening in Miami today will be in your community tomorrow" (Tagle, 1991, p. 4). And, as Don Phelps noted: "If you think you are safe because you are in the suburbs, or because you are far from a large metropolitan center, you may simply not be paying attention. There are no safe ways to isolate oneself from the changes taking place in our major cities" (Phelps, 1991, p. 2).

In writing this book, we wanted to provide an update of information and document trends in college responses to at-risk students— some benchmarks in the history of our development. We did not intend to write a book on developmental education; the issues surrounding at-risk students are much too broad to define them so narrowly. These issues, although too often considered isolated problems that affect only special, identifiable student groups, impact the entire institution and must be addressed by everyone there.

We intended to focus on hopeful, potentially successful responses to the current challenges that at-risk students bring to higher education. The situation they create is neither impossible nor hopeless—not by a long shot—unless, of course, we choose to ignore it or underestimate the threat it poses. Yet, as Pat Cross observed in *Accent on Learning,* "The problems are clearer than the solutions" (1976, p. xi), and we too frequently dwell on those problems, thereby draining the critical energy we need to create and develop viable solutions. While we did not intend to paint the situation with a rosier hue than it deserves, we did try to provide a more balanced perspective by describing viable, successful strategies and programs.

We intended to write a readable book. As Page Smith observed in *Killing the Spirit,* there is a "strange, almost incomprehensible fact...that many professors...feel obliged to write dully," afraid that if their writing and lectures appeal to emotions they will appear unscientific or unobjective (1990, p. 211). We find that we remember best the information that is delivered with enthusiasm and laced with interest-generating companion ideas. Moreover, human creativity is more likely to be supercharged by the ideas of others, whether or not the ideas are palatable or believable, when the individual is actively engaged in learning about them.

We wanted to write a book that generated an interest in our readers for reading what others are writing about this subject and related issues associated with teaching and learning for all students. No one can argue with the notion that teaching and learning strategies that are successful with at-risk students are equally successful with more traditional students. Many of the articles, chapters, and books that we reread for review, as well as those we read to sample broadly the more current market, are well worth additional attention. Sometimes we noted that was so, but the absence of such a recommendation for an individual selection should not suggest that further reading would not be useful. Moreover, readers will observe that we pulled from sources—*Alice in Wonderland,* for example—that undoubtedly some will consider curious in a discussion of such a serious subject. And, we had our favorite sources, many of which were incredibly critical of contemporary teaching strategies. We held firm to our belief that a healthy combination of divergent and convergent thinking is required for creative and effective problem solving.

We wanted to showcase some programs that had been recognized as successful with at-risk students and, essentially, with all students. It is in learning about the successful strategies of others that we can avoid reinventing the wheel and maximize the opportunities for improving the designs that others have created.

Finally, the most exasperating activity we confronted was deciding what to omit; we acknowledge that some readers will think us negligent in ignoring some subjects, issues, or notions that might be on their list of top priorities and that other readers will think we paid too much attention to less worthy issues. In addition, while personally and by reputation we knew about many excellent programs that had not received formal awards for their success, we chose to limit this study to those that had been so identified, reserving the others for different studies.

The efforts that we made to achieve our goals are represented in the following chapters.

Chapter One—"Focusing on the Problems: America Between a Rock and a Hard Place"—describes the serious economic, technological, and demographic imperatives that provide tremendous impetus for American community colleges to make good on the promise of opportunity through education.

Chapter Two—"Back to the Future: Getting Here from There"—provides a brief history of the community college that brings us to an incredible present and future, including the increase of at-risk students, the proliferation of programs and strategies for responding to their needs, and the criticisms that surround the situations they create. The chapter concludes with a description of the 1992 study, a list of the participants, and the survey questions.

Chapter Three—"Designing Programs to Work: Shifting Paradigms for Changing Times"—reviews the attitudes toward "second-chance" opportunities and some of what we know about college at-risk student programs: their goals and objectives, their achievements, and their places within the institution. With this chapter, we begin to address the award-winning college responses to the targeted survey questions.

Chapter Four—"Selecting and Developing Faculty: Getting to the Heart of the Matter"—reviews some of what we know about faculty responses to all students, but especially to those at risk. It discusses what we know about excellent teachers by reviewing the findings of studies about them, describes strategies for identifying and selecting faculty, and characterizes the particulars of their professional status.

Chapter Five—"The Door Opens with Identification, Orientation, and Involvement: Who Am I? and What Am I Doing Here?"—reviews the problems of at-risk students historically, discusses their decisions to try the higher education route, and explores the importance of orientation and involvement in the life of the college, as well as the issues of assessment and placement.

Chapter Six—"Instructional Strategies: Identifying Some Realities of 'How' to Get There"—reviews some of what we know about learning and discusses some of the institutional strategies that support instruction.

Chapter Seven—"Program Evaluation: The Proof of the Pudding"—reviews the complexities and the critical nature of effective program evaluation. Included in this chapter are descriptions of current state and national legislative initiatives for evaluation and strategies for identifying criteria by which programs and strategies might be evaluated.

Chapter Eight—"Through the Looking Glass: Toward a Vision of Student Success"—is written from our own perspectives from 25 years of teaching and researching the at-risk student, primarily in community colleges across North America, interspersed with examples from the award-winning programs. Included in this chapter are our recommendations for college responses to the needs of at-risk students, and we hold firm to our belief that what is acceptable practice for those students who are characterized as at-risk is equally so for those who are characterized as traditional. We can and should do better at meeting the needs of all students.

We accept all responsibility for errors in this manuscript and accept the fact, or perhaps a corollary to a Murphy-type law, that only when more than 10,000 copies of any document have been printed will those errors become immediately visible to the naked eye. The attention and care of those who provided critical assistance should not be judged by how well we ultimately completed the publication process. We recognize that a project such as this could not have been completed without the support and patience of some very significant others.

Linda Gibbs, a graduate student in the Community College Leadership Program and our research associate whose internship in this project met the formal research requirements for her Ph.D. in Educational Administration at The University of Texas, carried several major responsibilities—collecting and organizing the submissions by each program director; researching and framing the contemporary economic, social, and educational scene as depicted in Chapter 1; and providing critical document support for the discussion of evaluation. Organized, calmly efficient, and extremely patient with at least one author who demonstrated few such qualities, Linda expertly juggled her other student assignments with those of the project, always willing to make "just one more library run," locate just one more "misplaced" document, and ask once more, "Is there anything else you need for me to do?" Her tolerance for ambiguity—created by authors who were always having "one more good idea"—earned her numerous good conduct awards. Linda brought a sterling combination of charm and serious commitment to a task that, in process, many vow to do only once in their lifetimes. We hope that her experiences with us in this endeavor have convinced her that it is a task worth repeating.

Sheryl Fielder, currently NISOD administrative assistant, was and is an editor extraordinaire. Always a willing reviewer, Sheryl brought a talented eye to "wordsmithing" and was never shy about making editorial recommendations. She has an uncanny ability to ferret out even those "invisible" errors that numerous others had passed over; and by her frequent rereading of every chapter, she earned her reputation: "It's not right until Sheryl *says* it is!" Among numerous other assignments, Sheryl read and reread every word of the manuscript, standardized formats and terminology, rode herd on the computer files to keep the various stages of corrected chapters out of the hands of well-meaning but less talented users of the technology, and accepted final responsibility for all of the dreaded bibliography checks. For the ability to keep her head on those occasions when all others about her were losing theirs, and for other talents too numerous to mention, we pay our special respects to Sheryl.

While she arrived somewhat late to the project, Julie Leidig, a graduate student in the Community College Leadership Program, brought another accomplished, professional eye to the editing process. She frequently was asked to have chapter reviews completed "yesterday," but they were always accomplished in record time and with the same high level of commitment that she brought to her own manuscripts for her graduate work throughout the semester. Her good-natured responses—especially, "You want it *when?*"—were welcome distractions during some tedious processes.

Finally, the study would not have been possible without the colleges and the individuals who responded to our requests for information about their award-winning programs. The program directors were kind to join in the study and answer our initial questions, then to take phone calls and provide follow-up details, and finally to proof the final drafts of program descriptions that were sent for their approval. They are as follows: Donna Fung, A STARTING POINT Minority Transfer Program, De Anza College (California); Lisa Brady, Athletic Academic Advising Program, William Rainey Harper College (Illinois); Arves Jones, the Academic Information Monitoring System, Highland Community College (Kansas); Susan Rogers Strand, QUEST (Quality Undergraduate Education for Student Transfer), Illinois Central College (Illinois); Marzell Smith, the Black/Hispanic Student Opportunity Program (BSOP), Miami-Dade Community College (Florida); Evelyn Clements, the Freshman Seminar and Course Clusters Program, Middlesex Community College (Massachusetts); Lynda Edwards, Counseling and the Advantage Program, North Lake College (Texas); Angie Runnels, who provided the original information about the program but took a position at another college and was replaced during the study by Perry Carter, Developmental Studies Program, Richland College (Texas); Jack Friedlander, Transfer Achievement Program (TAP), at Santa Barbara City College (California); Paul Fornell, Student Success Model, Santa Fe Community College (New Mexico); Randolph Manning, the Eastern

Campus Retention Program, Suffolk County Community College (New York); and Charles Bohlen, who provided the original information about the program but took a position at another college and was replaced during the study by Donna Adler, Developmental Skills Education Program, University of Toledo Community and Technical College (ComTech) (Ohio). During every conversation, we were met with enthusiasm and candor; the energy and interest that these professionals shared with us provided very special support during the research and writing process. Our experiences with them will remain as very special recollections of an important task.

And, to those friends, family, colleagues, and students who listened with great interest and patience to months of discussions about "the book," we owe a collective thank-you and a promise to require less of them during future studies. But for their forbearance during this one, they are especially appreciated.

Austin, Texas   John E. Roueche
January 1993   Suanne D. Roueche

Focusing on the Problems:

America Between a Rock and a Hard Place

It is...the America of all of us that is at risk...It is by our willingness to take up the challenge, and our resolve to see it through, that America's place in the world will be either secured or forfeited.
— *A Nation At Risk*
April 1983

The stark realities of changing demographics, the demands of a burgeoning technology, and a faltering public education system have America caught somewhere between a rock and a hard place. These realities, any one of which is capable of critically affecting progress toward a quality of life that we call the American dream, are not entirely new challenges to our nation. In fact, sitting in the 1990s and taking a cursory look at these realities and society's responses to them as they emerged over the last several decades, one cannot help but be reminded of Yogi Berra's observation, "It's déjà vu all over again."

Community colleges have long been caught between a rock and a hard place—trying to provide access and opportunity to *all* who can profit, while maintaining academic standards in the face of increased student underpreparedness. Borrowing from an old phrase coined to explain a religious phenomenon, we propose that if the public community college did not exist in times like these, society would have been forced to invent it. And what a mission it has been given! Today's community college student is at risk in a number of ways that complicate and make obsolete the old definition of college student. By *at-risk*, we are describing students who are not only underprepared for college, but who are also working 30 or more hours each week, who have little if any support from key family members, who are first-generation college attenders, who have what some have described as "failure expectations," and who have little academic success as they begin their postsecondary experience. These harsh social, economic, and educational realities have merged to create an unprecedented pressure on community colleges for effective basic skills training—a need that creates such a daunting challenge to American community colleges that some have called their response nothing less than a "mission impossible."

Perhaps our collective vision was too near-sighted, too narrow, or too optimistic; perhaps the view too fragmented by single-issue, limited-views-of-the-world policies. But, *how* we arrived at this place where there is little or no "wiggle room" will not be the primary focus of this book, although some plausible explanations could not be ignored. Rather, the focus will be on *where* we are and *what* we are doing about extricating ourselves from this extremely uncomfortable and totally unconscionable place. This chapter identifies a significant number of the most current problems that will not go away without serious and successful interventions.

The Problems of Illiterate and Unskilled Populations

The ability to write one's name rather than signing with an "X" was once the mark of a literate individual. Since 1840 literacy rates have been reported by decade on the basis of school attendance data gathered and disseminated by the Bureau of the Census. Early on, those figures told us how many citizens had attended any school and, later, how many years they had completed; these were the earliest common identifiers of "literate" citizens. Accepting the military's benchmarks of fourth- and fifth-grade designations as the point at which one could be considered literate, the Census of 1979, in reporting very low literacy figures, actually reported attendance in school, not reading and writing abilities (Harman, 1987). However, studies of schooling in the 1950s first generated suspicions that educational experiences through these grades did not necessarily produce literate people, and studies in the 1980s and 1990s confirm the suspicions that remaining far later into the public school experience does not necessarily increase the probability of literacy. Yet the Census still reports literacy data against "school-leaving" or school-attendance numbers.

As life has become more complex, not only are definitions of the past inadequate, but there are still no standard definitions of literacy to which all organizations and researchers can agree. Perhaps one standard definition would turn on the alphabet—either an individual knows the alphabet or does not; perhaps that is the only constant definition that can draw a distinction between a literate and illiterate person. Beyond that simple definition, however, there is uncharted territory. The definition, for example, of functional literacy is complex and turns on a multitude of factors—assumptions about knowledge, vocabulary, community, and other particular circumstances (Harman, 1987). And because there are no standard definitions of literacy, the approaches used to measure illiteracy or literacy in this country (or in the world) are not standardized either.

Of the most recognized approaches to studying literacy, two perhaps most quickly come to mind. One approach is that taken by the military, which looks at the reading materials required in its various occupations and assigns them, through readability analysis, grade-level equivalencies; it has determined that the desired levels are somewhere between eighth and tenth grade (Harman, 1987; Sticht and Zapf, 1976).

The other approach is that taken by the Bureau of the Census and by The University of Texas at Austin; it ignores the grade-level definitions and proposes that "objective" tests of reading tasks that are practical and necessary requirements for most Americans are more useful indicators of literacy levels. The Texas study, completed in 1975, is perhaps the most widely cited and offers the most widely accepted figure— that one in five, or 20 percent, of American adults today are not functionally literate (Northcutt, et al., 1975). The study documented that between 23 and 57 million adults are functionally illiterate; the Census, however, identifed between 17 and 21 million. The disparities in the numbers clearly reflect the concerns about the reliability of literacy statistics in general (Harman, 1987). But what these studies do is identify enormous numbers of Americans who are not functioning at basic skills levels that allow them to be successful in many everyday tasks, such as reading grocery labels and bus schedules or calculating their change due in a minor purchase. Such limitations profoundly affect their ability to adequately care for themselves and their families and to work productively. The researchers noted that, indeed, such individuals are condemned to a perpetual struggle for survival—one that becomes more and more difficult and from which there seems to be no escape. These two studies brought national attention to serious literacy problems, although the particulars of their estimates and definitions have not been resolved, nor have any new studies been completed that effectively challenge their findings or improve their research techniques.

Educational Testing Service's highly detailed survey on illiteracy in America documented the abundant evidence that 440,000 young Americans—or roughly 2 percent of the 21 million people aged 21 to 25—could not read well enough to be tested. For those who could be tested, the picture was little better: almost 6 percent, or 1.25 million young Americans, could not read at the fourth-grade level (Meisler, 1990). Another six million, or almost one-third of those measured, did not function at the level required to write a letter to a store about a billing error or to balance a checkbook. Earlier in America's history, each succeeding generation was better educated than the one preceding it, and general educational levels of the majority of the population corresponded closely to the demands of daily life. In recent years, however, these demands have become much more complex, far outstripping the ability of public education to prepare young adults to meet them. The fact that so many adults lack basic skills appears even more critical in light of the numerous predictions by labor market experts that the new jobs of the next century will call for well-developed skills in communication, simple mathematics, and critical thinking.

Indictments and Defenses for the Public Schools

In *Trends in Academic Progress* (1991), the National Center for Education Statistics reported the results of the National Assessment of Educational Progress (NAEP); the mathematics, reading, and writing skills of America's students were shown to persist at the same levels that caused alarm in the 1970s and again in the 1980s. In reading achievement, the report noted: "Significant improvement during the 1970s has been all but eradicated by commensurate declines during the 1980s" (National Center for Education Statistics, 1991c, p. 3).

And, in mathematics achievement, the results of the 1990 NAEP Mathematics Assessment as reported by the National Assessment Governing Board (under the new standard-setting process employed to adapt definitions of achievement to subject matter and content—that is, the NAEP data were reported in terms of what students "*should* be able to do") indicated that just over 60 percent of the students in grades 4, 8, and 12 were performing at or above the basic level (partial mastery), but less than 20 percent of students in these three grades reached proficiency level (central level, solid performance and competence) or beyond (superior performance). Students performing at or above the advanced level ranged from 0.6 percent in grade 4 to 2.6 percent in grade 12. Regrettably, more than one-third of the students assessed performed at levels *below the board's lowest identified level* (Bourque and Garrison, 1991, p. vii).

Alison Sprout of *Fortune* (1990) asked the provocative question, "Do U.S. schools make the grade?" Her answer is a regretful "No." She concluded that, indeed, there is a basic skills crisis in the U.S. when only half of the nation's high school seniors can adequately solve problems with fractions and decimals and fewer than 15 percent of eleventh graders can write and think analytically in English. Although 75 percent of American high school seniors are theoretically qualified to go on to college, they are clearly not equipped to do regular college work.

Conceptually, the U.S. educational system is more open than almost any major system in the world; yet the system's product is clearly inadequate, both for American society and when compared with other systems. On indicators such as hours spent on homework, spending on education as a percent of GNP, number of days in the school year, and scores on science tests, Sprout's "report card" ranks the United States between a poor fourth and ninth. In fact, the only category in which the U.S. ranks first is the number of hours of television watched per day by teenagers.

The enormity of the crisis is further revealed when results of skills tests are scrutinized by ethnic groups. While 80 percent of Anglo young people passed the letter-writing and checkbook-balancing tests in the Educational Testing Service study, only 40 percent of young African Americans and 60 percent of young Hispanics did so (Meisler, 1990). This disparity in functional levels is the result of the high correlation among poverty, undereducation, and minority status, as documented by such sources as education author Jonathan Kozol (1991), the Business-Higher Education Forum (1990), and the National Center on Education and the Economy (NCEE) (1990).

Characterizing the home surroundings of one in five children as "Third World," the 1990 NCEE study identified some of the more critical ways in which poverty affects educational opportunity: inadequate health care and hunger limit a child's learning ability on both a daily and a long-term basis; a life in which drug abuse and violence are common-place can impair the learning process permanently; perpetual emotional and physical insecurity drain youth of the energy and focus required for success in school. Needing more attention to compensate for other disadvantages, the poor child is instead more likely to receive less; needing supplementary materials, staff and programs, poorer schools are more likely to receive less because of their low tax bases. Low attendance and high dropout rates in poor schools take their toll in lost federal funding, completing the vicious circle of educational disadvantage.

Author Kenneth Labich (1992) proposed that the U.S. must ask both more and less of its schools: more of quality and achievement of genuine educational goals and less of what he calls such "codswollop" as social skills and raised consciousness—citing, as an example, the California legislature's mandate that their schools teach "true comprehension of the rights, duties, and dignity of American citizenship, including kindness toward domestic pets" (p. 65). He argues that transmission of social values, previously accomplished by families and churches, now falls increasingly on the public schools, to the detriment of basic skills development. He describes America's schools almost as catch-all institutions that are called upon to fill whatever responsibilities for disseminating whatever information the public deems important whenever they decide it. Labich quotes education expert Chester Finn, as he cautions parents against expecting the impossible from schools. He observes that by the age of 18, a typical American child has spent only 9 percent of her or his life attending class. Finn aptly points out that much learning must occur outside the classroom during the remaining 91 percent of the child's life and that parents are "passing the buck" to an educational system that is overburdened.

It would appear that public education is experiencing a "mission blur," the almost inevitable result of trying to be all things to all people. Once divided among parents, extended family, church, community, and schools, the many tasks of rearing children—e.g., socialization, development of value systems, establishment of health and hygiene practices, development of work ethic and self-discipline—are increasingly regarded as the responsibility of the schools. It is no wonder that focus is often lost and that the system's product is of questionable quality.

Societal factors beyond the control of the schools and outside the purview of the agencies that fund and regulate public education are contributing to ineffectiveness. Journalist Haynes Johnson, in "Why Johnny Still Can't Read," referred to an educational problem that "only a cave dweller could deny" (1990, p. A2). The U.S. is falling behind in producing large numbers of highly skilled, flexible workers who can competently fulfill the technologically demanding positions of tomorrow's job market. In fact, the overall scholastic achievement levels of college-bound students, in the very early 1990s, were "below what they had been 20 years ago" (p. A2). The decline of the inner cities has created an increasingly volatile environment that is reflected in an equally tense classroom climate. Single parents have difficulty just supporting their children, much less finding time to give the personal attention, encouragement, and interest in children's activities that foster motivation to succeed in school and in life. In its study of minority life in the U.S., the Business-Higher Education Forum (1990) observed that those minority individuals who have joined the middle class primarily have been the products of the intact two-parent families of previous generations. The individual who has been successful without the strong support and encouragement of family is the exception.

The reality is that the public education system is not delivering a literate and well-informed student/product. The challenge for community colleges is clear. As the institutions most likely to admit the underdeveloped majority of high school graduates as well as the alternatively certified students and the returning adults, community colleges must fill in the skills gap.

Contemporary Issues for Economic Development

Demands for the Work Force

America is changing the way it works, and the changes are combining to raise the minimum basic skill levels for workers. Much of America's economic strength has been built on the factory model of work organization originated by Frederick Winslow Taylor and made famous by Henry Ford near the turn of the century. The purpose of the factory model was to accomplish complex tasks with low-skilled workers, and it was highly successful in achieving this end. Underlying the model is the simple premise that complex jobs can be divided into numerous simple, discrete tasks that can be performed on an assembly line by many laborers working in a machine-like fashion (National Center on Education and the Economy, 1990). This system was ideal in a time in which most workers were unskilled because it required relatively few "thinkers" at the top, supported by a hierarchy of middle management and administration. The most desired characteristics for the vast majority of workers were reliability, willingness to work, and willingness to follow directions; education was not required.

This system of work organization reached full flower after World War II, when farmers migrating to America's cities joined immigrants in providing a plentiful supply of low-skilled labor, which in turn fueled the domestic market and further encouraged the growth of mass production. So successful and so ingrained into the nation's society did the factory model become that it can also be seen in the organization of schools, offices, banks, and hospitals. The decline of the Taylor model has been precipitated by a number of factors, chief among them the simple fact that other nations can now implement it better than the U.S., due to their lower wage levels and the incredible advances in communication technology (National Center on Education and the Economy, 1990).

Economic development requires an educated work force. The Business-Higher Education Forum and the Public Agenda Foundation report that when leaders and labor market experts look ahead to the information society of the twenty-first century, they predict that those nations that have the best educated "bottom third"—nations that have developed all of their citizens—will be the strongest global competitors (Immerwahr, et al., 1991). America's previous industrial success was built with the nation's tremendous natural resources upon the foundation of its stable, yet flexible society, and it was driven by the ingenuity and optimism that have always typified American attitudes. However, the successes of the past are no guarantee of future achievement in a world that is rapidly moving away from the old industrial model toward an economy powered by superior knowledge. Such an economic climate requires ever more sophisticated skills from those nations and those individuals who wish to prosper; and, in light of this, many analysts fear that if the U.S. work force is not better trained, America will soon prove unable to compete in the world marketplace.

Already, one out of every four American youths drops out of school before entering the work force, while by contrast, some 96 percent of all Japanese youths arrive at their first job with a high school diploma in hand. Naisbitt and Aburdene (1990) state the equation positively: "In the new economic order, those countries which invest most in education will be the most competitive" (p. 198). While this may be true, it also may be an oversimplification that does not take into account the debilitated state of America's work force and the educational systems that serve it. Far from striding toward futuristic goals, the nation seems to be more in a position of "catching up" with neglected work force development needs. Projections now show that the number of functionally illiterate Americans will swell far into the next century, just at the time when more capable workers are needed. Not only have those who will comprise the work force of the year 2000 already been born, but most have completed their primary education, receiving, at best, a mediocre academic foundation. Along with many members of today's work force, they will require considerable training, not only in occupational skill areas, but also in basic academic skills.

As critically important as it is to improve or reform education in grades K–12, it is clear that reform is a long-term strategy. The economic effect of such improvements will not be felt by society for another 10 to 20 years, when the students who have benefitted from them become part of the work force. Can America wait? Are the needs of today's workers and today's underprepared students to be ignored? If so, at what cost? A growing number of leaders believe that the nation cannot afford to focus its efforts solely on reforming grades K–12 to the exclusion of developing its work force. Former Xerox CEO David Kearns characterizes the education problem as an economic and global competitiveness issue. To illustrate his concern that by the year 2000 America will be "out of qualified workers," he reports that in World War II a submarine required 1,700 men educated to about the eighth-grade level for its operation. Today, the equivalent cruiser requires 700 individuals educated to a level of two years beyond high school. "That's American business," he says. "It's exactly the same" (Kearns and Flanigan, 1990, p. 46).

Increasingly, bureaucracy is being eliminated in the U.S. in favor of "flatter" organizations in which design teams have greater decision-making latitude and in which more complex tasks are performed by fewer better-trained people. As a result, the 1990 Workplace Literacy Survey, conducted by the Society for Human Resource Management and Commerce Clearing House, reveals that many workers hired several years ago would now be ineligible for employment due to changes in job requirements. Fifty-five percent of the survey respondents indicated that job applicants with high school diplomas do not have adequate basic skill levels for employment; some went further to say that even recent college graduates could not perform acceptably (Pilenzo, 1990).

Using a strategy called "deskilling," some companies attempt to compensate for the lack of basic skills in the work force through the use of graphic symbols. Chrysler Corporation was forced to resort to such symbols because so many assembly-line workers were unable to read the words "bad hood fit" on the button they were supposed to push when they detected a defective part (Collins, 1990). Symbols on cash register keys and universal product codes perform a similar function, ensuring a level of accuracy that would not be attainable otherwise with today's work force. Picture posters and symbols for chemical and mechanical dangers are also being used with increasing frequency (Pilenzo, 1990).

Deskilling strategies, however useful in specific situations, are no solution for the ongoing basic skills crisis. According to Immerwahr, Johnson, and Kernan-Schloss in their study for the Business-Higher Education Forum, America's leaders realize that it will take years and tremendous investments of human and financial resources to upgrade the skills of American students and workers. Thirty million illiterate adults must be assisted in learning to read, and students and workers must be assisted in developing the complex yet flexible skills they will need for high-tech workplaces (1991).

There *will be* new unskilled and semi-skilled jobs in the work force of the future: M. Ross Boyle (1990) states that approximately 45 percent of the anticipated 21 million jobs to be created between 1986 and 2000 will fall in these least-skilled categories. However, the majority of these new entry-level jobs will lead nowhere. Instead of being the first rung on a ladder to the middle class, which was often the case in the 1950s and the 1960s, these are dead-end jobs in the low-paying service sector.

Journalist Stanley Meisler (1990) uses "Bailey," a 53-year-old worker in a Georgia textile mill who has recently confronted technology in the form of a computerized spinner, to describe the problem. Low-paid, unskilled, and non-union, Bailey fit the bill perfectly when first employed, and he successfully learned to operate and maintain his mechanical spinner. Unlike his old machine, however, the new one will flash a diagnostic message on a computer screen to signal a problem—a message Bailey will not be able to read. A third-grade dropout, Bailey nonetheless read the handwriting on the wall: two years ago he began taking reading classes in a company-sponsored program, and he has now progressed beyond the reading level needed to use the new technology (Meisler, 1990). Similar scenarios are being played out all over the nation, although most lack the happy ending. Many of America's illiterates are now employed, but their basic skills are so limited that they will not be able to adapt successfully to the demands of new technology.

Although the skilled, sub-professional share of the work force comprised 33 percent of the 1986 job base, it now accounts for only 25 percent of the positions yet to be created. Further, success in high school and in community college is becoming a clear prerequisite for those on this path to the middle class, as the skilled, blue-collar jobs that could once be attained by hard work and on-the-job training disappear forever. Although these jobs accounted for more than 12 percent of the work force in 1986, they currently represent less than 8 percent of the new jobs to be created in the 1990s. Requiring more formal education to handle a myriad of new technologies, the rapidly growing skilled sub-professional sector also demands stronger skills in communications and critical thinking (Boyle, 1990).

Dale Parnell refers to "occupational half-life," the time period in which one-half of a worker's skills will become obsolete (1990, p. 227). Citing the National Research Council, he maintains that this period, which was once seven to 14 years, has declined to a mere three- to five-year span. At all levels of the work force, individuals will need basic skills and problem-solving ability to become lifelong learners, repeatedly adjusting to new work situations as their skills become outdated. Naisbitt (1990) observes that although the information economy will create many well-paid challenging jobs, workers must have the skills to perform them. The outlook for the unskilled is bleak; they have so little to contribute that is valuable to the new economic order. He sees that in the very near future most jobs will require such high degrees of competence that there will not be nearly enough American workers qualified to fill them.

As tragic punctuation to this reality, Boyett and Conn's discussion of *Workplace 2000* (1991) provides this example. Deming's 14-points outline his thinking on the quality process; his "Cease dependence on mass inspection" (Deming, 1992, p. 28) is increasingly being implemented through "statistical process control," or SPC, as it is often called. It involves training employees to observe and keep detailed records of variations in product quality. Such records usually consist of complex graphs and charts, requiring critical thinking skills that are far beyond today's average worker. The estimated cost for training an American worker in SPC ($200) contrasts sharply with the cost for similar training of a Japanese worker ($ .47): The Japanese worker is given a book to read, while the American must be taught to read it (Boyett and Conn, 1991).

Boyett and Conn note yet another fundamental change in the workplace that requires even higher skill levels—the ability to profit from an exchange of ideas and, thereby, to formulate new concepts. Once considered the basis of power, physical strength and ability are now valued less than their mental counterparts. Brute strength no longer rules the world; in the new economy it will be the thinker who rules. The forces of technology and the quality movement have dramatically increased the requirements for higher work force skill levels: In order to bring decision making closer to the level at which decisions are implemented, workers must be given considerable operational and problem-solving responsibilities. These workers must be committed and discerning, capable of self-improvement, able to work well with others, and, often, to take leadership in their task group (Boyett and Conn, 1991).

Finally, the mathematics of the high-wage economy is illustrated well in Massachusetts where, between 1985 and 1987, almost 75,000 jobs were lost in the manufacturing sector, a percentage loss that was five times the national rate. Yet, during this same period, numerous high-skilled, high-wage information jobs were being created; the result was a rise in the state's per capita income that was 40 percent faster than the national average for the same period (Naisbitt and Aburdene, 1990).

Public Responses to Workplace and Work Force Changes

The unemployment rate for college graduates is 1.7 percent; for high school dropouts it is 9.4 percent and rising, a difference of nearly six-fold (Naisbitt and Aburdene, 1990). These figures come as a surprise to many, as evidenced by public opinion research described in Immerwahr, et al., (1991) and published by the Business-Higher Education Forum and the Public Agenda Foundation. Their inquiry was conducted to identify the American public's perceptions of problems and solutions relating to work force skills and quality of public education. While the researchers noted that their findings were preliminary and should be tested with further research, they were able to document great disparities between what the public believed about the relationship of work and education and what experts and leaders were trying to tell them about that relationship. These disparities may explain the apparent lack of public enthusiasm for closing the "skills gap."

They discovered that virtually none of those interviewed understood the importance of the productive side of the economy, and, in addition, few interviewees saw the need to increase the country's productivity; almost none saw any connection between the country's economic health and the skills of its work force (Immerwahr, et al., 1991). They also found that the public's preoccupation with jobs and motivation prevented its accepting the need for work force training. Many reasoned that retraining is a waste for those who have jobs and that those who do not have jobs are lacking in motivation, not skills. The prevailing wisdom appeared to be that, after all, there are plenty of menial jobs around for those who really want to work (Immerwahr, et al., 1991). Characterizing public resistance to upgrading skills as a "legacy of the Great Depression," researchers found an almost universal belief that the biggest danger to the nation's economy is too few jobs; leaders, on the other hand, were aware that the critical issue in the "new unemployment" will not be too few jobs, but too many people without the skill levels to perform the available jobs (Immerwahr, et al., 1991).

Future Demands for the Work Force

The at-risk population cannot be ignored; not unlike the violence and drugs that have captured our national attention, this population has the power to threaten the very fabric of our society. The at-risk population is not just personally at risk, but it creates a risk for society as a whole; if these individuals are not empowered to contribute, the nation's economic future is gravely endangered (Parnell, 1990). The gaps between existing skills and skills required for employability continue to widen for this population, "contributing to a growing underclass of individuals who are mired in a cycle of conditions producing permanent poverty and dependence" (McCabe, 1992). The links between national productivity and education are obvious. The NCEE Commission on the Skills of the American Workforce noted that during the last two decades, our productivity growth "has slowed to a crawl," and it predicted a future where "[e]ither the top 30 percent of our population will grow wealthier while the bottom 70 percent becomes progressively poorer, or we all slide into relative poverty together" (1990, p. 1). Because the development of a permanent underclass of people can both destabilize and debilitate a society, the nation's future may very well depend on our ability and willingness to prevent it.

Previously neglected segments are becoming increasingly important to the economy. Indeed, indications are that the work force of the future will have to be recruited from groups that have hitherto been neglected: the undereducated, minorities, and women, as well as returning or older workers. As Justiz observes in the fifth annual Harry S. Truman Lecture to the American Association of Community Colleges, we as a society are most likely to act in our own self-interest. Perhaps it is for this reason that the most persuasive arguments for adult literacy often emanate from a perspective of economic development and/or avoidance of the cost of burdensome social programs (1990).

In looking ahead to a future in which the efforts of three workers will be required to support each retiree, Justiz asks, "Where will the money for social security retirement come from?" (p. 20). Emphasizing that one-third of the nation is undereducated as well as underrepresented in educational institutions, he points out that a generation that acquiesces to the underdevelopment of such a large segment of its population would appear to be jeopardizing its own future, as well as limiting its current growth. Justiz describes the current generation's relationship to future generations as "reciprocal dependency," in that what this generation does affects what others can and will do in the future (p. 21). To disenfranchise the "contributors" to this generation's retirement is a mistake that could prove costly in many ways. Self-interest, national security, and competitive ability are all compelling reasons to provide a quality education for the nation's growing minority population.

Entire segments of society cannot be abandoned and their educational needs ignored, if for no other reason than that advanced by Carnevale, Gainer, and Meltzer (1990): the demographic reality of a shrinking 16- to 24-year-old cohort. This age group has previously provided new workers for the American labor market; to compensate for the scarcity of "traditional" workers, employers will need to recruit from the ranks of those whose development has traditionally been neglected—minorities, women, and older workers.

Reporting on school enrollment in 1990, the National Center for Education Statistics reported that between the ninth grade (1986–87) and the twelfth grade (1989–90), 24 percent of students had dropped out. An additional 5 percent who were enrolled in the twelfth grade during 1989–90 failed to graduate, which means that a total of 29 percent of this cohort of students discontinued education during their high school years. The same statistics for the twelfth-grade class of 1989–90 indicate only a minor change in the numbers: Slightly more than 23 percent dropped out between ninth and twelfth grades, with an additional 5.5 percent of twelfth graders failing to graduate. Although an additional group of about 3 percent annually completes high school through alternative options, this does not lessen the tragedy of losing nearly one-third of each student cohort: indeed, the picture is even more bleak if it is considered that these figures do not take into account those students who dropped out before the ninth grade—a significant group in both rural and highly urbanized areas (National Center for Education Statistics, 1992). For the year 1990, an overall high school completion rate for 19- to 20-year-olds of 82.8 percent masks the disproportionately low completion rates of minority students. Of Black, non-Hispanic youths aged 19 to 20, only 77.6 percent had completed high school or its equivalent, and only 59.7 percent of Hispanics had completed either type of program. While in the next cohort, 21 to 22 years of age, Blacks reported a 83.3 percent completion rate, the Hispanic rate increased less than 2 percent to 61.1 percent. Among Hispanics aged 23 to 24 years, the completion rate falls to 55.6 percent, rather than rising as might be expected with the passage of time (National Center for Education Statistics, 1991b).

In the years since 1973, the percentage of Blacks aged 30 to 34 years who have completed high school has risen from approximately 62 percent to just above 80 percent. During the same period, Hispanics in this age group also have evidenced a rising completion rate: From approximately 42 percent in 1973, their completion rate has risen to the current level of 57 percent (National Center for Education

Statistics, 1991b). The importance of these statistics is twofold: the disparate completion (or dropout) rates for the three ethnic groups examined reflect, in part, a persistent inequity in educational opportunity in the United States; and this educational disadvantage combines with the greater likelihood that these individuals are classified as poor to effectively condemn them to a minimally productive life.

In an article written during the Gulf War, journalist James Flanigan draws a parallel between the United States today and Britain in the 1940s. Following World War I, Britain had neglected postwar reform, preferring to return as soon as possible to "business as usual." However, during World War II, with the people of Britain once again involved in fighting, the leadership began to plan for the needs of postwar society. Their goal was to create "a nation fit for heroes." Flanigan continues that the United States, whose disadvantaged citizens were overrepresented on the front lines in the Gulf War, has a similar obligation to plan for opportunity and economic development in its postwar society. The author advocates societal investment in education "because the needs are pressing" and because it offers "a measurable payoff." In addition, the magnitude of the nation's losses attributable to undereducation is such that eliminating this drain "would be like paying off the national debt" (Flanigan, 1991, p. D3). Citing a cost of $4,600 per year per dropout, due to lost tax revenue and spending for social programs, calculations are that over a lifetime each class of high school dropouts costs the country $240 billion. The author concludes: "Count on it: the nation that found the money to fight for freedom overseas will find a way to pay repair bills for the good society here at home" (Flanigan, 1991, p. D3).

Poverty and Undereducation: Inextricable Linkages

Poverty and undereducation are inextricably linked; together they present an almost insurmountable obstacle to personal advancement for a growing American underclass. Despite Flanigan's optimistic outlook, the facts remain that one in every five children in America is born into poverty and that this group will comprise one-third of the future work force (National Center on Education and the Economy, 1990). The children of poverty are, by definition, at-risk personally, educationally, and societally. While there is some debate as to which is cause and which is effect, there is considerable evidence of a link between poverty and undereducation. Some believe that illiteracy virtually guarantees poverty. Others will contend that this type of reasoning confuses cause with effect, that most illiterates are so because they were poor when they went to school.

Kozol (1991) has documented the "savage inequalities" of school finance in the United States and the system's legacy of underachieving, undereducated young people. Scoffing at the idea that schools that spend less are *not necessarily* of lower quality, he points to disparate achievement scores and disproportionate dropout rates, as well as to the underrepresentation of minorities in postsecondary education, as evidence that an inequitable system produces inequitable results. Poor academic functioning is only one legacy of the third-rate education that has been provided for minority individuals.

A more insidious outcome is that many such individuals have ceased to believe in education as a path to a better life. Their expectancy of a return on effort expended in school is so low that lack of motivation often becomes at least as much a factor as skill level. The children of affluence see the relationship between education and possessions, between education and quality of life. The underprivileged young person lacks such daily object lessons. While possessions are only a small part of the reason for pursuing education, their immediacy and tangibility can provide a strong motivation for achievement, especially in these times of instant gratification. It matters little what is said—the young believe what they see. If the education/advancement equation is the lesson America wants the young to learn, it must be hammered home with real-life examples (Molnar, 1992). Raspberry (1990) characterizes the lack of belief in the long-term benefits of schools as a "special educational deficit" of the poor child, and it is one that would not necessarily be eliminated by school reform alone.

While there will continue to be jobs for unskilled or illiterate workers, "there will be very few jobs *paying a decent wage* for those persons lacking basic reading, writing, and computing skills" (Boyle, 1990, p. 7). The implications are enormous: Great numbers of workers will be unable to provide adequately for themselves and their families. The children of these families are desperately at risk of becoming yet another generation of illiterates. Today's undereducated adults are the parents of tomorrow's dropouts.

During the past decade, college-educated males aged 24 to 34 gained 10 percent in real earnings, while those with only high school credentials lost 9 percent in real earnings. Those with less than a high school education lost 12 percent in real income. More than 60 percent of White, non-Hispanic families have incomes over $25,000 per year, compared to Hispanic and Black families, who are in this category 49 percent and 36 percent respectively. The stage is set for increasing inequities in American society (National Center on Education and the Economy, 1990).

Today's dropouts are tomorrow's parents; one in six babies in the United States has a teenage mother, and one in four babies is born out of wedlock (Caminiti, 1990). In the inner city, two out of three children live in a household headed by a single parent, usually a female, contends Parnell (1990); he continues, characterizing teenage pregnancy as "the feeder system" which creates the single-parent households, springing as it does from a "lack of hope and few positive life options" (pp. 107–108). A teen parent can look forward to only half of the lifetime earnings of a woman who postponed parenthood until age 20, which probably condemns her children to an impoverished youth. Today, reversing a long-time trend, children are the poorest segment of society, with 23 percent living in poverty, as compared to 14 percent of the entire population (Parnell, 1990). It will require aggressive action to reverse these directions.

Research indicates that per-pupil expenditures, class size, teacher salaries, and school location are all less important in a student's education than the motivation that is provided by parents. "The influence of the parents appears to be of overriding importance in determining how seriously children will take their education, how well they will do, and how far they will go" (Boyett and Conn, 1991, p. 283). Yet that critical interest and influence are severely limited in parents who have not themselves been successful in education. Literacy experts Sticht and McDonald emphasize the critical role played by parents' educational levels in the academic success of children throughout their years of schooling. They describe a cross-generational effect in which educated parents positively influence children's education, resulting in student success that ultimately produces more highly literate adults; these adults, in turn, produce children who are more readily educated and who are likely to be successful in education. So the process continues, leading the authors to describe the education of adults as the "leverage point" for activating this cycle (Sticht and McDonald, 1990, p. 3). Born illiterate, children are inculcated by home and community cultures with an understanding of the forms of literacy and its functional uses while also acquiring a value for literacy. If this process does not occur or is not completely accomplished, a child is already behind on the first day of school. The strong influence of parents on children's literacy stems largely from their provision of the early environment—surroundings that may or may not contain such literacy artifacts as magazines, books, and writing materials (Sticht and McDonald, 1990). The modeling of literacy behaviors by parents also helps the child understand how literacy skills fit into everyday life.

Sticht and McDonald discuss in detail the significant effects of the mother's educational level on each stage of a child's development, prenatal through high school. Given the pervasive influence exerted by the mother, they conclude that the single most cost-effective strategy for reducing adult illiteracy is to focus educational resources on the development of women and girls, particularly those who are about to become mothers. Such expenditures are described as "double duty dollars"; they contribute both to the development of the woman and to that of her expected child (1990, p. 6).

Community Colleges and the At-Risk Population

The nation's tightening economy threatens the critical support that community colleges need to serve the growing numbers of the at-risk population. Community colleges are being threatened with a double-edged sword as economic conditions tighten budgets and shrink pocketbooks—their enrollments continue to increase, but they are financially stretched to maintain, much less improve, current services. As Americans assign increasing value to a community college education and perceive colleges to be serving all segments of the population well, more and more students are enrolling. However, with such increases in student populations, these colleges may be stretched beyond their limits to provide adequate services. So financially stretched, colleges may begin to assign more value to some segments of their populations than others and decide that programs for those less valued should be eliminated or severely curtailed. Programs and courses for at-risk students remain question marks for many in higher education: Should we be in the business of remediation at this level? Can we really effectively address the remediation problem? The questions may well drive answers to limit, if not abolish, remedial efforts in favor of putting limited funds where the quantities are better "known"—the more traditional student—and the results more certain. However, such decisions would not address the basic questions: What would happen to this growing at-risk population? What would happen to society?

McCabe has argued that community colleges have gone through a period during which they have been "overlooked, thought of after the fact, underfunded, and systematically undervalued." Yet, he has detected "the beginning of an understanding by national leaders" that community colleges could well be their best hope for radically improving the social and economic conditions that threaten America with an established underclass dominated by minorities and a work force that cannot compete globally (McCabe, 1992, p. 4).

This is the decade that Dale Parnell characterized as a "window of opportunity for colleges and universities to help the disadvantaged and undereducated gain an economic foothold in a society that most of this population have never seen" (1990, pp. 110–111). And, yet, looking about him and ahead, Brad Butler, the former chairman of Procter & Gamble, foresees the creation of "a Third World within our country" (National Center on Education and the Economy, 1990, p. 23), and, for those who were transfixed by the images on their television sets in May 1992, the prediction seemed to be coming true in Los Angeles. If, as Martin Luther King, Jr., said, "A riot is the language of the unheard," (Minerbrook, 1992, p. 36), then it would appear that the Third World is here.

Conclusion

Regrettably, the "déjà vu" experiences of the last decades have done very little to encourage us to get serious about educational, economic, and social issues in any meaningful ways. The news apparently has not been tragic enough—*yet*. In the minds of most, these issues were traveling at more or less parallel speeds along different highways; but the highways have merged, and unbelievably they did so at an intersection devoid of even one yield or stop sign. The result is a collision of such magnitude that viable repair cannot occur in the foreseeable future— many forecast that it will take decades to accomplish.

High school dropouts and underskilled high school graduates make up increasing portions of the population. Clearly, one-third of the nation's youth is educationally at risk. In 1983 Terrel Bell, secretary of education, and David Gardner, chairman of the National Commission on Excellence in Education, issued *A Nation at Risk: The Imperative for Educational Reform,* which proclaimed:

> Our Nation is at risk. Our once unchallenged preeminence in commerce, industry, science, and technological innovation is being overtaken by competitors throughout the world....We report to the American people that while we can take justifiable pride in what our schools and colleges have historically accomplished and contributed to the United States and the well-being of its people, the educational foundations of our society are presently being eroded by a rising tide of mediocrity that threatens our very future as a Nation and a people. What was unimaginable a generation ago has begun to occur—others are matching and surpassing our educational attainments.
>
> If an unfriendly foreign power had attempted to impose on America the mediocre educational performance that exists today, we might well have viewed it as an act of war. As it stands, we have allowed this to happen to ourselves (National Commission on Excellence in Education, 1983 p. 5).

The call for reformation of the public education system went out loud and strong, and states responded. But sadly, Bell reported at the 1991 Leadership 2000 conference, the reform movement had indeed failed. Not only had it failed, but the situation had deteriorated further by every possible indicator. The nation *was* at risk!

Add to that youthful group the returning older adults who are unemployed or underemployed, in need of retraining or redirection, and the numbers swell. Although underrepresented in the postsecondary population overall, minorities tend to choose community colleges in disproportionate numbers for reasons relating both to economics and to academic preparation (Parnell, 1990). In 1986 almost 47 percent of minorities entering higher education enrolled in community colleges (Business-Higher Education Forum, 1990). Their growth in actual numbers and their increasing percentage rate in the general population make them a special target for proactive institutional response. Added to these American populations are the increasing numbers of immigrants who are arriving in this country with skills that put major gaps between them and employment at any level.

The power of the ancient Chinese curse, "May you live in interesting times," will be determined in the future by the responses that society and education will make to the interesting times in which we live. Put simply, community colleges are caught between a rock and a hard place as surely as is America. As literacy requirements in both college curricula and society escalate at a frightening pace, students are falling farther and farther behind in basic academic (and many would add, human) skills that are critical for success in college-level courses and in social and economic circumstances. Contemporary and future economic, technological, and demographic imperatives provide tremendous impetus for American community colleges to make good on the promise of universal opportunity through education. Moreover, it is these institutions that are most capable of providing the bridge from an unfocused and inadequate secondary education to a full and productive adult life.

Back to the Future:

Getting Here from There

Histories are stories we tell one another. With them we try to understand ourselves, to sustain our traditions and institutions, sometimes to raise doubts and disappointment, to urge new direction. History is written many times from different points of view, with different plotlines and different meanings.
—**McGrath and Spear,** 1992

In the Universal movie *Back to the Future,* Michael J. Fox portrays Marty McFly, a young man who is propelled by a faulty time machine not into the future but into the past— back to his parents' high school days. He becomes a participant in the events that are moving toward his future. Several times it appears he will be the catalyst for a decided change of events—a change that will alter dramatically the future as he knows it. Marty must move strategically, if not frantically, to keep events rolling consistently toward what he *knows* (and wants) the future to be. Sometimes the events turn so quickly that the audience wonders if the future can be saved! But, what was to be was to be: his parents marry, their children are born, and the rest is the future! Along the way, Marty makes some interesting observations. Not surprisingly, he discovers that the stories he had *heard* or *imagined* about "those days" were not exactly the way that he *learned* they were as he lived them.

The years before we were born or before we were old enough to have clear recollections of events and people can be sources of great curiosity. To satisfy that curiosity, we must rely on reports of the "facts" from history books and the written and oral histories that others compile. In any history we can point to actual events that the majority of history books will document with consistency—for example, legislative acts, wars, population explosions, and establishment of colleges. They are undeniable facts. However, the recounting of human behaviors associated with those documentable events will vary given the nature of individual human proclivities for exaggeration or understatement, negativism or positivism, as well as the time and distance the tellers were removed from the event and the intensity of the involvement (e.g., whether the teller was a casual observer or was sitting in the eye of the storm). As anticipated, the reported histories of higher education and the community college movement include some interesting variations.

We acknowledge that even as we drafted this historical perspective of American higher education, we realized that we could not do justice to the rich histories that are written every day, and so we agreed only to draw an admittedly broad-brush but useful picture of how we got here from there, so that we can now better appreciate the ideas and events that have crafted the future as we know it. Thus, we offer a backdrop—a reporting of the events that unquestionably occurred and some perspectives on those events that were crafted both by participants and observers—thereby tracing ever so briefly the coming of age of what has been called an American social invention (Gleazer, 1963, p. 3), the community college, and its critical role in meeting America's newest challenge, the at-risk student.

Institutions of Higher Education: Some Perspectives on Castles and Moats

The earliest notions of the university as an "ivory tower"—a place designed to accommodate but a few who were admitted only by special permission, and where only the loftiest ideas were entertained—was simple, cleverly crafted, and apt. One might well observe, developing the "edifice" analogy, that over the last 150 years the tower has remained essentially unchanged, and a rather sizable, substantial castle has been erected as well. The obligatory drawbridge and moat have remained—these images from the past help describe the access and opportunity issue that has brought us to the future as we know it.

To the best of our knowledge, Cross (1974) first chose to describe succinctly three periods in the growth of institutions of higher education: the aristocratic, the meritocratic, and the democratic (or egalitarian). Each period turned on the question of access—who should go to college and, in more recent years, what college they should attend. Others have used the terms almost as a shorthand language to identify an age of access policies and as a way to compare and contrast institutions. For example, Zwerling pointed out that the first in the series of "people's colleges"—the land-grant colleges created by the 1862 Morrill Act—within one decade of their establishment began to "resemble the aristocratic colleges to which they were supposed to provide an alternative" (1976, p. 56).

Historically, higher education in the U.S. was reserved for the privileged few. In the early nineteenth century, the classical college, established primarily to preserve and transmit culture and tradition, was the only institution of higher education. Most students were the children of aristocrats who would inherit both their family's money and social status. Going to college was considered a requirement for maintaining their station in life. There was, in fact, no other basis for selecting students to attend what were private and very expensive colleges. The majority of the students were young men; it was agreed, in fact, that the poor, the ethnic minorities, and women would not need a college education. However, some "finishing colleges" were established to provide training for those wealthy young women who, as the aristocratic young men, were destined to assume and serve in their aristocratic positions.

During this century social forces began to drive the establishment of not only additional colleges, but different types of colleges. The free-school movement began with the notion that education was the responsibility of the state, women were afforded educational opportunities, the lyceum movement began and became the forerunner of what we now know as college extension services, and the demand increased for trained personnel and technicians to support expanding industrial development. By the mid-1800s it was clear that America's rapidly expanding needs could not be served by traditional institutions of higher education.

As the demands for a broader curriculum and a wider range of subject choices gathered momentum, they were joined by a tremendous press for adding business, technical, and agricultural courses to existing educational offerings. The Morrill Land Grant Act in 1862 and in 1890 extended educational opportunities to all people (Boylan, 1988; Vaughan, 1983). The acts "reached a stratum of students for whom higher or even intermediate training would not otherwise have been available" (Ross, 1942, p. 133), and the former aristocratic notions of education for the privileged few were well challenged. The land-grant colleges that developed out of these acts contributed significant new ideas to the American educational system: establishing laboratories as teaching tools, offering extension services, and focusing research activities on practical everyday problems that consumed average people. In effect, the acts were written to legitimize teaching "applied" subjects in colleges. And while the land-grant colleges initially were called the "people's college" and embraced a more diverse clientele of students than higher education had ever known, they still did not admit minorities, offered few opportunities for women, and were geographically inaccessible to many students.

Yet even as these new colleges were being established and holding out the first hazy notions of egalitarianism, they began to turn toward more selective admissions, assuming many of the characteristics of the colleges of the aristocracy. As advocates of these new colleges were looking to embrace populations that had never before been considered for admission, they were working simultaneously to design procedures for identifying which segments of those new populations should be so embraced. They stuck on the notion that because they had no past performance by which to predict future behavior, college admission should be based upon academic merit—that is, only those young people who exhibited the most promise for doing well were to be admitted. But the ideas that were called up and took life when the first "people's college" was established did not go away, and instead they fueled new notions of another kind of college.

The Junior College

Not until just after the birth of the twentieth century, in 1902, was the first ancestor of today's comprehensive community college established—Joliet Junior College, an institution considered by many to be the first independent public junior college designed to prepare students for the university (Henderson, 1960, p. 13) and to sort out those students who were not qualified to enter the more challenging university-level curriculum (Brubacher and Rudy, 1958). William Rainey Harper, then president of the University of Chicago, first established the concept of the junior college within the University of Chicago in 1892 (Griffith, 1976), literally dividing the four years in half, calling them "Academic College" and "University College"; then in 1896 the names were changed to "Junior College" and "Senior College" (Eells, 1931). When he recognized that this break did not accomplish what he had initially envisioned, he encouraged the superintendent of the Joliet schools to establish the "junior college" by extending Joliet High School for two more years to give the high school graduates additional time to prepare themselves socially and academically for the "senior college." His initial ideas that there should be a distinction between upper- and lower-division work and later that extension services should be instituted to serve the community may be the signal reasons that he is viewed by many as the father of the American junior college. Almost simultaneously, Alexis F. Lange, dean of the School of Education at the University of California at Berkeley, and David Starr Jordan, president of Stanford University, were joining forces to press for the California legislation of 1907 that authorized public school districts to offer the first two years of college work. A serious break with the university had been established.

Other advocates of the junior college openly urged its establishment to provide some "buffers" between growing numbers of high school students who had begun to seek higher education—that is, the first glimmers of an expanding and heretofore unexpected population—and the more specialized university. And, as Zwerling (1976) (and others) argued, the founding fathers of the junior college may not have had this larger segment of the population in mind, nor had they been following a vision of expanding educational opportunities, but rather they were creating the two-year college to "divert" more and more students away from the university, to allow the pure university the freedom to pursue its preparation of a professional elite. Other advocates saw the junior college as "providing particularly for that class of men who are mechanically minded and of women who are domestically minded, the opportunity to improve their abilities" (Eells, 1931, p. 289).

> The junior college has popularized education. Where a local junior college is established, probably the number of people who "go to college" is at least doubled. It would be unwise and unfortunate if all of us tried to enter a university and prepare for professions which in most cases are already overcrowded, and for which their talents and abilities in most cases do not fit them (Eells, 1931, p. 289).

As junior colleges embraced larger segments of the population and literally developed in their midst, it appeared to be a natural progression to think of them as fixtures in the community. Some advocates put these progressive ideas into words, asserting that the junior college should in fact be a community institution—it should meet community needs, provide adult education, and offer educational, recreational, and vocational activities, placing all of its facilities at the disposal of the community (Hollinshead, 1936).

Laid as the foundation for all of this institutional growth were two driving forces—the conviction that higher education was the right of any person who could profit from it, and the accompanying belief that colleges existed to serve the American people. The comprehensive educational system that fostered the development of community colleges was a direct outgrowth of some basic democratic philosophical assumptions (from Roueche, 1968, pp. 7–8):

> 1. **Education is necessary for the maintenance of a democracy.** That an educated citizenry will profoundly affect the destiny of a democratic society has been a long-held belief in this country. Thomas Jefferson, an early craftsman of the thoughts and the language describing American ideals and goals, admonished those who argued that education is for the few: "If the nation expects to be ignorant and free, in a state of civilization, it expects what never was and never will be" (1816).
> 2. **Education is essential for the improvement of society.** History records education's valuable role in resolving some of America's most serious social problems: for example, the Americanization

of large groups of immigrants in the 1890s and early 1900s, and the assumption of educational responsibilities for these women and children formerly trapped in exploited labor practices in U.S. mills, mines, and factories. In truth, the manpower retraining function of American education still strengthens the status as a national necessity.

3. **Education helps to equalize opportunity for all people**. The concept of individual worth, upon which this nation was founded, fuels the American dream that every individual should be permitted to seek an education to the highest level of his potential. Talents and motivation should be the only limits to an individual's opportunities and achievements. Thornton emphasized the individual purpose of education when he noted that the American people were learning what older cultures have learned, that the schools are the social elevators in a hardening social structure (1966). Education continues to be the vehicle by which individuals can achieve personal and social advancement.

The "open door" to higher education had been well established by the time enrollments began to rise sharply with the passage of the 1944 G.I. Bill of Rights; while opinions varied about whether so many returning veterans would have come to college were it not for the special funding, the fact remained that they did flood college campuses. And with the Truman Commission on Higher Education's 1947 declaration that postsecondary education through the fourteenth grade should be provided to all citizens regardless of race, sex, religion, color, geographical location, or financial condition, the community college's role as a major force in American higher education seemed assured. The commission advocated the establishment of locally controlled colleges that would put education at the doorsteps, or at least within reasonable commuting distance, of most Americans. In fact, much attention was directed toward determining the actual size of that group capable of profiting from the services of these colleges. The President's Advisory Commission on Higher Education in 1947 estimated that 49 percent of the population could profit from at least two years of post-high-school education and that about 32 percent had the capacity for a normal four-year college course of study. In 1952 Hollinshead's report for the Commission on Financing Higher Education concluded, "Perhaps 35 percent of youth might be expected to profit substantially from formal full-time, post-high-school education of the kind given at present by such institutions" (p. 138). While these commissions were providing some encouraging numbers about the percentages of potential students, they would discover that within the next 20 years their estimates would appear remarkably shortsighted.

The stage was set for a growth and development that would never again be witnessed in higher education. As Vaughan would later remark, "Indeed, the merging of the various forces that shaped the community college was not the clash of town and gown for which American higher education is famous; to the contrary, it was more like love at first sight" (1983, p. 8).

Yet, even as the egalitarian notions of including larger and larger segments of society in higher education were spinning out in junior colleges, simultaneously the meritocratic notions of access were being strengthened. In fact, Cross referred to the 1950s as "the heyday of educational meritocracy" (1976, p. 26). Concluding remarks from a study by the Commission on Human Resources and Advanced Training pointedly and bluntly testified to the prevalent view:

> The democratic ideal is one of equal opportunity: within that ideal it is both individually advantageous and socially desirable for each person to make the best possible use of his talents, but equal opportunity does not mean equal accomplishments or identical use. Some men have greater ability than others and can accomplish things which are beyond the powers of men of lesser endowment. The nation needs to make effective use of its intellectual resources. To do so means to use well its brightest people whether they come from farm or city, from the slum section or the country club area, regardless of color or religious or economic differences, but not regardless of ability (Wolfle, 1954, p. 6).

The events of the day turned dramatically upon the last five words in this statement of philosophy—"but not regardless of ability." The aristocracy had designed its curriculum for and limited its enrollment to a small and elite segment of the population, and the colleges operating from a meritocratic view of education believed that a larger, but still only a limited, segment of the population would be capable of benefitting from their curriculum.

Historical antecedents tugged again; admissions policies were carefully drawn to define the limits of accessibility within the newest population. Where policies had been rewritten to admit only those students who could best profit by instruction, policies were now to be rewritten so as to admit only those who could best profit by a *particular* instruction. During the late 1950s and early 1960s, colleges and universities attempted, primarily through testing and high school records, to distinguish between those students who could profit by remediation and those who could not—that is, sorting out those who were regarded as low-achievers or underachievers (those who may have had good ability as indicated by test scores but lacked either motivation or study skills, which was most apparent in poor performance, or poor grades, in the classroom) (Cross, 1976). Concern about wasting public and private monies on students of low ability was dramatically expressed: "During these times, the great importance of not allowing conditions to deteriorate to a point where qualified instructors are forced to dissipate their energies on undeserving students can hardly be overemphasized.... A college cannot do very much for students of low academic ability" (Pittman, 1960, p. 426).

The 1970s were years of controversy. The meritocratic and the egalitarian philosophies presented an unpalatable combination of circumstances and criteria. A headline in *Time*, 1970, read, "Open Admissions: American Dream or Disaster?" The 1970 President's Taskforce on Higher Education recommended financial aid to "students of all races who have the desire and the ability to profit from post-high-school education." In that same year, the City University of New York was opening its doors to all New York City high school graduates without regard for their previous academic performance, even in the face of the Carnegie Commission's latest report that only at community colleges should open admissions be allowed. And John Gardner's questions a decade earlier in his highly acclaimed *Excellence: Can We Be Equal and Excellent Too?* (1961) loomed even larger. In that book, Gardner admonished the educational system to offer opportunities to all who could contribute to society, to embrace the growing diversity. His message was humorously but painfully clear: Unless we were willing to equally respect both philosophers and plumbers, we would be a nation in which neither our theories nor our pipes would hold water. Other questions served to fuel the meritocratic/egalitarian fires: "What happens to the value of the college degree when everyone has one? Is there some fixed concept of 'college' that permits us to say you should attend? Should higher education serve those who can profit from traditional offerings, or is there an obligation to change the offerings to meet the needs of those who wish to attend college?" (from Cross, 1974, p. 4).

Early efforts to describe and delineate the purposes of the junior/community college could only dimly forecast the burgeoning array of assignments these colleges would eventually be handed. While the transfer function was its earliest and primary assignment, by 1947 the President's Commission on Higher Education proposed that less attention be given to the transfer or preparatory function and more attention to the occupational function. In fact, the commission's major concern was for the education of technicians and semi-professional workers—specifically recommending: 1) training for the semi-professions and occupations requiring no more than two years of post-high-school work; 2) general education for students terminating their formal education at the end of two years; 3) adult education; and 4) college-parallel work for those students who wished to transfer (1948, pp. 68–69). In 1950 Jesse Parker Bogue, longtime executive director of what was then the American Association of Junior Colleges, expressed the conservative ideology of junior college leaders when he wrote what came to be regarded as the foundation of what was to become a major mission of the contemporary community college—training individuals for semi-professional fields of employment: "Democratic cooperation means more than topflight leadership. So to speak, it also means intelligent followership" (p. 60). In 1956 the Yearbook Committee of the National Society for the Study of Education concluded that the major purposes of community colleges were: 1) preparation for advanced study; 2) vocational education; 3) general education; and 4) community service (including adult education as one of the various services) (1956, p. 69). In 1958 Hillway, in *The American Two-Year College*, summarized the functions as: 1) democratization of higher education through the extension of greater opportunity to all youth; 2) community services; 3) vocational training for the semi-professions; 4) more effective adult education; and 5) guidance and rehabilitation (1958, p. 83). And in 1962 an even more comprehensive statement of purpose was offered by AAJC President Edmund Gleazer: "It is the purpose of the community college to make readily available programs of education beyond the high school which match a wide spectrum of community needs and which relate economically and officially to the total pattern of educational opportunity in the area" (Wattenbarger and Godwin, 1962, p. 2). [By the 1970s the term *community college* was applied typically to colleges that were lower-division branches of private universities, privately supported two-year colleges, and the more comprehensive, publicly supported institutions (Cohen and Brawer, 1982).]

By the 1960s these colleges were responding to the egalitarian notions gathering momentum during the decade. They offered a wide range of programs in general education, vocational-technical education, transfer education, developmental education, and community education. Medsker (1960) described the reality of their situation well: "No unit of American higher education is expected to serve such a diversity of purposes, to provide such a variety of educational instruments, or to distribute students among so many types of educational programs as the junior college" (p. 4).

Moreover, while institutional goals were closely related to the concept that individuals should be provided the opportunity to progress as far as their interest and abilities would permit, they did not support the notion that every student should have the same education, or that an array of diverse educational programs should be available to all. The colleges were responding as rapidly as possible to the unmet needs of a society that had set major goals for itself, goals drawn from the prevailing and growing interest in equality and economic prosperity.

The view that such a multipurpose institution could achieve all of its goals turned on the belief that the goals of access and excellence did not have to be compromised. "Fortunately, the demand to educate everyone up to the level of his ability and the demand for excellence in education are not incompatible. We must honor both goals. We must seek excellence in a context of concern for all" (Rockefeller Brothers Report, 1958, p. 22).

An early evaluation of the transfer function—still the major academic focus—indicated that community colleges were training their students to enter and compete successfully in four-year institutions. Three decades ago, a well-known longitudinal study followed more than 7,000 students transferring from community colleges to a variety of four-year institutions in 10 states and documented that 62 percent graduated with bachelor's degrees in three years. The researchers forecasted that a minimum of 75 percent would go on to graduate (Knoell and Medsker, 1965). By the late 1970s, however, the traditional university-parallel program was no longer the vehicle by which transfer was made; rather, occupational and technical programs were issuing more than half of all community college degrees and significant numbers of those students transfered to four-year institutions (American Association of Community Colleges, 1979). And, by the 1990s the transfer function is still documentably less prominent in the enrollment figures, and graduation rates of all students in all programs of study have claimed the most interest.

Major recurring criticisms of community colleges turn on the notion that by attempting to serve everyone, regardless of interest, achievement, and ability, and that by spreading themselves thin along a continuum of programs and functions, these colleges serve all students less well.

According to Lynes (1966):

> Its functions are so diverse, its people so scattered, and its efforts to be all things to all students so determined that it escapes identification...In general it has been looked down upon by holders of B.A. degrees as a refuge for the stupid, and it has been avoided as a place to teach by most serious scholars (pp. 59–60).

In 1968 Roueche, following the first national study of community college remedial programs, documented that the majority of colleges did not evaluate these programs and that those who did discovered that they fell woefully short of their goals. However, it was clear that even without solid evidence to support their claims, educators across all program areas were boasting about their achievements with the increasing numbers of nontraditional students. Cohen admonished these colleges for their overall "lack of genuine self-appraisal" and their characteristic "mixture of defensiveness and self-congratulation" (1969, p. viii). In 1970 Jennings derided, berated, and then challenged the community college to make good on its promises by making "its only viable mission the matching of its pretentions with performance" (1970, p. 24).

> It strives for continuities and creates fragmentation. It delivers less than what it so generously promises. It often fails the students who need most help. To those who seek direction, order, goals and purpose, it offers the jigsaw puzzle of an all-purpose curriculum. Its all purpose curriculum is useless (1970, p. 18).

In 1970, after researching the increasing numbers and the college experiences of those he termed high-risk students who had been drawn to the "open door" and placed in college remedial programs, Moore pronounced these students badly treated and no better off after the remedial experience, if in fact they survived it at all. Roueche (1968) asked if remedial education could ever be effective in college if public education had not been able to accomplish it. And Jencks (1968) pessimistically viewed the likelihood that equality of educational opportunity could ever occur:

> Consider the case of the junior college[s]...They offer a variety of curricula, including some designed for the academically apathetic or inept students. Yet the existence of these colleges has not improved the competitive position of the poor in any dramatic way (pp. 304–305).

In 1972 Karabel argued that getting into college was not as critical an issue as what happened once students got there. Among other things, he described what he believed was a socioeconomic and racial tracking system within the community college that was as real as the tracking system in the social milieu outside its walls—a veritable message of prevailing, albeit obscured, notions about privilege and limited opportunities. In 1976 Zwerling proposed that the community college was not really a lever of opportunity at all, but rather a social filter, a place for "cooling out" the aspirations of students to more "realistic" levels, and a diffuser of potential social discontent (pp. xviii–xix). Moreover, he noted the system "not only keeps certain people out, it also tells them that they never had what it takes to get in" (1976, p. xxi).

As well, the community college's open door was blamed for a national decline in the general academic performance of high school students. Harvard University Professor David Riesman made this point:

To say there should be universal access to college seems fair. It seems egalitarian, but it's been destructive because students think you don't have to strive in high school. There's the illusion you can always recover so the whole level has dropped (as cited in Feinberg, 1984, p. A6).

The open door was also targeted for criticism by many community college faculty who felt betrayed by their institutions as they wrestled with expanding responsibilities:

The move to emphasize noncollegiate efforts combined with the increase in the need for remedial courses, the sharp turn of students to vocational programs, the diminishing role of the traditional liberal arts courses, and the decline in the rate of transfer of students to four-year colleges and universities to produce considerable uneasiness among many faculty in community colleges (Seidman, 1985, p. 8).

The transfer program enrolled a large majority of community college students well into the 1960s until enrollment in occupational-technical programs began a major upswing and remedial/developmental program enrollments were burgeoning. By 1987 Richardson and Bender criticized the community college's movement away from university-parallel curriculum, echoing past and forecasting future critics' concerns that academic rigor was being diluted and that colleges were moving toward pervasive remedial missions:

The preoccupation with remediating from 60 percent to 90 percent of their entering students, along with the need to provide social services, and with the need to prepare their clientele for immediate employment, leaves [community colleges] with little energy and few resources to offer challenging transfer programs to those who enrolled with the ultimate intent of earning a baccalaureate degree (p. 3).

And in 1991 McGrath and Spear drew out a history of the "remedialization of the community college." Echoing Karabel's charge that community colleges had established within their own walls tracking systems not unlike those in American society, they continued that "the educational practices offered to children of professionals at four-year colleges and universities are tougher, more rigorous, and denser than those offered to the non-traditional students for whom education means the most" (p. 54).

Since community colleges' inception, issues around whether they can offer open access, deliver educational opportunity, and maintain acceptable standards of educational excellence at the same time have created questions for discussion and drawn criticism from a wide array of educators, researchers, and legislators. They are heady issues with equally heady arguments. Access and opportunity are not synonyms. Access is simple and direct, and it makes higher education available to more segments of the population than ever before. But opportunity is complex; it is not just having the right to try—"educational opportunity means more than the right to meet minimal standards; it means the right to develop one's talents to maximum effectiveness" (Cross, 1976, p. 3). Educational opportunity depends on community colleges' abilities to understand their students, to design curriculum and instruction to address their needs, and to employ faculty who embrace philosophically and operationally this changing array of challenges.

The Students

As "democracy's college," the community college manifests the American dream of offering postsecondary education to all. The fact that community colleges were attractive to increasing numbers of students was obvious from their inception. By 1971 Medsker and Tillery were reporting that approximately one-third of all students entering institutions of higher education did so through the open doors of the community college. By 1992 more than one-half of all students enrolled in higher education were enrolled in community colleges.

What made community colleges so attractive to so many? The colleges determined early on that in order to serve greater numbers of students, they must be made more accessible. The accessibility issue was addressed by tackling the three major barriers to higher education: geographical, financial, and social. According to the findings from national studies in the 1960s, by building within acceptable commuting distances of potential student populations (Trent and Medsker, 1968; Cross, 1968) and charging reasonable tuition and fees (D'Amico and Bokelman, 1962; Cross, 1968), these colleges effectively addressed the geographical and financial barriers. However, it is the social barrier that has proven to be the most complex to describe and address, and that has generated the most controversy. In embracing unprecedented numbers and extraordinary diversity of student abilities and educational experiences, community colleges have been most challenged.

For the first two decades, junior college students were a rather select group; they had well-defined goals of completing their preparation for the last two years of college work. Researchers and educators looked historically to these students to draw the definitions and the characteristics of the "traditional student" population (Cross, 1968). Yet by the early 1960s, the community/junior college student was much more representative of the general population—mentally, socially, and economically (Fields, 1962, p. 58). And, because new phenomena do not arrive complete with new vocabulary for describing them, they can be described only in older, familiar terms. We knew who the "traditional" students were—students who historically had enrolled in college with fairly clear-cut goals. The students with whom we were not so familiar then could only be described as "nontraditional." As Cross noted in her first descriptions of the junior college student, only "traditional measures" were available "to describe a student who does not fit the tradition. The inevitable result is that we picture America's newest college student as being less adequate than his peers at the tasks of higher education—*tasks which have been developed over the years for a different type of student*" (1968, p. 53).

But describing them was essential to the task of addressing their needs. In the early 1960s research about junior college students provided a fairly well-defined set of characteristics: they had graduated from high school with a low C average or below, were deficient in basic skills (particularly in language and mathematics), had poor study habits, were weakly motivated, had no home support to encourage continuing in school, had unrealistic and ill-defined goals, were from homes with few advantages and minimal standards of living, and/or were the first of their family to attend college (Merson, 1961, p. 61).

In 1968 Cross identified the knowns and unknowns of their characteristics from a synthesis of the current available research (see Cross, 1968, specifically pp. 47–53, for a broader discussion of these characteristics). She wrote that we knew there was a high probability that large numbers of junior college students would achieve lower mean scores on academic ability tests than would comparably selected samples of four-year college and university students; what we did not know was much about the pattern of special abilities and aptitudes of these students. We did know that parents of junior college students tended to have lower socioeconomic status than parents of students entering four-year colleges and universities; we did not know much about the students' home environments and the student-parent relationships. We did know that the presence of a junior college in a local community appeared to make it possible for more young people from low socioeconomic levels to enter higher education, but it could not be determined if the cost factor alone prevented them from seeking a college education; we did not know what students and parents knew about college costs and about the amount of financial assistance available in junior and senior colleges and the effects on those students who worked and attended college at the same time. We did know that they were likely to be attracted to a college for practical reasons—for instance, it was near home or that training for a job would lead them to a higher income. As a group they appeared to have lower educational-occupational aspirations than students who began in senior colleges, their future plans were more unsettled, and they aspired to managerial and professional occupations more often than the skilled and semi-professional work force from which their parents may have come; we did not know much about the satisfactions and dissatisfactions of those who dropped out, about those with unrealistic aspirations, and what they knew about the various pathways that were open to them. We did know that their intellectual interests were clearly different from those who did not enter college or who attended four-year colleges and that they had a much more practical orientation to college life than did their peers in four-year colleges. As well, they were more likely to be less venturesome and flexible in their thinking, less likely to take chances. We did not know much about the personality characteristics of these students—specifically, their values, their feelings about themselves, and their relationships with others. We did know that they did not feel as well prepared for college as four-year college students, that they were less confident of their academic abilities and thought that their high school teachers would not rate them as good students, but they rated themselves a good deal higher on their nonacademic abilities than did their four-year counterparts; we did not know the range of activities in which these students felt exceptional—leading us to describe, therefore, junior college students as unsure and lacking in self-confidence.

By 1971 Cross was labeling these students as "New," further identifying them as ranking in the lowest third of high school graduates on traditional tests of academic achievement. She acknowledged that while the issue of test bias (particularly in regard to minority student performance) was controversial, low test scores were, of all indicators yet found to measure potentially poor academic performance, the most distinguishing measurement available, including race, sex, socioeconomic status, and high school grades (grades fluctuated so highly across the nation that they were especially unreliable). She continued that if students did not perform well the tasks required on traditional tests, it was obvious that they had educational problems; but even more important, it was highly likely that they would have difficulty performing those same tasks in the classroom—translated, tests are moderately good predictors of college grades and/or are as good for members of minority groups who are singled out as for majority youth (see Cross, 1974, p. 14).

Well into the 1970s the profile of the nontraditional student had not changed dramatically for more than 45 years—most were Caucasians from blue-collar families; substantial numbers of the rest were members of ethnic minority groups. Most had parents who had never attended college, they had not been successful in high school studies, and they were more likely to plan on entering community colleges or vocational schools than four-year colleges or universities. They viewed education as a way to a better life than their parents'.

But by 1973, even while Karabel was documenting the tie between low socioeconomic status and enrollment in community colleges, a new and significant student minority had surfaced. These students' fathers had attended college, and their families were not considered particularly disadvantaged in terms of socioeconomic status, but these students had learning problems and a history of poor academic performance, including feelings of school failure, that were strangely similar to those from less advantaged backgrounds (Cross, 1976). By 1977 it was possible to document that changes were continuing in enrollment patterns. Relationships were unclear between type and incidents of postsecondary enrollment and socioeconomic status, ethnicity, prior educational experience, and concomitant achievement level. In other words, the problem students were now representative of all society, and the relationships that historically had existed were not now so evident. In fact, it was now even clearer that preliminary attempts to define the disadvantaged or nontraditional student population had incorrectly targeted minority populations, when in fact low-achieving students entering open-admissions community colleges were composed of all socioeconomic groups at varying levels of abilities (Roueche and Snow, 1977).

A wide variety of terms were being coined to identify/describe these students: disadvantaged, disprivileged, nontraditional, underprepared, remedial, developmental, high-risk, low-achieving, and the like; but whatever they were called, they were perceived as less likely than their better-prepared counterparts to succeed in their courses and to complete a schedule of study (Romoser, 1978). They lacked a solid educational base for success (Kraetsch, 1980). They had fallen farther and farther behind during their elementary and secondary school years, and were most likely ranked in the bottom one-third of their high school class (Campbell, 1981). In 1981 Breneman and Nelson pointed out that "compared to students in other sectors of higher education, those in community colleges are more likely to be, on average, less wealthy, members of minority groups, older, part-time, working, and less well-prepared" (p. 22). Cross (1981) noted that students were entering from the ghetto, the barrio, the reservation, and the suburbs; they were 20, 30, and even 70 years old; they were single parents preparing for careers; they were unsure of their skills; and they were hopeful students who were the first ever in their families to attend college. It was rather universally agreed that these basic characteristics of community college students would make it especially hard for them to persist in school (Astin, 1982, p. 183).

In its 1990 report, *Serving Underprepared Students*, the League for Innovation in the Community College noted that while a disproportionate percentage of these students were minorities, especially in urban areas, there remained incredible diversity within the category of "high risk"— recent high school graduates, returning adults, high school dropouts, illiterate adults, immigrants, and students with limited English proficiency. They also were disadvantaged by the same characteristics that have more traditionally described the developmental student: weak self-concepts, a history of academic failure, uncertain or unrealistic goals, and family and economic difficulties.

Early on, most researchers agreed that of all his characteristics, the nontraditional student's disbelief in his ability to be successful was perhaps the most threatening of all to his persistence and performance. The manifestations of a weak self-concept made him especially wary of the new educational surroundings. As a result of his prior schooling, he had learned to fail and had become, in psychological terminology, failure-threatened and therefore a failure-identifier. The failure-identifier would approach learning situations quite differently than would the more traditional and academically stronger student:

> The picture is not unlike that of a strong and a weak swimmer thrown into downstream currents above a waterfall. The strong swimmer soon swims to calm waters and begins to focus his attention on how fast he can swim, while the weak swimmer is dragged into such swift currents that his only concern is to keep himself from going over the waterfall. In the language of psychology, the strong swimmer becomes achievement-motivated while the weak swimmer becomes fear-threatened. Future learning is structured differently for the two swimmers (Cross, 1974, p. 22).

This student has little confidence in his ability to learn, generally suffers from a low self-image, and rarely participates in class (Friedlander, 1981–82). "They unconsciously regard themselves as educational failures on their way to fail again. That self-fulfilling prophecy is predictable from their behavior. They often come to class without pencil or paper, put off purchasing a text, sit near an exit, do not complete initial assignments, become erratic in attendance. One day they simply vanish" (Weber, 1985, p. 1).

In Cross's 1970 questionnaire on developmental services, mailed to a 20 percent random sample of the two-year colleges listed in the 1969 American Association of Community Colleges's *Directory*, "lack of effort, has quit trying" ranked as the *major obstacle* to learning for low-achieving students (Cross, 1974, p. 192). [Note: In 1970, 49 percent of the respondents listed "lack of effort" as the primary obstacle; in the same survey, conducted in 1974 with a similar sample, it dropped to third behind "poor elementary and secondary schooling" and "poor home background" with a 28 percent response (Cross, 1976, p. 234).] Holt (1970), in *How Children Fail,* observed:

> Children [who feel failure]…may decide that if they can't have total success, their next best bet is to have total failure…. Incompetence has [an] advantage. Not only does it reduce what others expect and demand of you, it reduces what you expect or even hope for yourself. When you set out to fail, one thing is certain—you can't be disappointed. As the old saying goes, you can't fall out of bed when you sleep on the floor (pp. 85–86).

According to Cross, the "great future task is to investigate whether, and in what ways, the junior college student differs in *kind,* or in pattern of abilities, rather than in *degree* from the traditional college student" (1968, p. 53). It is obvious that we do not know nearly enough about these students. What we do know is that they offer serious challenges to present educational systems. As Cross recommended in the swimmers' analogy, programs must do more than keep students from going over the waterfall, but rather they must be designed to change the students' narrow view of their options.

In our graduate classes at The University of Texas, by intensive discussion and scenario we ferret out and then graphically display the essential differences between students enrolling for the first time in a public university and those enrolling in a community college. The university of choice in our classes will serve well for purposes of discussion here (see Figure 2.1).

University freshmen can be expected to have strong family support, backed by years of high expectations for their success and their future. The community college freshmen can be expected to come from families that provide little psychological and financial support, if any; moreover, they are likely to be first-generation college students, with no relative available to "show them the ropes" or explain what they might expect once they arrive on campus or in the classroom. University freshmen, in addition to family, likely have other mentors from high school, the community, or even the university who have some knowledge of or interest in their whereabouts and can advise them about courses and professors. The community college freshmen do not have advisers or mentors and must decipher on their own what the expectations are and what paths to take to be successful.

University freshmen have strong self-concepts and images, backed by years of successful or at least satisfactory academic and personal

---

Figure 2.1
Entering Freshmen

The University of Texas	*A U.S. Community College*
• Family expectations/ support	• First-generation learners/little support
• Connectability/mentor	• Pathways to success unknown
• Strong self-concept & image	• Poor self-image
• Have a "worldview"/ traveled	• Have not left neighborhood
• Success experience/goal-oriented	• Failure/self-defeatism/ unreachable goals
• Adversity-free/low work levels	• Work 30 hours per week/ social ills
• Age range 19–22	• Average age 28
• Youthful women/recent high school graduates	• Returning women
• Majority student population	• Large minority student population
• Small percentage of foreign-born students	• Increasing numbers of foreign-born students
• Economic security: $70K	• Economic insecurity: one-third students below poverty level
• Competitive/motivated	• Desperation/economically driven
• Academically talented	• Academically weak
• High school GPA 3.6+/top 10 percent	• Top 99 percent of high school graduating class
• SAT = 1100	• Poor or low test scores/GED

experiences, experiences further enhanced by the ongoing recognition of family and friends. As a result, they are more likely to be goal-oriented, having had success experiences that have strengthened interest and belief in future possibilities. They are also more competitive and motivated to succeed. Community college freshmen have few, if any, experiences that can provide a base for developing a strong self-concept or an image of themselves as learners or as potential successes in any arena. They are failure-identifiers and have a rather narrow view, if any, of reachable, achievable goals. And, they are motivated not by success, but by failure, driven by stringent economic realities.

University freshmen have had more opportunities for travel and, thereby, for developing some worldview. Most community college freshmen have not been far out of their neighborhoods or their communities; they view the world through their limited experiences.

Although in the 1990s they are working more hours while going to school than ever before (Cage, 1992), university freshmen typically have outside means of support that can help make their academic work more adversity-free, as represented by few hours required in the workplace, leaving more hours for study. As well, they are economically more secure because their family can provide some support, and they are in more advantageous positions, given past academic performance, to seek opportunities for scholastic scholarships. As a group they are young, typically 19 to 22 years of age, compared to the average age of 28 for their community college counterparts. At community colleges, the freshman class is more likely to include greater numbers of returning women, minorities, and foreign-born students than would the university class. The older the group of students, the more likely that family-support responsibilities will exacerbate the difficulties in balancing work and school commitments. Community college freshmen typically work 20 to 30 hours a week and are in tight economic situations, where frequently decisions between work and academic responsibilities result in decreased numbers of hours available for study. They are critically insecure economically; it is estimated that one-third of community college students live below the poverty line.

Although many universities and four-year colleges are openly recruiting minority students, or "students who are at risk, in order to diversify their student bodies" (Cage, 1992, A30), entering freshmen at community colleges are more likely to be minorities and returning women. While data have indicated community college enrollment increases over the last decade for both groups, current, more widely accepted figures indicate that more Blacks and Hispanics are enrolled in community colleges than in any other institutions of higher education. Moreover, in many sections of the country, a growing number of immigrants are finding their way to the open door.

Academically, university freshmen as a group have SAT scores that meet university entrance requirements (average 1100) and have demonstrated academic talent in high school, earning a high school GPA of 3.6+ and graduating in the top 10 percent of their class. Most community college freshmen have poor or low SAT or local entrance test scores, and many have earned a GED rather than a high school diploma. Community college students are more likely to be in the bottom one-third and have poor academic records.

These characteristics most distinguish what we choose to call the at-risk community college student from the typical university and four-year student. The unbelievable variety and magnitude of academic, social, and economic circumstances makes this student more likely to succumb to failure in future academic pursuits.

The Programs

Institutions of higher education have literally been in the business of remediation for more than 150 years. In 1828 developmental studies at Yale University prompted an article in the *Yale Report* that was uncomplimentary of the university's practice of enrolling students with "defective preparation" (Pintozzi, 1987). In 1849 the University of Wisconsin established the nation's first documented remedial program (Brier, 1984), a college preparatory department offering remedial courses in reading, writing, and mathematics; by 1865, of 331 students registered at that institution, only 41 attended regular classes (Brubacher and Rudy, 1976). By 1880, following attacks brought on by embarrassment of its existence on campus, the department was abolished (Wyatt, 1992). Over the next 10 years, this college preparatory model was widely adopted by other higher education institutions (Boylan, 1988).

In 1869 Cornell University President Andrew Dickson White complained that students' "utter ignorance" in the "common English branches" was "astounding"; in 1872 the *Vassar Miscellany* referred to such students as "inferior forms," and in 1882 as "a vandal horde" (Brier, 1984). In 1871 Harvard University President Charles Eliot noted that Harvard freshmen displayed ignorance of even the rudimentary rules of grammar, punctuation, and spelling. He called for the establishment of an entrance examination, and half of Harvard's applicants failed that exam, but many were admitted "on condition" (Weidner, 1990, p. 4). In 1874 the Harvard faculty instituted freshman English to remedy the writing deficiencies demonstrated by upperclassmen and established the notion that freshman English courses always would be considered college preparatory (Maxwell, 1979). Brier cites "hearings" in the late 1800s to review the academic qualifications of those students with "defective preparation," conducted by "Committees on Doubtful Cases" (Brier, 1984); in 1882 "[u]nhappy instructors were confronted with immature thoughts set down in a crabbed and slovenly hand, miserably expressed and wretchedly spelled" (Weidner, 1990, pp. 4–5). The University of California at Berkeley began its first remedial writing course for underprepared students in 1889 (Boylan, 1988). Wellesley College offered a remedial course in 1894 through the dean of students' office that focused primarily on study skills (Cross, 1976). In 1894 over 40 percent of the entering students in colleges in the U.S. were preparatory students (Levine, 1978). In the latter part of the nineteenth century, with the signing of the second Morrill Act, more and more underprepared students were enrolling in higher education, and increasing numbers of preparatory courses were established.

By the turn of the century, competition for students became more keen, and colleges were more willing to accept freshmen who historically had been questionable. Eighty-four percent of all colleges and universities in the U.S. had preparatory schools similar to that established in 1849 at the University of Wisconsin (Abraham, 1991). By 1915, 350 institutions of higher education offered college preparatory programs (Maxwell, 1979), and 70 community colleges offered the "equivalent of the first two years of college courses combined with a large menu of preparatory courses" (Boylan, 1988, p. 4). That number increased five years later to more than 200.

In 1927 William F. Book at the University of Indiana "began to laud rather than condemn the practice of assisting underprepared students" (Wyatt, 1992, p. 12). He discovered in 1926 that one-half of the Indiana freshmen had not met their course requirements and 16 percent had failed all of their courses; he observed that reading and study habits seemed to be their primary problems and that apparently intelligence was not a factor. He responded to the dilemma by establishing a "How to Study" course that was keenly futuristic: he stressed the importance of using actual content material in the teaching of reading and linking the instruction to how readers would put the information to use in the real world (Book, 1927). In the late 1930s and early 1940s, the how-to-study courses continued, and remedial reading courses were introduced to the curriculum (Charters, 1941; Triggs, 1942). The reading courses, however, primarily focused on eye movements and eye span, which were believed to increase reading rate; typically, the skills, which included skimming, organizing, and vocabulary studies, were taught in isolation from context (Charters, 1941).

The remedial education courses offered in the 1950s and 1960s in most colleges were intended for students with high ability who performed poorly in some phase of academic work. During these years, as enrollments increased, remediation became a major agenda at universities and public institutions. While many major public universities turned to even more selective admissions policies (meritocratic attitudes regarding college admissions were still prevailing influences), others combined selectivity with a simultaneous offer for so-called catch-up, preparation courses to be completed during the summer sessions by those students identified as not meeting academic admission standards but with demonstrated potential for eventual academic success.

With the passage of the Higher Education Act of 1965, colleges were admitting increasing numbers of nontraditional students—educationally disadvantaged, minorities, and women. In 1968 the most frequently offered remedial course was English; other courses included reading, courses with some sequence of life experiences, and mathematics. Less-offered courses were in social sciences or business. Primarily, terms such as "salvage" and "second chance" were used to describe these courses. But by the mid-1960s colleges were faced with some fairly clear indicators that remediation could not be approached just by tackling poor study habits or teaching reading skills in isolation from other courses; the students were bringing an unbelievable variety of problems to the classroom that could not be addressed in a simplistic manner.

Cross's 1970 and 1974 developmental education surveys indicated that in four years "total push" programs had increased from 20 percent to 36 percent in community colleges; they were usually federally funded programs emphasizing a unified approach to recruitment, counseling, and financial aid, combined with carefully designed remedial efforts under the leadership of a full-time director. Special counseling programs for these new students increased from 61 percent to 72 percent, and remedial or developmental courses increased from 92 percent to 98 percent. Data indicated that the trend was toward offering courses and programs that were characterized by broader and more integrated approaches to serving the nontraditional student.

Between 1970 and 1977 there was an 80 to 95 percent increase among two-year colleges offering learning assistance and a 50 to 77 percent increase among four-year colleges; more special programs, courses, and services were found in community colleges than in comprehensive four-year colleges, but nearly 90 percent of U.S. colleges and universities provided remedial/developmental instruction (Roueche and Snow, 1977). By 1981 the number of preparatory courses offered in colleges had risen by 22 percent in public institutions and by 25 percent in private colleges and universities (Roueche and Clarke, 1981).

In 1984 we completed the first national study of its kind of college and university responses to low-achieving students. We surveyed all community, junior, and technical colleges, as well as all senior institutions, awarding traditional associate, baccalaureate, and graduate degrees. Of the 2,508 surveys mailed, 1,489 were returned and 1,452 were usable responses. Of that total, 160 institutions reported they had no basic skills programs, courses, or alternatives for low-achieving students; however, we noted that of those 160 institutions, several had been featured in professional articles describing their developmental efforts, and several of their faculty and staff had been quoted regarding their personal and institutional concerns about the growing national literacy problem and its effect on their own institutions. We could only speculate as to why these institutions chose to deny awareness of or institutional response to the problem, but the conflicting reports did answer the major research question—few institutions were escaping the literacy problem (Roueche, Baker, and Roueche, 1984).

As the number of nontraditional students grew, there was a simultaneous decline in SAT scores of high school graduates; between 1972 and 1979 the verbal SAT scores of college freshmen declined 40 points and math SAT scores declined 18 points (Trow, 1983). In that same study, it was discovered that the majority of freshmen entering community colleges were reading below the eighth grade level, a decline of at least two grade levels since 1971. In 1972 the Learning Assistance Center at Stanford University was established with the objective of meeting the needs of underprepared students, and by 1976, 50 percent of the freshmen were receiving assistance in reading and study skills (Maxwell, 1979).

In 1984 between 30 and 40 percent of entering freshmen in two-year colleges were reading below a seventh grade reading level, and the forecast was that "there is little hope that they will show any noticeable improvement for the next two decades" (Roueche, Baker, and Roueche, 1984, preface). In a 1984 survey by Lederman, Ribaudo, and Ryzewic (1985) of 1,297 U.S. colleges and universities, 85 percent of the four-year college faculty believed that freshmen had poor academic preparation, and 90 percent of the two-year college faculty felt the same. Yet, even as late as 1985, Hodgkinson was reporting that while the majority of colleges were offering academic support programs for underprepared students, the level of institutional commitment to these programs was unclear.

The National Center for Education Statistics (1986) reported that in fall 1985 one-fourth of all entering college freshmen were enrolled in preparatory courses in English, reading, or mathematics. In 1987 Abraham reported that 82 percent of all institutions and 92 percent of all public institutions were offering at least one preparatory course. In 1988 there were more than 2,500 learning assistance centers in American colleges and universities. A decline in basic skills had occurred at all levels of ability and socioeconomic classes, and it was obvious that the changes could not be attributed directly to the demographic characteristics among the entering students (Boylan, Bingham, and Cockman, 1988).

In 1988–89 the Southern Regional Education Board (SREB) surveyed all institutions of higher education in its 16-state region to identify a remedial/developmental profile of first-time freshmen and institutional practices in college-level remediation; 826 institutions were surveyed, and 606 responded (Abraham, 1991 and 1992, respectively). Findings from this survey reflect national trends, as indicated by the results from a similar survey conducted in a similar time frame by the National Center for Education Statistics. Remedial education was defined as any program, course, or activity designed for first-time entering freshmen who had basic deficiencies in any skills the institution deemed necessary to begin college-level work. The survey documented that over 90 percent of the public colleges and universities had remedial/developmental programs, and one in three first-time freshmen were enrolled in at least one remedial course; at two-year colleges this number reached 42 percent. On two-year campuses, more Hispanic students than Blacks were enrolled in remedial courses, and enrollment rates for Blacks and Hispanics were consistently one and one-half to two times those for White students (in sheer numbers, more White than Black students took remedial courses). Gender differences were small. More students needed remedial work in mathematics than in writing, and more needed remedial work in writing than in reading.

Of particular interest in the SREB findings was the discovery that of those six states that had mandated statewide assessment and placement programs, there were consistently higher reports of students needing remediation in all three basic skills areas. "While several factors might help explain these differences, including which institutions participated in the survey or the use of different placement standards, the presence or absence of statewide standards for admission and placement appears to be the most significant variable" (Abraham, 1991, pp. 5–6). The researchers proposed that higher numbers reported in those six states may signal that other states simply do not recognize the magnitude of their problem.

As compared to the same survey conducted four years prior, the trend in remedial enrollment was now directed toward increases in *all* institutions; among two-year colleges, the increase was 67 percent, the highest of any other institutional type. Institutions were asked to explain why they believed these increases had occurred; their answers by response rate were: (1) overall increase in enrollment, (2) more accurate assessment, and (3) change in placement policy.

Institutional practices among SREB colleges that responded to the 1989 survey included:

- Four-fifths of the colleges and universities had written policies to govern placement of academically underprepared students; 45 percent or more of all public institutions reported that they are guided by state or system policies.
- Almost 125 combinations of about 75 different tests in reading, writing, and mathematics were used to place students in either degree credit or remedial courses.
- Degree credit for remedial studies had been almost totally eliminated; most awarded institutional credit only.

- Three-fifths reported permitting simultaneous enrollment in remedial and regular college courses, with restrictions; one-fifth permitted it with no restrictions.
- About one-third had summer remedial course enrollment requirements; nearly 25 percent required summer enrollment as a condition of admission.
- The traditional academic department was the most frequent means of delivering remedial education; nearly one-third used separate divisions to offer remedial courses.
- Nearly one-third of all institutions that had remedial education reported that ongoing training was available for remedial instructors.
- More than 90 percent reported that remedial courses were supported by general institutional funds allocated through regular budgeting processes (Abraham, 1992, abstracted highlights from pp. 3–4).

In 1991 the National Center for Education Statistics published the findings of a Fast Response Survey System (FRSS) of colleges on remedial/developmental programs offered during fall 1989, conducted to provide information at the national level on the extent of remedial education and the characteristics of remedial programs; 473 institutions responded, for a weighted total of 2,874. The survey generally provided national estimates of institutions offering remedial courses; the reading, writing, and mathematics remedial courses offered; students enrolled in and passing remedial courses (included in this chapter under Evaluation of Remedial/Developmental Programs); and faculty teaching remedial courses. In addition, it provided information on the characteristics of these courses and programs and the retention and baccalaureate graduation rates for students who enrolled in remedial courses (included in this chapter under program evaluation). This study was the first conducted since the 1983-84 FRSS survey on the same topic. (Racial/ethnic breakdowns were not reported because the percentage of institutions that maintained and provided these data was too low to provide any basis for a computation of national estimates.) Remedial studies, for the purposes of this study, were defined as any program, course, or other activity—in the area of reading, writing, or mathematics—for students lacking those skills necessary to perform college-level work at the level required by the institution and the activities were referred to throughout the questionnaire as "remedial/developmental." The highlights cited for this study were:

- Three out of four colleges and universities offered at least one remedial course in fall 1989.
- Sixty-eight percent offered mathematics, 65 percent writing, and 58 percent reading.

- Both in institutions with a predominantly minority student body (less than 50 percent White) and institutions with a predominantly nonminority student body (greater than or equal to 50 percent White), 74 percent of the institutions offered at least one remedial course.
- At least one remedial course was offered in 91 percent of public colleges, 90 percent of two-year colleges, 64 percent of four-year colleges, and 58 percent of private colleges.
- On average, colleges with remedial courses provided two different courses in a given remedial subject; on average, 15 people per college taught one or more remedial courses in fall 1989.
- Thirty percent of all college freshmen took at least one remedial course in fall 1989. Twenty-one percent took mathematics, 16 percent writing, and 13 percent reading.
- At institutions with a predominantly minority student body, 55 percent of freshmen enrolled in at least one remedial course. At institutions with a predominantly nonminority student body, 27 percent of freshmen enrolled in at least one remedial course.
- Approximately 17 percent of institutions were unable to provide enrollment data for freshmen in remedial courses. About 30 percent of institutions that provided remedial course enrollment data were unable to provide racial/ethnic breakdowns.
- About 20 percent of colleges offering remedial education had a separate remedial department or division; 98 percent offered at least one support service, such as peer tutoring and counseling; and 97 percent conducted at least one evaluation of remedial programs, such as reviewing student completion rates in remedial courses.
- Approximately 20 percent of colleges awarded degree credit for remedial courses. About two-thirds awarded institutional credit, which counted in determining full-time status but not toward degree completion. One-tenth awarded no credit at all.
- Remedial courses were required for students not meeting institutional standards, with 68 percent of colleges offering remedial writing, 63 percent offering remedial mathematics, and 54 percent offering remedial reading.
- About 90 percent of institutions providing remedial courses used placement tests to select participants; remedial-course exit skills were based on regular academic-course entry skills by 86 percent of institutions for remedial mathematics courses, by 81 percent for remedial writing courses, and by 70 percent for remedial reading courses.
- One-third of colleges providing remedial education allowed students to take any regular academic courses while taking remedial

courses; in only 2 percent of colleges could students take no regular academic courses while taking remedial courses.

• Forty percent of colleges providing remedial courses were not engaged in any activities to reduce the need for remedial education. Fifty-four percent communicated with high schools about skills needed for college work, and 19 percent participated in or organized workshops for high school faculty.

• Forty-seven percent of institutions were unable to provide retention rates to the second year for freshman who had enrolled in at least one remedial course, and approximately 66 percent of institutions were unable to provide these rates by race/ethnicity.

• Institutions offering one or more remedial courses in reading, writing, or mathematics decreased from 82 percent in 1983–84 to 74 percent in 1989–90 (National Center for Education Statistics, 1991a, pp. iii–iv).

What are the actual national trends regarding numbers of students entering institutions of higher education needing some remediation? Because public and private four-year colleges and universities have more restrictive admissions policies, and because most colleges and universities define remediation and identify students for these courses along different dimensions, there can be only speculation about rather broad trends based on national and some regional studies, such as the SREB survey in 1989. But since the early 1970s, forecasts as to students entering community colleges in some need of academic remediation have included percentages as low as 25 (Cohen, 1973) and as high as 70 (Gold, 1977; Barshis, 1982). In 1979 Lombardi predicted that at least 50 percent of entering students will need some remediation in the 1980s; Roueche (1982) noted that even such an unconscionable prediction might be too low. In the late 1980s available data from national and large regional studies indicated that the forecasts had not been unrealistic: as late as 1989 between 30 and 32 percent of all entering college freshmen took at least one remedial course; in institutions with a majority of minority students, the rate was as high as 55 percent; in two-year colleges the rate was as high as 42 percent.

Trends in remedial/developmental education provide us with some measures of how far we have yet to go. A 1986 Texas study, *A Generation of Failure*, by the Committee on Testing, reported that of the 110,000 freshmen students who entered Texas public colleges and universities each year, 30,000 could not read or write at levels needed to perform successfully in those institutions. The study reported that 40 percent of entering freshmen students appear to need remedial courses. Many of them, however, complete college without much improvement. Sadly, from 1984 to 1986, of the approximately 30,000 students in Texas four-year colleges and universities who took the pre-professional skills test to qualify for admission to teacher education programs (usually after 60 hours of college work), 30 percent failed; and of those who took the test more than once, approximately one-half continued to fail.

SREB has set as one of its educational goals for the year 2000 that four out of every five students in SREB states will enter college prepared for college-level work. With more than one-third of their students presently entering higher education in need of remediation, the numbers must effectively be reduced by one-half to achieve that goal. While changes in educational systems are attacking the problem, the year 2000 appears to be too near for such an accomplishment to be realized. Indications are that the forecasts cannot even hint at a decrease in remedial/developmental efforts within the foreseeable future, unless of course there are widespread decisions to weaken the pull of historical antecedents of tightened admissions policies.

Remedial or Developmental: Questions of Terminology

Early on, *remedial* generally referred to those college courses designed to bring students to academic skill levels needed to successfully negotiate beginning college-level work. The programs were indeed designed to remediate, i.e., to strengthen that which had been diagnosed as weak or was not up to some accepted standard. Cross argued that in the 1970s we were still concentrating on trying to make nontraditional students, or "New Students," into traditional students so that we could serve them in our traditional educational ways. We were most concerned about creating access models to education to make these new students eligible to participate in *traditional* higher education, and remedial courses were designed to remove "academic" deficiencies (Cross, 1974). But with the increasing numbers of at-risk students who did not bring the more traditional focus to their goals and who had such a wide array of life experiences, colleges began to recognize that the remedial function, as it was defined and implemented, was too narrow.

By the late 1960s and early 1970s, it was clear that college responses to the at-risk student were in evolution. Research and evaluation began to challenge the earlier, more simplistic notions that single, usually disjointed remedial courses designed to improve specific basic skills were the best approaches to addressing at-risk students' academic problems. It was proposed that remediating academic deficiencies, as was the goal in the first documented remedial programs, was more likely to be successful when the goals and objectives of the college and student were more focused and limited and all other life experiences were more or less equal. Moreover, questions about the impossibility of the task suggested that perhaps these issues were more complex than any strategies yet devised to address them. The at-risk student was bringing a plethora of problems to the classroom that called for a total, interconnected program of basic academic skill and human skill development. The earlier courses and programs were too disjointed, and their ties to other programs, courses, and experiences were too blurred (Roueche, 1968; Cross, 1974).

Also, by the late 1960s and early 1970s, the term *remedial* had assumed severely negative connotations—primarily as a result of links with poorly performing, low-status programs; further indications were that affixing the term to programs and students on college campuses was negatively prejudicial (Roueche and Pitman, 1973; Roueche and Snow, 1977). In 1985 Harvard University required a remedial writing course for those students whose placement test scores indicated a skill deficiency. The resentment felt by faculty and by students required to take it made its way to the student newspaper; however, changing the course title from "Basic Writing" to "Introduction to Expository Writing" improved atittudes, eliminated questions of its appropriateness to the curriculum, and attracted some students who chose to take it voluntarily (Armstrong, 1988). Many educators moved away from using the term to describe their courses and programs, but the term did not disappear altogether from course and program titles or from general program descriptions. And while a variety of titles were assigned to the newly developing programs—titles chosen, apparently, to better describe what the institution believed to be the mission and goal of the effort (e.g., "Basic Studies," "Guided Studies," "Advancement Studies," and the like)—the literature continued to refer to such courses and programs in such generic terms as *remedial*, but even more frequently *developmental*, *developmental education*, or *remedial/developmental education*.

Thus, over the years, although the terms *developmental* and *remedial* have been used almost interchangeably, researchers have attempted to draw some subtle distinctions and differences in order to better define what the terms actually represent on college campuses. One definition assigned the term *remedial* to efforts designed to strengthen basic skill deficiencies in order to prepare a student to enter a program of work for which he was not currently prepared, and the term *developmental* to a broader development of skills and attitudes that were not necessarily designed to make the student eligible for a particular program of study (Roueche, 1968). Cross proposed that a more useful distinction between the terms could be made by identifying the goal or purpose of the program:

> If the purpose of the program is to overcome *academic deficiencies*, I would term the program remedial, in the standard dictionary sense in which remediation is concerned with correcting weaknesses. If, however, the purpose of the program is to develop the diverse talents of students, whether academic or not, I would

term the program developmental. Its mission is to give attention to the fullest possible development of talent and to develop strengths as well as to correct weaknesses (1976, p. 31).

Researchers have cited such cognitive theorists as Piaget and Bruner, and such developmental theorists as Kohlberg and Perry, as providing the foundation upon which the major tenets of developmental education were constructed. "The notion of *developmental sequence* is the kingpin of developmental theory...A goal of education is to stimulate the individual to move to the next stage in the sequence" (Cross, 1976, p. 158). Others cited the strength of the "whole person" approach in psychotherapy, developed by Carl Rogers (1961), in convincing proponents that only by addressing the "whole" student could significant educational experiences be achieved by underprepared students (Barshis and Guskey, 1983). But while the theoretical support for a movement toward developmental education and, conversely, away from remedial education as it was traditionally offered, was drawn rather clearly in the language of the authorities on cognition and development and psychotherapy, these distinctions were not so clearly drawn by either program developers or faculty on college campuses. Simply speaking, the movement from the narrower view of remedial to the broader view of developmental—that is, from a narrow focus on academic skills to a broader view of strengthening academic and human skill weaknesses and talents—was a series of responses to the educational realities of the complex dimensions of at-risk students. Current usage of these terms, *remedial* and *developmental*, in the literature and in research reflects a melding, if not a blurring, of their former distinctions and their histories; many studies merely report that they will use the two terms interchangeably, or if they define them, they always refer to "institutional definitions." The terms may have mellowed with age as the issues surrounding evolution of the courses and programs become hazier and as the efforts to which they refer become commonly identified with the larger issue of how best to serve the at-risk student.

However, because basic skills were the most visible and appeared to be the most pressing problems for the first underprepared students that higher education encountered, it is understandable that this would be the arena where the battle to improve their performance in college would begin. Their academic problems were approached from a traditional instructional mindset and with the strategies and tools that were currently at hand—in hindsight, too simplistic an attack.

Evaluation of Remedial/Developmental Programs

Early efforts to evaluate remedial courses reported similarly favorable results. Entwisle (1960) concluded from her review of research

from the 1940s and 1950s that "uniformly favorable results...are strik-
ing, when one considers the wide variation in the kind of course leading
to improvement, and the disparate kinds of students enrolled" (p. 250).
Yet Cross (1976) identified major research flaws in the studies Entwisle
reviewed that would have rendered the findings questionable: poorly
formulated criteria for success, naive research designs, weak data interpretations and implications for improvement, and lack of adequate control groups. For example, she explained that while it was common for
investigators to report that the students who signed up for the study
skills courses (that were voluntary and carried no college credit) made
better grades than those students who were equally unprepared and did
not take the study skills course, they did not factor in the concept of student motivation, which has been determined to be, according to numbers of researchers (for example, Lesnik, 1972; Roueche, 1973), one of
the most influential factors in student success. Simply put, students who
are motivated to do well will make more effort to seek help than those
who are less motivated to do so. Finally, she identified the use of standardized reading tests to measure improvement from pre-test to post-
test. Without adequate control groups and using a pre-test and post-test
design, the investigators would frequently cite any gains by initial low
scorers as directly attributable to the effects of the remedial course. All
in all, Cross concluded, the research of the 1940s and 1950s may well
have been "half-hearted," given the prevailing lack of any real concern
about remediation, the perception that the courses and programs were
only services for the student, and the lack of seriousness around the
notion that the programs needed to be held accountable for meeting
their objectives (1976).

In his first national study of remedial education programs,
Roueche (1968) documented that the results were devastating to educators who had touted remedial education programs as significant forward movements in embracing this new segment of the population. He
concluded:

> There is a paucity of research on the efficacy of remedial pro-
> grams in the junior college. Indeed, with few exceptions, com-
> munity colleges neither describe nor evaluate their endeavors in
> this critical area. Available research will not support the con-
> tention that junior colleges offer programs that in fact remedy
> student deficiencies. Programs are certainly offered, but the
> entire issue of remedying deficiencies has not been sufficiently
> researched to date (p. 47).

He further discovered that few students who were initially placed in a
remedial course ever completed the class requirements, and as many as

90 percent failed or withdrew from these courses. Sometimes the courses were required, but the results were disastrous. The critics then turned to calling the open-door admissions policy a "revolving-door" policy—these early programs were poorly conceived, poorly designed, and even more poorly implemented. In 1968 evidence documented that the early remedial programs were mostly watered-down versions of regular college courses. There was no doubt that while millions of dollars were being expended annually on these programs, there was, with very few exceptions, little research to evaluate the effectiveness of either the programs or the instructors. In fact, Roueche finally concluded that "[i]ntuition rather than research appears to be the basis for most remedial programs" (1968, p. 42). The overwhelming conclusions led him to ask two critical questions: "Can a two-year college actually remedy student deficiencies?" and "Can a community college remedial course rightfully expect to accomplish in one or two semesters what public schools have failed to accomplish in 12 years?" (Roueche, 1968, pp. 47–48).

Serious evaluation of these programs in the 1960s was complicated further by the open admissions and civil rights issues, redirecting the questions from whether the courses were meeting their objectives to whether the more diverse student population could successfully negotiate college work. Jensen, in an unforgettable article in the November 1969 *Harvard Educational Review*, stated that Blacks were innately less able than Whites to learn. Educators involved in remedial education during this decade looked to defend the programs and issue statements about their successes (even without evaluative data) in an effort to challenge such accusations as those expressed by Jensen and by others not so publicly voiced. The emotionally charged times may well have mitigated against more serious evaluation efforts. The challenge to the success of both the programs and the institutions appeared overwhelming during a time in which it was too difficult even to hint that both the programs and the institutions could not do the job that they had set out to do (as cited in Cross, 1976). Even by 1973 Roueche observed the possibility that "community college leaders deliberately did not evaluate remedial programs because they knew beforehand how disastrous results of such an evaluation might be" (p. 26).

Yet by the mid-1970s, even as Cross was reporting that the emotions of the 1960s created by the exaggerated links between remediation and ethnic minorities apparently had subsided and that there had been a shift to the view that *all* students were involved in the problem, institutions still were slow to initiate evaluation processes. Unfortunately, most of the colleges in 1977 could not document evidence of student success in their remedial programs. They could not report how many students ever completed a required remedial program, nor did they know how many of these students persisted from the programs into regular college courses and whether they were successful there. In the majority of the institutions that were studied in 1977, evaluation was nonexistent. As a result of this inability or unwillingness to document results, researchers continued to lament that "remedial education has been and continues to be one of the least successful college programs in achieving its goal" (Lombardi, 1979, p. 67).

In the 1984 survey of college responses to low-achieving students in all institutions of American higher education, evaluation data furnished by the majority of institutions were neither consistent nor useful (Roueche, Baker, and Roueche, 1984). Institutions were asked to provide correct percentages to the categories of entering students assigned to basic skills instruction, students completing successfully after one semester/quarter, original group retained for second semester/quarter, original group after two semesters/quarters, and original group for third semester/quarter. What appeared to be an easy question at the outset was not so when the responses were returned. The percentages requested did not require program directors or faculty to have conducted longitudinal studies outside their own areas; rather they simply required standard in-house or in-department records. Gross percentages and/or identical percentages in every category, among other responses, indicated widespread inattention to such a basic evaluation question as "How are we doing in our own programs?"

In 1983 Boylan reviewed over 60 individual efforts to evaluate the success of program activities and determined that developmental programs tended to improve student GPA and short-term persistence. Kulik, Kulik, and Schwalb (1982) looked at reports from more than 300 programs and also concluded that participation in developmental programs was associated with improved GPA and increased short-term persistence. However, little information had been accumulated on the effects of developmental programs on cumulative GPA, long-term retention, or subsequent student performance in regular college courses.

In the 1992 SREB survey, less than half of the responding institutions were able to, or chose to, report retention rates for remedial and nonremedial students. The median percent of students retained to start a second year was 55 percent for remedial and 65 percent for nonremedial students (Abraham, 1992, p. 4).

The National Center for Education Statistics, in its Fast Response Survey System, found:

- Remedial courses were passed by 77 percent of those taking remedial reading, 73 percent taking remedial writing, and 67 percent taking remedial mathematics.
- Approximately one-fourth of institutions were unable to provide passing rates for freshmen in remedial courses, and about one-half were unable to provide passing rates by racial/ethnic breakdowns.

- Eighty-one percent of colleges did not maintain baccalaureate degree graduation rates for entering freshmen who enrolled in at least one remedial course, and 87 percent did not maintain graduation rates by racial/ethnic groups for these students (1991a, iii, iv).

Recognized Successful Programs

From a synthesis of 30 years of literature on remedial/developmental education, Cross drew five major conclusions and stated them as recommendations for designing effective programs (see 1976, pp. 42–45 for fuller discussion):

1. Skills training must be integrated into the other college experiences of the student. We have known for years that 'transfer of training' does not take place automatically.
2. Cognitive skills training must be integrated with the social and emotional development of the student...In short, academic achievement or lack of it is not a purely cognitive matter.
3. Staff working with remedial students should be selected for their interest and commitment as well as for their knowledge about learning problems.
4. Degree credit should be granted for remedial classes. Initially at least, the major 'reward' that education has to offer these students is college credit.
5. Remediation should be approached with flexibility and open-mindedness. There is still much that we do not know. We do not even know which skills developed to what level are important to academic survival...We do know that self-confidence is a major ingredient of success.

In 1973 Roueche and Kirk concluded that indeed community colleges could effectively serve nontraditional, high-risk students. They cited several common denominators, or components of success, of the five programs that they studied in that investigation (see pp. 62–79 in Roueche and Kirk, 1973, for a fuller explanation). These programs documented good student persistence to program completion and solid evidence that students were learning to read, write, figure, and study well enough to enter and succeed in college programs. They employed only faculty who volunteered to teach these courses, and they involved students by immersing them in the process—that is, students were spending most of their time in the activities of reading, writing, and figuring. Results were significant in documenting that low-achieving adults possessed the abilities and the motivation to be truly literate, but simply had never been taught before.

In 1977 Roueche and Snow identified successful programs in both community college and university settings; 139 community colleges and 134 senior colleges were surveyed. These colleges had developed program goals that were tied to students' learning successes, had written statements to students about their belief that students "could learn," and had indicated that they were assessing academic skills of all entering students to place them properly. Successful colleges had learned that the open-door admissions policy should not imply nor infer that students had open access to college-level courses.

In 1982 Noel, Levitz, and Kaufmann reported that while approaches of successful developmental programs varied from college to college, there were some basic requirements for establishing a strong developmental effort: administrative support and stable funding; adequate facilities; ongoing assessment of learners; an atmosphere conducive to adult learning; and a competent, committed, and dedicated staff—that is, faculty and other personnel who had a genuine concern for the success of their students and who enjoyed their work.

Successful programs, as identified by responses to the 1984 national survey conducted by The University of Texas (those programs reporting 50 percent or better retention in developmental courses), appeared to have at least 11 common elements:

1. *Strong administrative support.* Board policy manuals, college catalogs, and student handbooks carried written statements as to institutionally shared responsibility for student success, which translated into student assessment and placement in appropriate courses.

2. *Mandatory counseling and placement.* Students were tested for basic skill development and then were enrolled in courses appropriate to the outcomes of that assessment and not allowed to enroll in courses where those skills are required until they are developed to appropriate collegiate levels. Many colleges required the testing and subsequent placement as conditions for enrollment and successful completion before enrolling in other courses.

3. *Structured courses.* The size of the institution was a major factor in determining the programmatic structure of the effort—where the developmental courses were housed—but the courses met regularly, and there was careful monitoring of student attendance and progress.

4. *Award of credit.* Early on, the issue was controversial, but without exception the courses were awarded transcript credit, although institutions differed as to whether the credit was elective and counted toward specific degrees or was transcript credit only.

5. *Flexible completion strategies.* Students were allowed to complete the prescribed work in the number of semesters required to earn a satisfactory grade. Persistence without observable and profitable progress was met with career alternatives and academic counseling.

6. *Multiple learning systems.* From an analysis of their written assessment, students were engaged in learning activities drawn from performance-based objectives, using self-paced modules of instruction, engaging group instruction, and using pre- and post-tests to indicate sequential movement through work. Instructional strategies were varied for meeting the diverse student interests and learning styles.

7. *Volunteer instructors.* Only those who volunteered to teach basic skills, usually after meeting predetermined curricular and instructional criteria, chose to accept the special demands that are made on faculty by at-risk students.

8. *Use of peer tutors.* Usually selected by performance criteria, further trained to work with at-risk students, and regularly evaluated, peer tutors increased the individual contact during class sessions and out-of-class time blocks and increased the number of intervention strategies required to monitor at-risk students' attendance and progress.

9. *Monitoring of student behaviors.* Excessive absences, failure to produce assigned work, and failure to produce acceptable levels of work were intervention signals. Intervention strategies included calling absent students, bringing them up to date on assignments, and providing tutoring or other academic services whenever necessary.

10. *Interfacing with subsequent courses.* The faculty of basic skills courses conducted modified needs assessments to determine the requirements of generic and specific-discipline courses and used the results to design their own course content and learning strategies. They designed exit criteria that reflected these assessment demands for successful completion of their own and of the next level of courses.

11. *Program evaluation.* Improving data collection procedures for program evaluation and for developing improved retention strategies was recognized as a priority by administrators and teachers of these successful programs. Further, there were plans to improve pre-assessment strategies for identifying low-achieving students and improving the intervention strategies during the first months and semesters, as well as to refine exit interviews for determing problem areas as yet unidentified (Roueche, Baker, and Roueche, 1984).

The Faculty

The growing numbers of at-risk students, often 50 percent of the freshman class, challenge the resources and commitment of the educational process, and most particularly the commitment of the faculty. Faculty currently are similar in demographic composition to earlier periods, except that they are growing older and have more teaching experience. Full-time faculty members account for less than half the positions and teach three-fourths of the courses, while part-time faculty members have steadily increased in numbers and in involvement with college and professional issues and interests.

Historically, faculty were hired from various disciplines from other colleges and universities, from business and industry, and frequently from local high schools. For some faculty coming directly from master's and doctoral degrees who had looked forward to careers in academia with some emphasis on research, the community college clearly would offer some professional disappointments with its emphasis on classroom teaching and with its expanded mission to serve the academically underprepared. Slowly, over the years, more graduate courses and programs in community college teaching and administration have been developed; some community colleges encourage and/or require that staff development include some of this training. These graduate experiences and individual institutional staff development programs are preparing more and more professionals who may better understand the mission and be more prepared for their experiences.

In 1966 Bossone found that 55 percent of the instructors who taught remedial English in California public junior colleges had two years or less teaching experience; many did not indicate any knowledge or understanding of the basic objectives of the remedial courses they taught and believed their "primary objective" was to bring the student up to the level of the college course (p. 14). Kipps (1966), too, discovered that the most inexperienced instructor was the one most often found in the remedial classroom in basic arithmetic courses. In 1968 Roueche documented that in departments where remediation was part of the department's function, instructors typically were assigned at least one remedial course as part of their regular teaching load. The "pecking order" in most departments, based almost entirely on seniority and institutional tenure, gave tenured instructors first choice in teaching the advanced or specialized courses and left less-experienced and untenured instructors assigned to the remaining classes. There appeared to be "a real gap between what the junior college instructor views his role and function to be and what his role and function must be if the community/junior college is to make good on its promise of providing educational opportunity for all" (Roueche, 1968, p. 18).

Among the recommendations from the first national study of remedial programs in 1968 was this admonition: Because teacher attitudes are probably related to student achievement, no teacher should be arbitrarily assigned to teach a remedial class if he or she would rather not teach that class, nor should any teacher be assigned who is only mildly interested in doing so; uninterested teachers cannot be expected to motivate students who are typically characterized by a lack of motivation (Roueche, p. 51). Moore, in 1971, reported that many faculty believed the effects of cultural deprivation to be irreversible.

In 1976 Cross concluded that "[s]taff working with remedial students should be selected for their interest and commitment as well as for their knowledge about learning problems" (p. 43). Further, she noted that "academic achievement or lack of it is not a purely cognitive matter. The faculty member who claims that his or her responsibility is limited to the 'mind' of the student should not be working with New Students. Indeed, such a parochial view of the teaching function is so unrealistic in the light of everything we know about human learning that it is hard to defend even for highly motivated graduate students" (pp. 42–43).

In 1978 Brown found that community college faculty attitudes toward disadvantaged students—students enrolled in developmental coursework—differed significantly from attitudes toward the general student population. While the faculty-at-large had negative attitudes toward disadvantaged students, female instructors and developmental course instructors had significantly more positive attitudes toward these students.

In 1980 London, in a community college case study, reported that there was a high degree of faculty ambivalence toward the community college mission—translated, to help at-risk students. Faculty generally believed that student weaknesses could be attributed to deficiencies in character, mind, or social background, and that students should be entirely responsible for their own success or failure.

Roueche and Mink (1980) called for instructors to change their attitudes toward the curriculum and students, to move from a subject orientation to a student orientation. The instructor's responsibility extended to motivating the student by specifically emphasizing the functional use of knowledge. Roueche and Mink noted that instructors were the key in this process because they controlled the content of the curriculum and the way it was presented, and that the selection of content and its presentation reflected their own attitudes toward their students. Moore and Carpenter (1985) also called attention to the need for a change of faculty attitudes. They observed that while there were increasing numbers and diversity of underprepared students on campus, "There are little data to suggest that those who deliver instructional services will be able to successfully accommodate this reality. Most of what we believe to be truly innovative have little to do with one particular teaching method or another, but with attitude. Will academic personnel voluntarily change their attitudes or, at least, some of their practices with regard to who is qualified to teach or be their colleague, which students deserve and are eligible for or entitled to their services, and which activity—teaching, research, or service—will receive priority?" (p. 106).

By 1989, reporting on the general characteristics of community college faculty, Keim found that most considered themselves to be very effective instructors, were satisfied with their jobs, and intended to remain in their current positions. While the proportion of part-time faculty has increased and full-time faculty members have become older, apparently job satisfaction has not diminished. Data from the 1989 national survey of instructors by the Carnegie Foundation for the Advancement of Teaching (1990) indicated that faculty at community colleges were predominantly interested in teaching, not in research; moreover, they felt that teaching effectiveness should be the primary basis for promotion. In addition, they generally assigned more importance to shaping student values than did their four-year college counterparts. The survey indicated that 47 percent showed more enthusiasm about their work than when they first began teaching, and only 38 percent reported that their job was a source of stress in their lives.

There is much about the continuing challenges of addressing the needs of a diverse and often underprepared student body to keep alive discussions and debates about faculty roles and responsibilities. Perhaps this reminder of the critical role that the individual faculty member plays in affecting the outcome of any endeavor should remain at the heart of these discussions: "25 percent of the students in a class will fail if the teacher thinks they should, no matter what the program is" (Canfield, 1967, p. 19).

Some Perspectives on the Absence of Drawbridges and Moats

The history we have sketched has seen the weakening of both faculty and student expectation about what counts as rigorous academic work. Intellectual activity became debased and trivialized, reduced to skills, information, or personal expression—for students who look to education as their chief hope of advancement. The remedial and developmental practices that now largely constitute the academic culture of community colleges are far too weak to elicit the powerful transformations needed to really make a difference in students' prospects (McGrath and Spear, 1991, p. 54).

Over time there have been disheartening signs and ample criticism that community colleges have not planned well enough or implemented institutional programs strong enough to manage the great impact that diversity can have on access and opportunity.

In 1979 the National Institute of Education provided funding for Arizona State University and The University of Texas at Austin to conduct in-depth longitudinal investigations of literacy development activities in selected Arizona and Texas community colleges. Of importance here is that these parallel university research studies were looking at literacy strategies in *all* community college programs and courses, not just those in required remedial curricula. The studies were conducted independently of each other, but the major findings were remarkably similar. Both found that students would be expected to read, write, and figure more in remedial courses than they would ever be required in regular community college courses. In sum, the two studies documented that students in American community colleges are rarely expected to demonstrate literacy skills that are normally associated with college-level courses and programs (Roueche and Comstock, 1981; Richardson and Martens, 1982). Many of the students in these studies never purchased the required textbook or lab manual for a particular course or program because they had discovered that reading and comprehending those materials were not necessary for successful course completion. Many of the instructors never mentioned the textbook name; many of them never made reading assignments in the text. Much of the teaching was regurgitative at best; teachers would give orally or in one- and two-page handouts the bits of information that students would be expected to memorize and feed back on the next examination. The most prevalent teaching and evaluation procedures were at the lowest level of cognitive development, rarely requiring students to do more than recollect and produce such fragmented, disjointed pieces of information.

The joint finding that teachers in community colleges rarely talk to each other about the literacy requirements of their individual courses and programs was particularly discouraging. For example, the verbal requirements in courses like accounting, science, electronics, automotive mechanics, nursing, and various technology programs were among the most demanding and difficult in the college curriculum, usually requiring an entry-level reading ability of at least grade 12 or higher. Researchers found that the required math and English courses were typically taught in isolation from the regular college curriculum, most frequently taught as "ends" in themselves. Many of the basic skills instructors were surprised to learn how demanding the verbal skills in the technical and vocational courses were; in effect, the skills needed by career students were not being taught in required literacy development courses, and the skills being taught were in slight, if any, demand in other college courses. Finally, the instructional localization of basic skills—i.e., reading, writing, and math—encouraged other college instructors and administrators to pay little attention to or ignore them altogether. Both studies observed that most of the instructors lacked training in basic instructional methods and learning theory or in strategies in teaching nontraditional and adult populations. Therefore, the literacy problems that the more nontraditional students brought to the classroom created instructional problems with which most instructors were unprepared to deal. Most of the faculty finally ignored such needs and required the mastery of only very low-level cognitive skills—for example, memorizing rules of grammar or mathematics. The University of Texas study concluded by suggesting that colleges should not talk about *how* to teach without first deciding *what* is being taught, *why*, and to *whom* (Roueche and Comstock, 1981).

In 1987 *Access and Excellence* (Roueche and Baker) documented the success of Miami-Dade Community College and its Systems for Success model that turned a college from protecting and continuing the status quo toward organizationally scrutinizing reality and admitting that things were not at all as they should have been. In 1978, after a three-year study and investigation of college policies and procedures, the college began instituting reforms to accommodate both the open door and high academic standards: it put in place a directive program that included assessment after admission, a required general education core, and standards of academic progress that students must meet in order to remain in good standing in the college. It increased feedback to all students and support for those who needed assistance. The program relied heavily on computer technology at all of its levels. After the three-year study and three years of interaction with community and staff, referred to by at least one staff member as "the war," changes were in place—the faculty and staff at Miami-Dade believed education simply had to be better.

By 1985 the college had data indicating that the programs were a success. The reform began with the acknowledgment that the education system in general as well as the curricula at Miami-Dade Community College did not match the needs of society, that the very nature of work was changing and the college would not survive without a major reform process. Committed to the concept of open access, President Robert McCabe realized that the serious outcomes of open access reflected a devaluation of students by the institution. With possibly the greatest student diversity of any community college in the world—the largest number of foreign nations represented of any community college and more minority students than any other college in Florida—Miami-Dade's decision to meet the needs and to identify and correct the academic deficiencies of its learners was more serious and complex than perhaps at any other college. The four decisions made before beginning the reform efforts continue to be the hallmarks of the movement: 1) "open access had to be maintained; 2) if access were to be achieved, the college had to be much more directive; 3) the college had to be more supportive; and, finally, 4) high academic standards had to be maintained. These are the four principles upon which the success of the reforms at Miami-Dade rests" (1987, pp. 187–188).

After publication of *Access and Excellence*, Zwerling (author of *Second Best*, perhaps one of the most critical indictments of the community college movement) visited the four campuses of Miami-Dade Community College to gather impressions, essentially, about what Miami-Dade said about itself and what other researchers and reporters had said about it. After his visit, he concluded:

> My basic views about the community college movement had not shifted. Yes, Miami-Dade and a few outposts of excellence did exist about the country, but from my research and visits to dozens of other two-year colleges I was still convinced that most places were in fact too often *mis*-serving their students' potential. I came finally to feel, ironically, the Miami-Dade experience had reinforced my view that something *was* fundamentally wrong at our urban two-year colleges—especially if a place as large and diverse as Miami was able to accomplish so much. It seemed essential that what it had learned and what it could teach should be even more widely known. There was still certainly enough for despair, but there was also more reason to hope (1988, p. 23).

Conclusion

So what is this future to which we have returned? Larger numbers of remedial/developmental, at-risk students are entering colleges and universities each year; one-third to one-half of all newly enrolling students meet the standard definitions of at-risk. Institutions of higher education fall along a continuum of preparedness to meet the needs and expectations of these students. They are accepted into the institutions, pay their money or receive financial aid, and still receive some questionable services. Teaching basic skills at this level is still viewed by many educators, legislators, and taxpayers as a highly questionable endeavor; they believe that these skills should have been developed at more appropriate levels of education—specifically, in elementary and secondary schools. The basic skills development courses are often viewed by students (and frequently by their parents) as unnecessary delays in getting on with college work, or as efforts by the college to cool out students who do not appear capable of meeting goals that they have set for themselves or that others have set for them. The students who are identified as at-risk are still the subjects of controversy in and out of these institutions. Currently it is a less heated controversy, perhaps as a result of the stark light of current American economic, education, and social problems in which it is bathed, but heated nonetheless.

The question, "Who *should* come to college?" has been answered more broadly over the years as social and economic problems have critically affected what happens in colleges and universities. Many educators, researchers, critics, and others would respond that the question has been partly answered with yet another: "Who *is* coming to college?" Institutions must be more focused and diligent in preparing to answer this second question in the face of an incredible diversity unlike any we have witnessed. The answer to the question, "Who *will be* coming to college?" will stretch community colleges beyond all known limits.

The 1992 Study

In our 1984 study of college responses to low-achieving students, we surveyed all American colleges and universities by institutional type. A questionnaire was sent to every "senior institution" listed by the American Council on Education and to all colleges listed in the 1981 *Community, Junior, and Technical College Directory* published by the American Association of Community Colleges. The intent of our investigation was to determine both the existence and the extent of the illiteracy problem faced by American colleges and universities. We described the various approaches institutions employed to develop academic skills of these students, and we identified and described common elements among courses and programs that sought to prepare students for college-level work.

A decade later we seek to provide a status report of current information about exemplary college responses to at-risk students. We use the term *at-risk* (rather than another from the wide array of terms currently used in the literature and research—underprepared, high-risk, developmental or remedial, new, and others) because it most closely describes the reality of today's students, who possess an assortment of academic, social, and economic problems that collectively mitigate against success in college. We approach this update from a historical perspective, then turn to focus on current literature and research, and simultaneously showcase elements of 12 programs recognized as successful in serving the needs of at-risk students.

We recognize that community colleges employ a variety of organizational and programmatic approaches to embracing and serving at-risk students. The programs identified and featured in this study have each been recognized formally by one or more of the following national organizations that look critically at programs for at-risk students and for student success at the community college level:

American College Personnel Association
American College Testing
College Personnel Association
National Association of Developmental Education
National Council on Student Development
The Noel-Levitz Retention Program Awards

Neither the organizations, nor we, hold them up as models per se, but rather as being successful at what they do. Having targeted them for our investigation, we sent a letter of inquiry to the director or co-directors of each program and invited them to participate in our study. [Note: Not all of the programs that had been identified as award-winning chose to participate in this study.] The colleges and their programs featured in this study are:

De Anza College
Cupertino, California
A STARTING POINT Minority Transfer Program

William Rainey Harper College
Palatine, Illinois
Athletic Academic Advising Program

Highland Community College
Highland, Kansas
The Academic Information Monitoring System

Illinois Central College
East Peoria, Illinois
The Basic Skills Testing Program

Miami-Dade Community College
Miami, Florida
The Black/Hispanic Student Opportunity Program

Middlesex Community College
Bedford, Massachusetts
The Freshman Seminar and Course Clusters Program

North Lake College
Irving, Texas
The Advantage Program

Richland College
Dallas, Texas
Developmental Studies Program

Santa Barbara City College
Santa Barbara, California
Transfer Achievement Program (TAP)

Santa Fe Community College
Santa Fe, New Mexico
Student Success Model

Suffolk Community College
Riverhead, New York
The Eastern Campus Retention Program

University of Toledo Community and Technical College (ComTech)
Toledo, Ohio
Developmental Skills Education Program

We asked each program director to respond to the following questions (and supply any other information deemed appropriate):

1. What were the initial goals and objectives for this program? (Describe the extent to which they have been achieved)
2. How long has the program been in place and how does it fit into the organization of your college (e.g., where is it housed, how is it directed)?
3. By what criteria are students identified for program admission (e.g., test scores, recruitment)? Once enrolled, how are they oriented to this program?
4. How are faculty selected for the program and what professional development activities support their training (e.g., mentoring, supplemental instruction)?
5. What do you consider to be the program's most successful features?
6. What instructional strategies being implemented in the program have proven critical to retention (e.g., individualized instruction, CAI)?
7. What evaluation criteria are used to assess program success (e.g., retention figures, student feedback)?
8. Describe the current outlook for the program's future (e.g., proposed changes in structure or design).

The programs are not featured as case studies or as separate units of investigation; rather, their responses to our guiding questions are woven into the fabric of the fuller discussion of where we are as we approach the twenty-first century in responding to at-risk students in community colleges.

Designing Programs to Work:

Shifting Paradigms for Changing Times

> *Aspirations and hopes usually translate into effort, and effort makes something better than what otherwise would have been—for individuals, groups, and the nation.*
> *—Adelman, 1992b*

In 1970 Swiss watchmakers invented the digital timepiece; yet they decided that it had a limited—if any—future. Japanese watchmakers, primarily Seiko, adopted the invention; today, the digital watch commands 70 percent of the wristwatch market worldwide. But this is not just another story of Japanese ingenuity and hustle—taking someone else's good idea and "capitalizing" on it. Rather, this is an illustration of a mindset that narrows one's view to accept only those ideas that fit within an existing, or traditional, model or paradigm. It illustrates the dangers inherent in believing that there are limited numbers and types of paths to success, or that past performance invariably predicts future behavior.

The growth and development of the community college has turned on its flexibility and openness to new ideas. It has prided itself on these differences that, among others, separate it from its four-year college and university counterparts. Moreover, it has been touted as the institution that can best accommodate paradigm shifts and changing times. And, it has been advised to maintain its institutional integrity, not by raising admission standards, but by defining quality in terms that are compatible with its mission of maintaining the open-door concept (McCabe and Skidmore, 1983).

Attitudes Toward the Notion of Second Chance

Our society values equal opportunity and freedom of choice; those values support, then, the notion of a second chance—that everyone has a right to work toward achieving some level of success and to keep working toward that achievement if at first he/she fails. Most of us were reared hearing our parents or teachers applaud the simple virtues of perseverance and tenacity: "If at first you don't suc-ceed, try, try again." Failure definitely was not regarded as a virtue. Yet, as a society, we accept and accommodate failure, such as divorce or bankruptcy, in almost any human endeavor; at the extreme, our legal system is on record for giving murderers a second chance by releasing them back into society before their full sentences have been served, giving them time off for good behavior in prison, and telling them that their "debt to society" has been paid. Although admittedly we have more difficulty accepting some of society's sec-ond chances than others, we appear to have the most difficult time accepting failure in the academic arena, at any level. Because failure there is described in terms of the individual's performance when compared to other individuals or groups, it is a more serious blow to the likelihood of future opportunities. Typically, an individual of perceived low ability has fewer options than one who may have "failed," for example, in an intimate human relationship or a com-plex business effort.

However, if for no other reason, the dire warnings of our chang-ing times have required that as professional educators we take a second look at what second chances in college mean to society and to the indi-vidual. In 1968 Roueche found it curious that while many extolled the virtue of the salvage function, few writers, educators, and/or researchers justified salvage in terms of the value to the "human" in the "human resource." As recently as 1990 AACC President Emeritus Ed Gleazer, offering for evidence a collection of current advertisements declaring industry's interest in supporting public schools in order to develop "raw materials" and publicizing educational conferences fea-turing themes of "building human capital," asked a large group of com-munity college presidents and trustees: How did we come to develop the concept that education's primary role is to shape human "raw materials" to the needs of American business? Why have we not advanced to the notion that education is a means to human liberation and freedom? (1990, p. 4). And Greene, at Teachers College of Columbia University, warned against offering educational options tied only to the needs of the "contemporary structure," offering only "spaces where children are spoken of as resources rather than as human beings, where 'economic competitiveness' and the demands of technology become the driving forces behind education, where there is a fiercely widening gap between the rich and the comfortable and the tragically, undeservedly poor" (Greene, 1990, p. 47).

In sum, the idea of a second chance is only as good as it is *genuine* (Sever and Inbar, 1990, p. 238)—that is, students realize actual opportu-nities that were closed or remote to them before. Critics have suggested that "one way of testing the openness and flexibility of a social system is by exploring its second-chance mechanisms," that perhaps they are "among the better indicators of mobility and equality in the system" (Inbar, 1990, p. 2).

Some of What We Know About College At-Risk Student Programs

Organization. Historically, programs for at-risk students were low status, low priority, and isolated on a college's organizational chart. As the demand for developmental services became more acute, these programs became more prominent. A 1973 study by Roueche and Kirk indicated that the more successful programs were organized as single divisions or departments of developmental or basic studies. Cross discovered that between 1970 and 1974 there was a 16 percent increase (from 20 percent to 36 percent) in the numbers of colleges establishing separate divisions or departments of developmental studies; the trend was moving "toward remediation or developmental efforts embedded in a total *program* that includes cognitive, social, and emotional components" (1976, p. 27).

By 1977 a national survey on developmental studies programs identified three major organizational plans: isolated developmental courses in disciplined curricula; an interdisciplinary group of instructors; and a division or department of developmental studies. Less common plans were a combination of the three types, core disciplinary courses in occupational and continuing education frameworks, decentralization of developmental/remedial courses to fit into a sequential design of the departmental offerings, and offers of tutoring and individual help to all students through a learning assistance center. Moreover, nearly 50 percent of the community and senior colleges surveyed in this study had established a total program of recruitment, counseling, instruction, and evaluation; and all components were administered by a single director (Roueche and Snow, 1977).

The issue of separateness becomes critical to the program's effectiveness only when it widens the gap between the developmental effort and the rest of the college (and/or when it is associated with the negative aura surrounding academic "tracking"). Community colleges are so tightly enmeshed in developmental education that no one faculty member or department can afford to see himself or itself as outside of the problem. The arguments to support putting developmental courses into every department or literacy components into every course have been made for years. Cohen (1979) notes that fewer than 10 percent of the students in any community college are enrolled in courses for which there is a prerequisite; therefore, students with varying levels of ability and development are scattered in large numbers across the majority of college departments. He warns against continuing to promote separate departments of developmental education in the face of a trend that threatens to make community colleges an academic community of introductory and developmental studies courses only (Cohen, 1983). Others argue that the overwhelming diversity of student abilities and preparation are best left to those who both choose to address them and have the support to provide the "big picture" array of services that developmental students require (Roueche and Kirk, 1973; Cross, 1976; Roueche and Snow, 1977; Roueche, Baker, and Roueche, 1984).

Studies of organizational designs for at-risk student programs suggest that no one model will serve every institution equally well. The complexities of geography, budget, students, and staff variables, among others, demand unique configurations. However, the various studies of more successful programs have identified a critical characteristic that they share: each of them has made efforts to be compatible with the total college mission (Roueche and Roueche, 1977). These programs clearly sought through collaboration and service to become a significant *part* of the institution.

Institutional Commitment. A 1972 survey of community college programs and priorities discovered that there was weak commitment, as reflected in the priorities reported by college presidents, either to the development of programs for disadvantaged students or to solving social, economic, or political problems in the college's service area (Bushnell and Zagaris, 1972, p. 68). Yet, a 1973 study of successful programs for such students concluded: "Administrative leadership may well be the most important factor in the design of programs for nontraditional students" (Roueche and Kirk, p. 75), that a common feature of all successful developmental programs committed to serving the at-risk student was institutional commitment. Moreover, it documented that presidents who were able to articulate the goals and objectives for these programs were most frequently identified as the individuals responsible for the idea of establishing initiatives for serving the at-risk student population. Furthermore, these presidents sold the idea to their trustees, and, ultimately, committed the institutional funds necessary for program support. The administration's belief and expectation that these programs were meeting critical student and institutional needs were central to the individual program's ultimate success.

But, obviously, commitment to a new idea at the top of the organization can be risky, even disastrous, for the president who does not have the support of the faculty and staff. As Gardner reported: "Custom cannot stand up to machine guns, but it can raise the cost to the leader of every move that violates its tenets" (1987, p. 10). For the idea to have a future, the president must sell it by convincing the faculty that what is now in place is inadequate and that the new idea, or proposed change, will be worth the time and effort involved in its implementation. The process by which commitment is garnered is central to its survival; faculty who participated in the decision-making process will be more loyal, feel more responsibility, and will more actively support organizational goals than those who did not participate. "A commitment-building, participative decision-making process can be the primary means for encouraging staff to accept the philosophy and values which undergird the concept of the open door, comprehensive community college" (Richardson and Rhodes, 1983, pp. 194–195). The literature abounds with descriptions of strategies for encouraging participation and, thereby, increasing the likelihood of acceptance; but whether they are informal and simple, or formal and complex, productive exchanges of ideas and decisions-in-progress must occur for commitment to be solid and long-lasting.

Moreover, these exchanges should involve the largest group of potential supporters and transcend the greatest number of discipline and program barriers as possible. When Zwerling investigated Miami-Dade Community College's recognition as the "number one" community college in America, he discovered a faculty that talked about the "culture of change" at their colleges, but had little to say about their own role in shaping the changes that they believed had "kept us alive." Moreover, they did not identify administrative leadership as singularly responsible for those changes: "Some things come down, but they can go up, too" (1988, p. 19). He found it remarkable that "virtually all felt they had merely bent in the wind or responded to the inevitable" (p. 19). They were living in an environment where reform was patient and slow (taking years to plan, develop, and implement), where the president had made a "commitment" to surveying everyone regularly and responding to ideas and criticisms, where at least one major in-place reform initiative could be traced back to a faculty member's challenge to a new idea, and where all "[r]oads began to point toward the president's office." As one said, "[Miami-Dade President] McCabe has a way of sharing the glory and praise. Everybody knows it's him [sic], but feel they did it" (p. 21).

Goals and Objectives: A Continuing Controversy. On the occasion of his 90th birthday, comedian George Burns was asked about the personal goals he had set for the rest of his life. Burns smiled and replied that at his age *all* goals must be *modest*, by design! But, he went on to answer the question, concluding, no doubt with the familiar twinkle in his eye, that his final goal was to leave this world having been shot dead in bed by a jealous young husband. These humorous responses to a serious question identify at least three of the realities that significantly affect the process of goal setting: goals must be defined or described with great clarity—one must be able to identify where one is going and what one hopes to achieve; goals will be influenced by the times in which one lives; and goals will be the by-products of the degree of hopefulness or level of imagination that one brings to the definitions and descriptions.

In the best of all worlds, most would support the notion that "a man's reach should exceed his grasp" (R. Browning), that one should set goals that encourage achievements beyond those things that are clearly possible and that support aspirations for achieving those things that require extraordinary effort. As colleges that have agreed by open-door policy and by law to take essentially the top 99 percent of all individuals who might profit from postsecondary instruction, community colleges have been forced by their charge and their mission to set goals that by their very diversity and breadth are ambitious and immodest.

Some would suggest that organizations in general are innately unable to identify or pursue clear goals, that their leaders are too prone to describe current conditions and activities as the best possible for their organizations at that particular time (Perrow, 1982). And, history records some common criticisms and challenges to their ambitious notions and their immodesty—among them, that in attempting to be all things to all people, community colleges choose to wax eloquently in generalities about their objectives, and in so doing merely put off that occasion when they must admit that they cannot provide successful educational experiences for students of *all* abilities, as they claim.

Thus the criticisms and challenges raised more than two decades ago in *Salvage, Redirection, or Custody?* (Roueche, 1968) are still with us. In particular, there was no common definition of *remediation*; the goals and objectives of remedial programs were unclear; and definitions and goals were nebulous because there was no foundation upon which to build them—that is, there was no widespread agreement that remediation was even possible.

In fact, many remedial programs used the same nebulous terms to describe their goals and objectives as were used to describe the role and goal of the junior college—e.g., such terms as *salvage* and *second chance*. In tying these notions to remedial programs, junior college leaders acknowledged that these programs were essentially the keys to a second chance—low-achieving students were offered a chance to remediate their basic skills and increase the likelihood that they would be successful in college; they were being offered the opportunity to get from where they were to where they needed or wanted to be (Roueche, 1968). There was little argument (other than that raised around cost) that providing a second chance was unquestionably good for the individual; he would then have opportunities open to him that had been previously closed. As well, the idea of salvage as a function of the community college, and of the remedial program, was quite acceptable; it was tied to the economic development of this country—salvaging "human resources" for the good of society, increasing an individual's chances for meaningful employment, and decreasing the numbers on the welfare rolls.

While in the 1968 study the notions of *salvage* and *second chance* referred directly to what colleges said they were doing, the terms *redirection* and *custody* referred directly to what others reported actually happened there. While no one wanted to claim the idea that these colleges were "custodial" in nature, that they were only holding tanks designed to keep various individuals and groups out of the job market and off the street, others did claim the idea that they should redirect the students who had apparently made poor choices into more viable career and/or academic paths. Clark's term, "cooling out," has continued to be closely associated with the function of redirection. Borrowed from the gambler's terminology, this term describes the occasion during which the winner is responsible for allowing the person who has just lost the game, his money, his possessions, to face the reality of his situation. In education, the student is allowed to "discover" that he cannot continue in his program or courses of choice, that his abilities and his choices are incompatible, and that he must change his educational goals. Clark advocated advising students to take substitute courses that were not too different (particularly in status) from those in which they were currently enrolled or for which they were to register; they then would not feel a sense of failure, but rather a sense of relief that they had the opportunity to avoid or to rectify a mistake (1960). Yet, some noted that students were more typically moved to courses assigned significantly lower status, for example, either remedial, terminal, or vocational (Cohen and Brawer, 1982). Many argued that colleges did not want the responsibility of assisting students in making realistic choices when they first enrolled, and so the students either cooled out or dropped out—more frequently the latter (Roueche, 1968).

Both cooling out and dropping out were painted with the same brush; both were considered negative outcomes of a college experience gone awry, or maybe just gone bad. Early on, colleges either denied that cooling out was a function of their program or at least argued that it was certainly not an intended program outcome. And yet, even in the face of the negative responses to the process 20 years after coining the term, Clark, in describing the processes by which cooling out is effected, supporting the notion that it was an essential responsibility of the college, and re-examining his thesis, concluded: "The problem that causes colleges to respond with the cooling-out effort is not going to go away by moving it inside of other types of colleges. *Somebody* has to make that effort, or pursue its alternatives" (1980, pp. 23–24). He continued: "Any system of higher education that has to reconcile such conflicting values as equity, competence, and individual choice—and the advanced democracies are so committed—has to effect compromise procedures that allow for some of each. The cooling-out process is one of the possible compromises, perhaps even a necessary one" (p. 30).

The social arguments have not gone away, and many critics have challenged community colleges to disprove that they use cooling out to maintain society's class-bound status quo (Karabel, 1972; Zwerling, 1976; Pincus and Archer, 1989; Brint and Karabel, 1989). Adelman, in *The Way We Are: The Community College as American Thermometer*, argues that data from the National Longitudinal Study of the High School Class of 1972 (in which a generation of Americans were tracked for their involvement with community colleges from the time they graduated from high school into their early 30s) would "ultimately help us transcend this unproductive debate" (1992b, p. 25). He argues that the construction of variables and estimates used in pursuing this debate (e.g., who is on an academic/transfer track and who is not), the confusion and naiveté concerning an individual's aspirations and plans for attaining any degree (e.g., "plans" appear by far to reflect more honestly, than do "aspirations," an individual's realistic sense of his options), and the bizarre nature of the literature surrounding the economic outcomes of education (e.g., the charges and countercharges of critics and colleges based on implausible mixes and interpretations of research data) combine to provide us with little more than "hocus-pocus research" (1992b, p. 25). Moreover, he argues that Clark's cooling-out thesis could be explored, particularly with the data gathered around an individual's "plans," but that no one—neither defenders nor critics of the community college—have chosen to pursue the exploration (1992b, pp. 25–26). And, he concludes:

Lastly, our youthful aspirations and hopes exceed what actually happens to us, no matter what we do in between. Does that mean we should abandon them? If life itself is a 'cooling-out' process, does that mean we should spend most of it moping about what could have been or blaming 'the system' for what didn't happen to us? Do we adopt the position that only the 1 percent of the population at 'the command posts of the American occupational structure' (Karabel and Astin, 1975), only the movie stars, succeed in our society and that everyone else fails? everyone else is a victim? everyone else doesn't count?

And while we all gripe about our lives and fortunes, if that's all we do, we freeze ourselves out of efforts to improve the lives and fortunes of our children. The Class of '72 did not throw in the towel. We can't afford to, either (Adelman, 1992b, p. 32).

It is in that spirit that we asked the colleges in our study: "What were the initial goals and objectives for this program?" And it was with that hope that we requested: "Describe the extent to which they have been achieved." Because "place" and "fit" and "support" are important indices of the value that institutions assign to these programs, we asked: "How long has the program been in place and how does it fit into the organization of your college (e.g., where is it housed, how is it directed)?" Finally, we requested: "Describe the current outlook for the program's future (e.g., proposed changes in structure or design)."

What the Award-Winners Say About Institutional Fit, Goals, and Objectives

De Anza College's A STARTING POINT Minority Transfer Program was launched in January 1986, using two full-time staff: a counselor-director and a staff assistant. Since that time, one full-time counselor and one full-time academic adviser have been added. The program is viewed as a special counseling support program of student services, steered by a counselor-director who reports to the associate dean of counseling, who in turn reports to the vice president of student services. Some funding, thus some support for student performance reviews, in particular, has been lost due to current budget restrictions.

The program's initial goal was to address the college's "abysmally" low minority transfer rate to four-year institutions. The specific program goal, set in May 1985, was to increase the rate of transfer by De Anza students, "particularly minority students, by at least 10 percent" by June 1987, which would mark the end of the first stage of the program. The four populations targeted by A STARTING POINT were shown by statistical data to be severely underrepresented in numbers of transfers from the college, as well as in its retention rate. They were: Black/ African Americans, Latinos/Chicanos/Mexican Americans, American Indians, and Filipinos. In 1985, of 734 students who transferred to four-year institutions from De Anza, 12 were Black, nine were Filipino, six were American Indian, and 42 were Hispanic. These figures contrast sharply with the greater overall enrollment of these groups at De Anza College.

Prompted by these disparate success rates, the minority transfer program was developed. According to the director, "Our mission is to develop a meritorious pool of capable, energetic, and enlightened underrepresented minority students who intend to continue their education at baccalaureate-granting colleges and universities." The program's objective is to provide the targeted populations with the information and opportunities to become fully involved in academic, campus, and community life. Further expectations are that as students feel more secure on campus, they will take more risks and develop the self-confidence and social and intellectual skills to succeed academically. Program staff envision that participating students will enter the work force as educated, insightful, active, and enlightened leaders who will reflect the contributions De Anza College has made toward their success.

While A STARTING POINT remains true to the original intent to increase the transfer rate of underrepresented students, within that context it has developed a broader philosophical base, using strategies other than those originally conceptualized. Program staff also express a feeling of responsibility for offering services and activities that mainstream the members of the targeted groups and encourage intellectual, psychological, and emotional risk taking.

Program goals are:
- To acclimatize participants to the college milieu
- To teach participants to utilize student services
- To provide participants with the information and opportunities to become fully involved in academic, campus, and community life
- To provide participants with a "home base"
- To strengthen student academic achievement
- To strengthen student self-confidence and self-esteem
- To broaden student transfer options
- To assist participants in exploring and defining career goals and options
- To encourage students to consider advanced degrees
- To orient parents of participants to De Anza College and to the demands of college in general
- To increase faculty involvement with program participants and with program objectives
- To augment relationships with baccalaureate-granting institutions, near and far
- To develop an alumni program

Initially, three main services were designed to directly encourage faculty involvement: the Mentor Project, the quarterly Student Performance Review, and a monthly newsletter (see The Future).

The Athletic Academic Advising program at **William Rainey Harper College** was created in 1985 to provide academic advising services, promote the use of campus support services, and assist student athletes in defining and attaining educational goals. It is part of the student development department, with the coordinator reporting to the dean of student development and dean of physical education, athletics, and recreation. Athletes are encouraged to meet frequently with the athletic academic coordinator to discuss academic and personal concerns. A large number of athletes are referred to or seek out support services such as the Tutoring Center, Math Lab, Writing Lab, Learning Assistance Center, and Disabled Student Services. In an attempt to help student athletes make informed decisions regarding academic and personal issues, effort and time (either in informational meetings or one-on-one sessions) are spent exploring educational goals and explaining campus programs and college expectations for each individual as a student athlete.

Highland Community College's Student Support Services completed its second year of operation at the end of the 1992 spring semester. It is administered by the dean of academic affairs, fully funded by a TRIO grant from the U.S. Department of Education, and is under the direction of a full-time project director. The initial goals of the Student Support Services project were to identify and select 200 disadvantaged students as participants, 80 percent of whom were to be retained by the end of the next project year; to graduate, or to transfer as sophomores, at least 85 percent of all participants in the program at the end of the second year; to work toward an overall grade point average of 3.0 for project participants; to raise the percentages of disadvantaged students transferring to four-year institutions from 47 percent to 60 percent, the current collegewide standard; and to increase the retention of those students in the lowest quartile of GPA by 25 percent.

QUEST is the acronym for **Illinois Central College**'s (ICC) retention program, Quality Undergraduate Education for Student Transfers. Students respond to the recruiting brochure by affirming: "Yes, I'm interested in QUEST. I want to make the most of my education and my life." QUESTers are to accomplish this by joining the "community of learning," with personal support from the program's mentor/mentee system.

The QUEST program was developed by ICC Dean Ron Holohan following the recommendations of the national report, *Involvement in Learning: Realizing the Potential of American Higher Education* (National Institute of Education, 1984). It is administered by a QUEST director who reports to the dean of liberal arts and sciences, who in turn reports to the vice president of instruction and student services. QUEST attempts to develop the college's competencies by providing greater breadth of skills and knowledge, by integrating that learning into a more coherent curriculum, by providing more active modes of teaching that involve the students, and by creating a sense of group belonging and social integration.

The ICC curriculum defines 15 basic competencies to be developed by the time a student receives an associate degree in arts and sciences. Some of these competencies are skills (e.g., communications, mathematics, critical thinking, information gathering, effective group interaction), while some are bodies of knowledge (e.g., understanding society, the natural world, technology, and cultural heritage). Other competencies involve growth in attitudes and values, through self-examination and building a sense of one's own worth, enhanced by an appreciation of physical well-being. The program also cultivates tolerance, social responsibility, intellectual curiosity, and leadership. These competencies are developed through the academic courses as well as by involving QUESTers in organizing and working on such activities as College Information Fair, College Night, Transfer Afternoon, Fine Arts Festival, All-School Orientation, Scholastic Bowl, Campus of Difference, and an annual leadership conference.

Miami-Dade Community College initiated the Black Student Opportunity Program (BSOP) in 1987. The program is housed in the student services area in the Division of Education and is under the direction of the district director of minority student opportunity programs. There are several minority student educational initiatives housed in this division: College Reach-Out Program (recruitment), Comprehensive Opportunity to Pursue Excellence (retention), Challenge Center (retention), and Urban Community College Transfer Opportunity Program (facilitating minority transfer).

The goal of the Black Student Opportunity Program is to adequately prepare Black high school graduates to pursue and complete a college education and to provide these students with a financial headstart to earning a college degree. The specific objectives include increasing the pool of well-prepared high school graduates while placing special emphasis on programs that serve low-income students; assisting with better course selection in high school; encouraging parental involvement and role modeling; and providing mentor involvement and exposure to educational environments. Through fulfilling program objectives, BSOP intends to increase the number of high school students aspiring to a college education. The program staff seeks to motivate a greater number of participating students to enroll in college preparatory courses while still in high school, in an effort to develop strong information skills and higher levels of college readiness.

During the years that program participants spend at Miami-Dade, BSOP is available to facilitate student progress toward an associate degree and to assist students in successfully transferring to a college or university for completion of a bachelor's degree. Facilitation efforts include improvement of participants' basic academic skills as measured by standardized tests and all possible efforts to decrease the dropout rate.

The students are assisted with transferring to other colleges and universities through formal, contractual transfer agreements with other institutions. Such agreements detail the responsibilities of both the sending institution (Miami-Dade) and the receiving institution in the articulation process. For Miami-Dade such commitments include the monitoring of prospective transfer students and the ongoing provision of progress reports to the four-year college; the objective of both schools is to smooth the way for the BSOP student by ensuring that all prerequisites are in place, that skill levels are adequate for college junior-level work, and that the student is expected and welcomed at the receiving college.

In a typical agreement, the four-year college agrees to accept a specified number of program participants and their lower-division credits from Miami-Dade; the senior college further commits to match with grant support the "earnings" that the student brings from BSOP. Both institutions agree to monitor and maintain the articulation process, enabling students to transfer with no academic disruptions.

Participants in BSOP are able to begin earning scholarship dollars for their education as early as the tenth grade; they accomplish this by choosing from the program's list of recommended academic courses and by maintaining a B average or better. By ensuring that money will be available for college tuition and fees, Miami-Dade has transformed college education from an unattainable dream to a practical possibility for many Black students.

Freshman Seminar and Course Clusters have been developed at **Middlesex Community College** to foster group cohesiveness among entering students and to improve student retention. The Freshman Seminar began in fall 1988 and Course Clusters in fall 1989. Both programs resulted from Retention Committee discussion on developing initiatives that would encourage supportive connections among students and faculty and increase student retention. The committee was concerned that the large academic programs, such as liberal arts, liberal studies, and business, were the programs where students had the least connection with the college; and these programs did have, in fact, the highest attrition rates. The Freshman Seminar was approved by the Curriculum Committee for three years; after two years of extensive research, the results were presented to the Curriculum Committee and the Faculty Association in fall 1991, and the course was approved as a graduation requirement in liberal arts, liberal studies, and business. More than 40 faculty and staff were involved in teaching this course during the fall 1991 semester alone. The course is housed under student services and is directed by the dean of student development, who also chairs the Retention Committee.

The Course Clusters program, the second major initiative developed by the Retention Committee, has been offered to entering students as an option at registration each semester since 1989. Again the coordination of the program is the responsibility of the dean of student development. However, each cluster course is a part of its individual academic division. The dean of student development works closely with the academic division chairpersons and the dean of academic affairs to coordinate the program.

Both programs are firmly based on collaborative teaching among faculty of all disciplines, student services staff, and administration, an ideal that is often difficult to achieve. At a community college such as Middlesex, with different campus locations and where all students commute, establishing a high level of involvement among students is a great challenge. The philosophy and activities of both programs set a high value on collaboration and community building.

Additional goals of the Freshman Seminar are to familiarize students with various teaching styles through a team teaching format, to build communications skills, to increase appreciation of cultural diversity, to foster development of time management skills, to provide opportunities for and guidance in values clarification, and to assist in career planning.

The Course Cluster model has been designed to encourage connections between students and faculty, to identify and support potential high-risk students, and to build cohesive student communities within large academic programs. The clusters are actually block schedules of three major courses from different disciplines in addition to a Freshman Seminar. The cluster courses are offered at prime times during the day, and entering students can register for these blocks, if they choose, and select their electives from the master schedule. The goal of this model is to assist students in forming collaborative learning relationships, thus supporting both achievement and retention.

In the fall 1992 semester, four major clusters were offered with a designated Freshman Seminar:

- Cluster 1: Fundamentals of Math, Reading Strategies (Freshman Seminar) (emphasis on written word problems through interdisciplinary study)
- Cluster 2: Introduction to Psychology and English Composition (Freshman Seminar)
- Cluster 3: Introduction to Business and English Composition (Freshman Seminar)
- Cluster 4: Reading Strategies, Basic Writing (Freshman Seminar)

The goal is to create more in-depth interdisciplinary coursework in the cluster. Clusters are offered to both developmental and college-level entering students.

The Advantage Program at **North Lake College** has been in place since fall 1988. The full-time Advantage staff is composed of two counseling associates and one department assistant. Mentors (faculty), peer advisers (students with 15 hours and a 2.8 GPA), and student assistants work on a part-time basis. The Advantage Program staff now report to the director of counseling (previously to the vice president of student development). It is housed on the new, enlarged student development floor in an area with Counseling, Admissions, Special Services, Returning Adult Center, Financial Aid, Job Placement, and the Testing Center.

The Advantage Program's goal is to establish a system to enhance institutional effectiveness, retention, and student success. Educational research has shown that students are more successful when they are afforded the opportunity to establish rapport with college personnel. From the program's inception, the focus has been on "at-risk" students and the use of faculty mentors. The aim of the mentoring program is to establish more effective communication between students, faculty, and staff members, thus offering learners the opportunity to have a resource person answer questions, solve problems, and provide encouragement on a regular basis, if needed.

The Advantage Program is predicated upon the idea that a high-quality, proactive effort addressing student success and retention can have a significant impact. With this idea in mind, faculty developed the model for the Advantage Program during a year-long period of inquiry. The rationale of the program includes clear definitions of student success and at-risk students: student success is measured by persistence (completion of at least 75 percent of courses attempted in a semester) and academic achievement (grade of C or better in all courses completed). The at-risk student is defined as one who exhibits two or more of the following eight characteristics: reading assessment test score below college level; reading score below college level and enrolled in six or more hours at the 100 or 200 level; enrolled in developmental math or having assessment scores indicating computational skills below college level; younger than age 20 or older than age 40; enrolled in a telecourse; enrolled in a self-paced course; dropped or failed more than 25 percent of hours attempted in the last 12 months; registered during late registration.

The program implementation includes several components to address student success and retention. A mandatory orientation, consisting of a one-hour credit course, is required for all first-time college students who have graduated from high school within the last two years. Student success seminars are held for groups on a regular basis and include such topics as time management, stress management, and test-taking strategies. Academic monitoring is conducted at the end of the fourth and eighth weeks. Other services include academic advising, increased communication with students withdrawing from classes, staff development and training, and research and evaluation.

The developmental studies program at **Richland College** was one of the original instructional divisions when the college was established in 1972. A full-time division chair directs the program and has the same role and responsibilities that are assigned to all other college division chairs. The program includes in its services: instruction of reading, writing, math, and ESL; Center for Independent Study (tutoring services for students throughout the college); and instructional support services for the Special Services Division (which provides instruction for learning disabled and adult head injury students). Additionally, an Educational Personnel Program (Tech-Occ) is administered from this division.

The goals and objectives of the original division included providing instruction for students who enrolled lacking the necessary skills to succeed in college-level courses and providing instructional support services for faculty and students. Goals and objectives of the division have not changed significantly over the years, but the student population has changed both in age and ethnicity, and there are currently more students entering who are identified as at-risk than at any time in the college's history.

The Transfer Achievement Program (TAP) at **Santa Barbara City College** was initiated in fall 1988. The program has been supported in part by external grants from the state of California, private donations, and the Fund for the Improvement of Post-Secondary Education. A unit within the college's Transfer Center, TAP is directed by a full-time certificated coordinator whose sole responsibility is the management of this program. The TAP coordinator reports to the Transfer Center director.

TAP is designed to increase the number of underrepresented students who transfer to four-year colleges and universities. While not all underrepresented students are at risk, many of the students participating in this program would not transfer without TAP's assistance. Its major objectives are:

- To increase the number and proportion of underrepresented students who commit to transfer as an educational goal
- To increase the number of underrepresented students who complete the transfer-related activities as outlined on the Transfer Task Inventory
- To improve underrepresented student success and persistence in English and math classes through academic support groups
- To increase the number of underrepresented students who apply for, receive acceptance to, and enroll in a four-year institution to a level at least at parity with their proportion of the general student population

- To increase high school, community, and four-year institution involvement and collaboration in the delivery of pre-transfer outreach, support, and transition services

TAP was introduced to provide an integrated and cohesive set of services to underrepresented students who have the potential to transfer to four-year institutions. It was conceived and implemented with two major premises: that increasing student involvement and responsibility in transfer-related activity will increase student persistence and goal attainment, and that collaboration among students and among college services will increase transfer rates more so than would individual and fragmented efforts. With these premises as its foundation, TAP's efforts have resulted in a significant increase in minority student involvement in transfer-related activities, improved academic progress, and increased transfer rates of underrepresented students.

Santa Fe Community College's (SFCC) Student Success Model is designed with an overarching goal of success for all students (see Figure 3.1). The model begins with recruitment activities or with the potential student's first inquiry about the college. Each potential student is asked to define success in personal terms. This definition becomes a goal, and around this concept other interventions and services can be provided as appropriate.

"Definitions of success" generally fall into four categories in this model, and the first of these is personal enrichment, an approach to education that many students use intermittently throughout their lives. The transfer goal is a second definition, applicable to those who want to complete two years at SFCC before enrolling at a four-year institution. A third group wishes to obtain a degree or certificate to qualify them for an occupation or a career, while a fourth group defines success as improving job skills in their chosen occupational areas. All four definitions are clearly different in their requirements for support, and making this distinction about a student's definition before undertaking the advisement process allows college staff to treat students appropriately.

Santa Fe's Retention Program: Intrusive Counseling Supports Student Success. The Retention Program, in place since the college opened in 1983, is still driven by its original goal of supporting student success at SFCC through a campuswide intrusive counseling model. Housed and directed by the Guidance Services Department, the Retention Program is for *all* students, mirroring the college's Student Success Model; in this model, at-risk students receive support while they continue to function in the general student population. An intrusive counseling program is based on the assumption that a college cannot be passive and wait for students to seek advisement and counseling. Rather, intrusive counseling is a proactive approach in which the counselor takes

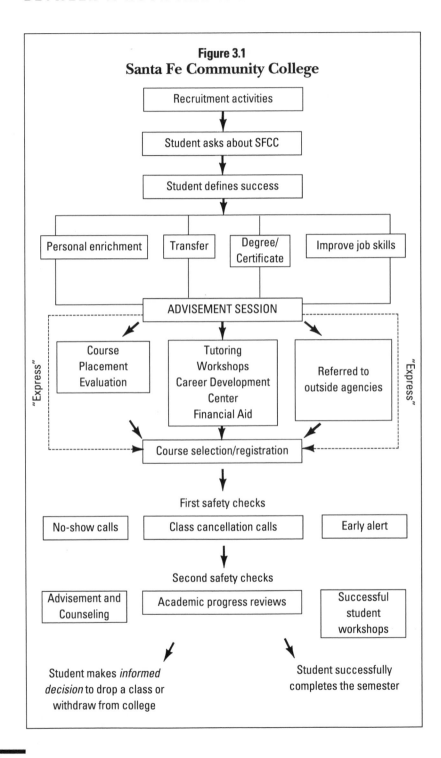

Figure 3.1
Santa Fe Community College

responsibility for establishing contact with students and addressing their needs before they become problems.

Students are initially identified for program activities and services based on the goals they have set individually, by defining student success according to their own needs. Accordingly, different follow-up strategies are then employed to support degree-seeking and nondegree-seeking students. The philosophy of student success advisement is that it is intended to foster student self-reliance. The adviser and student are responsible for working together to clarify the student's goals and objectives and develop the student's educational plan.

Santa Fe's Challenge Program: Mentoring for Student Success. SFCC's Challenge Program began in the 1991-92 academic year as a part of the Student Success Model; it is housed and directed by the office of the dean of students. The goal of the Challenge Program is to mentor and involve new, full-time students. It is based on the philosophy that new students are more successful at college when they exhibit several characteristics, the first of which is full-time status. Total student success requires a total commitment to the job of successful studies. It is a full-time vocation, and the most successful students are those who are aware of this and who make this degree of commitment. Another characteristic of successful students is broad involvement with the college; use of all the resources and experiences that are available at college enriches learning while building success. It also encourages one to "give back a little" for others, perhaps beginning a lifetime pattern of community service.

A third characteristic contributing to student success is guidance and mentoring provided by a caring person who is devoted to the student's concerns and needs. Such commitment by a mentor says to the student, "I value you and am invested in your success." An ongoing relationship with a mentor can be a source of strength to a student, preventing the feelings of isolation and alienation that can develop when things are not going well. The fourth characteristic believed to contribute to success is that the student be a scholarship recipient: the confidence and investment of others seems to inspire self-confidence in the student.

Santa Fe Community College's Developmental Studies Program. Established when the college was founded, the Developmental Studies Program is administered by a division head and is a department in the Division of Instruction. The program is designed to meet the needs of the underprepared college student and those students who have not yet completed a high school program by enhancing basic academic skills and developing human potential. The credit component provides reading, writing, and math courses in both traditional and self-paced formats. The Developmental Studies Center also provides free tutoring, workshops, and learning materials in support of these courses and the rest of the college curriculum. The noncredit component offers Adult Basic Education (ABE) and services provided by Literacy Volunteers of Santa Fe.

Santa Fe Learning Support Lab. The Office of Special Services and ABE offers a Learning Support Lab, which meets twice weekly for two hours. During the first hour, students who are experiencing learning problems can receive one-on-one tutoring in a particular subject or in an area where remediation is indicated. The second hour is a group session, which focuses on developing techniques and skills in the areas of concentration, memory, problem solving, study and organizational skills, and so forth. Students are encouraged to attend one or both hours.

Suffolk Community College Eastern Campus has successfully designed and implemented an effective retention program built on the belief that access for students does not necessarily lead to success. The multifaceted program is woven into many aspects of a student's college experience and is designed to improve retention in the general college population.

The process of designing and implementing this program began with answering the key questions: What does this college mean by "retention"? Why is retention an issue? The answers indicated that the program should be targeted to the entire college population, with special emphasis on those students at highest risk, and should focus particularly on providing them with skills and supports necessary to achieve their goals and/or graduate.

The retention program's objectives required the establishment of some key operations. Among these operations are
- Training of key personnel
- Faculty workshops on basic tools needed for student success, curriculum designed specifically for the required one-hour course titled Freshman Seminar
- Mandatory orientation, universal testing, academic advisement to identify all students' academic skill levels and assign them an adviser
- Developmental courses prescribed for students whose test scores indicate need for skill development
- Early warning and early notification by which faculty identify students in need of additional help and support
- Computer prerequisite blocks that do not allow students to register for courses for which they are unprepared
- The College Skills Center—available for all students, but scheduled hours required of students enrolled in developmental courses

- Exit interviews with all students, and a requirement that students withdrawing from a course or from the college without completing a certificate or a degree must complete a questionnaire citing the reason(s) for the withdrawal

Decades ago, the faculty of the **University of Toledo Community and Technical College (ComTech)** saw the need to serve the underprepared student and responded, beginning in 1960, with a few courses for "remedial" students. However, in 1983 the Strategic Long-Range Plan of the College called for the "enhancement of developmental education." Over the next few years, an organization evolved. Because some developmental courses were already in place and offered within two departments, Tech Science and Math, and General Studies, the faculty felt ownership of the curriculum, with full-time faculty teaching the courses. Not wanting to disturb the positive foundation that had been laid, a directorship was established that would facilitate growth of the program but would not change the reporting responsibilities the faculty had to their respective departments. The assistant director and nonfaculty staff report to the director of developmental skills education. This director holds one of three such positions in the college—has staff but no reporting faculty, large programmatic responsibility but no direct curricular responsibility, budgets to manage, and facilitating responsibilities. The director sits on the cabinet, along with department chairs and deans, and ultimately reports to the dean for instruction. A Developmental Skills Education Advisory Committee (DSEAC) is essential to the smooth operation of the program; it meets at least four times a year, makes policies for developmental education program issues, and establishes the annual goals for the program. Two deans, faculty (three coordinators and faculty at-large), the Learning Assistance Center manager, a premajor adviser, a community resource person, and the director, who serves as chair, serve on the DSEAC.

The program goal is to serve underprepared students by providing a meaningful curriculum and a set of services to enhance their preparation for college. On the heels of the long-range plan came the Mission Statement for Developmental Education and later a Mission Statement for the Learning Assistance Center. Both of these missions include the goal of enabling students to become successful to the point of graduation.

A third goal is to provide a balanced developmental program. Whereas 10 years ago the developmental education program at ComTech included only coursework, today's components include a mandated placement testing program, a mandated set of prerequisite courses, a sequential developmental curriculum, a premajor adviser for underprepared students, a learning assistance center with multiple services, and workplace literacy programs.

More recently, the university has prepared a Strategic Plan for the Year 2000. In response, Developmental Education has included more emphasis on serving business and industry with literacy programs. The Developmental Education Goals for 2000 are as follows:

- Provide a comprehensive model curriculum for underprepared students—administered through the departments of General Studies and Technical Science and Math—which enables participants to develop the prerequisite academic skills for success in the curriculum of their choice
- Provide instructional assistance and academic support services—administered through the Learning Assistance Center— that enable students to develop the appropriate skills for academic success
- Continue to develop intervention strategies for retaining students without compromising the college's academic integrity
- Develop a comprehensive, long-term computerized tracking system for underprepared students
- Conduct meaningful research data related to the success of developmental students in order to make effective decisions related to the curriculum and support services offered
- Promote a required orientation for incoming students
- Establish a comprehensive orientation program for part-time faculty
- Expand the relationship, including services and programs offered, to other departments
- Expand the programs of service to business and industry
- Promote comparable assistance services on other campuses
- Seek opportunities to serve the public

The Developmental Education program establishes annual goals through its advisory committee. These annual goals become the working document for the year.

What the Award-Winners Say About Goal Achievement

The success of **De Anza College**'s A STARTING POINT is represented in its student retention rates, transfer rates, internship involvements, and scholarships and special awards earned. During the pilot phase of the program (1986–88), research on retention rates for participants and nonparticipants (matched by ethnicity, educational objective, age, gender, time of entry, and completion of a college orientation course) indicated that participants maintained an 80 percent retention rate, compared to a 40 percent rate for nonparticipants. The study also indicated that participants accumulated more units and achieved higher GPAs than the control group. The study was conducted over a period of four consecutive quarters.

As of November 1991 more than 179 program participants have been accepted for transfer. Twenty-four students have been accepted to various internships—experiential, educational, or service programs. Students are often active in college clubs, student government, as well as serving as collegewide peer advisers and student ambassadors. And, finally, more than $22,000 in scholarships and recognition awards have honored A START-ING POINT students. A minimum transfer rate of 50 to 60 students is expected annually, and there is currently a waiting list of 250 students.

At **William Rainey Harper,** success of program goals is best indicated by the identification of students who are making unsatisfactory progress and the large number of student athletes contacting the coordinator to discuss academic and personal concerns, as well as seeking advice and information through other program channels.

Highland Community College's Academic Information Monitoring System has completed its second year of operation and recorded the following achievements of program goals. The full number of participants—200—were selected, enrolled, and served during the project year. Slightly more than 82 percent (goal of 80 percent) were retained from the first to the second project year. In the current project year, over 96 percent of the participants were retained from the spring to fall semester. Eighty-six percent (goal of 85 percent) of the participants graduated or transferred as sophomores at the end of the second year. During the fall 1991–92 semester, the project participants' average GPA was 2.54 (goal of 3.0 average), as compared with the previous semester average of 2.37. This improvement compared well with a stable collegewide average of 2.71. Of the students who did not return after the first project year, survey results indicate that over 75 percent (goal of 60 percent) had transferred to four-year institutions. The retention rate of students within the lowest quartile of GPA was 80 percent (goal of 25 percent) between the first and second project year, and 100 percent between the fall and spring semester.

One indication of the success of **Illinois Central College**'s QUEST program is its enrollment; the program has doubled in size since its inception. A less quantitative, but more concrete, indication is the fact that QUEST graduates keep in touch by writing, visiting, and calling the QUEST personnel. A third indication of success is the impact QUEST has had on the regular college transfer program. This includes the newly established Transfer Center, a similar program for returning adults (the Adult Re-Entry Program), and a collegewide orientation program for incoming freshmen.

In terms of the curriculum, the two courses that were originally developed for QUEST in English have now been assimilated into the regular English program. Based upon their collaboration in developing and implementing QUEST courses, groups of faculty have gotten together to develop interdisciplinary courses, thereby achieving more integration in the curriculum in general. Even experiments that have been tried in QUEST and failed, such as the attempt to measure student achievement through pre- and post-COMP testing, have been useful lessons to the college.

Through QUEST, a number of bridges with four-year schools have been constructed. The dean of liberal arts and sciences, along with 30 faculty members, addressed early on the critical basic questions regarding the purposes and priorities of the first two years of undergraduate education. QUEST was conceived as a "total program"—or a "mini-college." It includes a special curriculum, special support services, counseling, and recruitment. The program is aimed at a specific population, that of the potential transfer student.

Miami-Dade Community College's BSOP was initiated in 1987. Of the 75 students selected as the first program cohort, 15 were high school juniors (all graduated), and 60 were sophomores. Of the 15 students who graduated from high school, 12 matriculated successfully at the college/university level, while the remaining three entered the armed services. The 15 graduates were replaced by 15 additional students who were high school juniors. A total of 90 students were placed in the first BSOP group of students, and only three dropped out at the high school level. Using the original 75 students as a base, the program records a retention rate of 96 percent. This contrasts sharply with the dropout rate in the Dade County Public Schools, as determined by the district's Educational Accountability Office: 29.5 percent for all Black students, as opposed to a 4 percent dropout rate for participants in BSOP. It would appear that BSOP has increased the pool of well-prepared high school graduates. The program staff are in the process of determining how many of the original 90 students are still in college and how many have received degrees at the associate or baccalaureate level.

A second group of 75 students was selected for the program in the 1989–90 school year. They have graduated from high school and are attending a college or a university. The program staff are in the process of determining how many of these students are still enrolled in those institutions. The 75 students who comprise the third group are now juniors in high school.

The Freshman Seminar and the Course Clusters at **Middlesex Community College** have helped to build collaborative communities among students and have enabled faculty and staff to provide early and consistent support. The results have been remarkable. In carefully measured matched sample studies, with six variables held constant, Freshman Seminar students have had a statistically higher retention rate (at the .05 level or higher) than nonparticipants during two years of study. For Cluster students, the retention rate has generally been much higher than that of nonparticipants.

Although the statistics are impressive, the positive reaction from faculty, staff, and students to these programs further reflects the impact they have had on the whole college community. Students in the Cluster courses, for example, have formed study groups and support networks outside the class. When someone is absent, fellow students will call to share class assignments and provide support. Likewise, in the Freshman Seminar courses, faculty have reported that students appeared to gain more self-confidence and develop a stronger commitment to their education. Students reported that they developed better connections with other students and faculty, and they commented at length about the impact the course had on their college experience. One student wrote in the course evaluation, "The most valuable thing I've learned from this course is that I am not alone." Another said, "I feel confident about college now and know I can succeed." When community college students lead such fragmented lives that demand commitments to work and family as well as school, the college must create support systems to encourage their involvement in the learning process. Freshman Seminar and the Course Cluster programs do just that.

North Lake College's Advantage Program has been fully operational for the past four years. Findings from data collection indicate that mentored students maintain significantly higher GPAs after involvement in the Advantage Program and have lower dropout rates when compared to control groups with similar characteristics. For example, the retention rate from fall 1990 to spring 1991 was 29 percent for the control group, 24 percent for the Computerized Analysis System for Educational Success (identified from registration information), and 61 percent for the mentored, or Advantage, group. As a result of the program's success, there have been significant increases in referrals, including students electing self-referral to Advantage mentoring.

The success of **Richland College**'s developmental studies division has not been measured with regularly scheduled or consistent research at the college level; however, research around program outcomes is conducted by the office of institutional research at the district level to determine the numbers of students retained in classes, their enrollment over successive semesters, and their progress out of developmental studies to college-level courses and beyond. Students are also asked to evaluate the courses and program each semester.

There are currently 750 students in **Santa Barbara City College**'s Transfer Achievement Program. The number of underrepresented students who have transferred to a four-year institution from SBCC has increased from 90 in 1989 to 114 in 1991. It is anticipated that the number of transfers will increase in 1992–93, and the goal is to transfer 153 underrepresented students by 1994–95. This represents a 70 percent increase from 1989 to 1994.

TAP students participating in the math study groups had a pass rate of 70 percent, compared to 40 percent for underrepresented non-TAP students enrolled in the same math classes. The course completion and college persistence rates of students in TAP were substantially higher than those of non-TAP minority students and for all matriculated students with a transfer goal.

Santa Fe Community College reports several notable achievements for its various Student Success Model programs: during the first three weeks of class, SFCC experienced only a 4 percent dropout rate, as compared to the national rate of 17 to 26 percent for the same period; after midterm exams, 82 percent of the Challenge participants were in good standing; and developmental studies students achieved significantly higher success rates in subsequent courses in the regular college curriculum than did those who had not taken these courses (e.g., 92 percent success rate for DS students in regular math course, compared to 72 percent success rate for non-DS; 81 percent success rate for DS students in regular English courses, compared to 73 percent success rate for non-DS). When data charting success rates of DS students in regular college math and English curriculum had been gathered for three consecutive years, the success rates for DS students were statistically equivalent to or higher than those students who went directly into college-level courses. Moreover, there appeared to be lower withdrawal rates from DS courses than, for example, arts and sciences courses.

Finally, after mandatory student orientation was implemented in the 1991 fall semester, data indicated that successful completion of the student orientation courses resulted in higher levels of student success, as measured by four factors: individual GPA, completion rate in all classes, rate of return to college the following semester, and group GPA. Of those students who successfully completed the orientation course, 87 percent earned a 2.00 GPA (compared to the noncompleters' 17 percent), 90 percent completed at least 70 percent of their classes (compared to the noncompleters' 8 percent), 83 percent returned to college the following semester (compared to the noncompleters' 35 percent), and the group's GPA was 2.90 (compared to the noncompleters' .73).

Suffolk Community College Eastern Campus continuously charts the success of the retention program and, ultimately, the students. A study of student persistence rates, or the percentages remaining to re-enroll after one semester (and indications were that the highest percentage drop out after one semester), over four years (or eight consecutive semesters) indicated a fairly persistent climb from 72.6 percent in 1985 to 88.9 percent in 1988. Interestingly, with the introduction of universal testing of all incoming students, the percentages began a significant climb.

The results of the **University of Toledo Community and Technical College**'s **(ComTech)** program can be measured not only by increased enrollment, participation, and program expansion, but also by student outcomes. Graduation rates, when measured over a six-year period, have risen from 8 percent to 24 percent. Just five years ago, only 400 student visits were made to the Learning Assistance Center. During 1991–92, the center recorded 6,000 visits from 1,300 students for tutoring alone. Data indicate that students who participate in supplemental instruction receive higher course grades and have higher GPAs than students who chose not to participate. Student outcomes in subsequent courses following a developmental course demonstrate, in about half of the pairings, that students who went through the developmental prerequisite course succeed (grades of A, B, and C) at as high a rate as students who waived the course. For the remaining pairs, the goal is to continue to improve the prerequisite curriculum to the point where a student is adequately prepared for the transfer-level course. (Faculty use the student outcomes data to make valuable modifications to the curriculum.) Similarly, retention rates for developmental students match the retention rates of nondevelopmental students. (This is true for both subsequent-quarter retention and one-year retention; it was not true five years ago.)

What Some Award-Winners Say About the Future

De Anza College, its sister college, and the district are faced with serious fiscal upheavals that will impact all programs and services. The extent to which A STARTING POINT will be affected is unclear at this time. However, the operating budget has been cut by 51 percent to a figure below its initial start-up amount, and the full-time and part-time hourly staff has been reduced from 13 to seven. Consequently, programs and services have been eliminated that required the clerical support or incidental expenses (e.g., postage, printing, paper) that could no longer be provided. These included the Student Performance Reviews, the monthly newsletter, the recognition ceremony, and the Directory of Transfer-Ready Minority Students. Outside funding will be sought to continue the ceremony and the directory. Even so, the workload for the remaining staff is staggering, and a meeting to downsize the program has been held to refocus and to identify some means by which the student reviews can be reinstituted.

Changes planned for the Athletic Advising Program at **William Rainey Harper College** include implementing a study group program to match students who are doing poorly in specific classes after the five-week grade cards are examined; holding a sport nutrition seminar; presenting a sports-related career seminar; increasing the number of student athletes who are maintaining satisfactory academic progress to 90 percent of all student athletes; updating transfer information available to student athletes in the Athletic Academic Advising Office, as well as continuing to make all student athletes and Physical Education Athletics and Recreation faculty aware of the existence of this information; and computerizing the Progress Monitoring System further.

The future of the Black Student Opportunity Program at **Miami-Dade Community College** looks promising. The president and the college have committed to providing administrative and clerical support, space and facilities, equipment, salaries and fringe benefits, and a dollar-for-dollar match of funds raised by the program director as well as funds that may be contributed by donors (up to $140,000). Recommended structural changes include stipends for students to attend Saturday tutorials, additional funds for parental activities and support, and college prep classes (math, science, English, social studies) for organized groups of BSOP students.

At **Middlesex Community College**, the syllabus of the Freshman Seminar has been revised and refined yearly since the course began. Although team teaching has remained a cornerstone of the course, some sections are now taught by individual, "seasoned," seminar instructors, as a way to contain cost. The majority of sections are still team-taught, however, and new seminar instructors are matched with a "seasoned" partner.

The Advantage Program at **North Lake College** is seen as a viable student development department because of the work of those involved in its development and implementation. With current funding concerns, it is probable that some downsizing will occur in Advantage staff. Program activities will be carried out by three full-time staff persons, three mentors, and seven advisers.

The Transfer Achievement Program at **Santa Barbara City College** has two remaining years of funding from the FIPSE grant. The college is gradually shifting the cost of the program from external support to its general fund. The math study groups are now funded by the college. The college hopes to establish an endowment to offset part of the funds required to operate this program. Current operations are considered effective, and no major changes are being planned.

The outlook for **The University of Toledo**'s **(ComTech)** Developmental Skills Education Program is captured in the Developmental Education Goals for 2000 (see Goals and Objectives).

Conclusion

The diversity of these award-winning programs provides a kaleidoscopic view of the current shifting paradigms and institutional responses to changing times. As a group, their goals and objectives describe holistic, student-centered approaches to serving the at-risk student who has a constellation of personal and academic needs and imperatives. These programs see themselves, and are obviously regarded by others, as viable and valuable contributors to achieving critical college goals.

At a time when most higher education institutions look to raise standards and reduce options for students who require complex responses to their complex problems, these programs demonstrate an increased understanding of the importance of recruiting and assisting all students; many focus primarily on recruiting minority students and supporting them through all stages of the educational continuum, a process termed by some as "building a pipeline." While many institutions assign total responsibility for tackling the trend of younger school-age dropouts to those at the elementary and secondary levels, these programs show a growing awareness of the importance of planting positive educational expectations in the minds of students and their families as early as the elementary years, in preparation for actual college recruitment efforts during the high school years—a key to identifying and encouraging the potential college student who may be the first member of the family to aspire to postsecondary education. While early on many institutions have addressed the more obvious problems for college freshmen, these programs have a new awareness that providing ongoing support throughout the community college experience can improve the chances for transfer upon receipt of the associate degree.

The efforts to address the changing times must be a collective and institutionwide assault. As one Miami-Dade faculty member expressed: "We're not at the graveyard yet. We've been driven by heavy winds. It's constantly changing. And that change has kept us alive" (Zwerling, 1988, p. 19). As Paul Gallagher, former president of Vancouver Community College in Canada, remarked to a large delegation of community college presidents and their leadership teams:

> In our own institutions and in our own communities, we have made remarkable differences. We can and should continue to make remarkable differences. We can and should shape our immediate surroundings. We can and should create the climate that will encourage our students and fellow citizens to function well in the less certain world of tomorrow rather than cling to the security of the past (1990).

Selecting and Developing Faculty:

Getting to the Heart of the Matter

In the final analysis, the task of the excellent teacher is to stimulate 'apparently ordinary' people to unusual effort. The tough problem is not in identifying winners; it is in making winners out of ordinary people. That, after all, is the overwhelming purpose of education.

—**K. Patricia Cross,**
1984

On a recent trip to Washington, D.C., we saw a sizable group of what we assumed to be public school teachers waiting for arriving passengers at the National Airport terminal. Many wore t-shirts painted with bright red apples and various popular teaching slogans and quips, but one quip in particular caught our eye: "What are the three best things about teaching? June, July, and August!" Its message was powerful! We were struck by the attitude it expressed and were saddened by the potential effect it must have on students, not to mention the incredible professional waste. While in Washington, we learned that a large annual conference of selected teachers and parent-teacher national representatives was in session. We met one of the PTA representatives who was attending that meeting, and when we mentioned the shirt we had seen, she told us of a teacher in her child's elementary school who had that same quip on a large sign prominently displayed on her desk. This teacher's walls were bare while her colleagues' walls were bright with colorful displays, her students were strangely quiet while her colleagues' students were orderly but involved with each other's work, and her attitude was "My classroom is off-limits" for parents and colleagues alike. "Beware of this teacher!" was an unwritten agreement among parents in the know at that school. After that initial experience, we saw the quip on mugs, wall hangings, and other t-shirts over the next several months, and each time the message was as chilling as it was that morning in Washington.

What is especially troublesome about that message is the individual who is sending it. As research consistently documents, the teacher is the key to making the education system work, affecting most directly the lives of her students and, thereby, the attitudes toward learning that they hold. The fact that this message of disinterest or disregard, or, even worse, disgust for the teaching profession and students is flaunted, without apparent embarrassment among one's colleagues, is telling as well. Moreover, if that message correctly mirrors or becomes the pervasive attitude of public elementary and secondary school teachers, the outcomes for public education will be even more disastrous.

Yet, there is a long history of faculty concern, if not outright hostility, about student underpreparedness and lack of educational experiences, and the problems they generate for institutions and for teachers professionally. In fact, some of the first indications of faculty discontent were drawn by those who helped create the junior college, when in large part the decision was made to divert students with academic problems away from the universities and four-year colleges and retain only those demonstrating more academic ability. As these underprepared students were pushed farther down the academic ladder and as admissions standards tightened at the higher levels, community colleges bore the greatest brunt of the academic and social problems of the widening student diversity.

With the burgeoning enrollments of the 1960s and the spiraling increases in the numbers of remedial/developmental courses and programs, the proliferation of vocational programs, and declining enrollments in the traditional transfer courses and programs, many researchers began to report a growing discontent among community college faculty. Faculty discontent was drawn across discipline lines and focused primarily on problems created by student diversity and college mission. Faculty found the academic problems of their students to be overwhelming: "All I want to know is why I have to hold my humiliating job—teaching [community] college students that sentences start with big letters and end with punctuation...Being hired to teach journalism at my college is like being hired to coach track in a paraplegic ward" (John Medelman, from Zwerling, 1976). Faculty saw their jobs as second best to those at four-year colleges and universities: "It's not a very attractive job from the college teaching point of view" (Claude Campbell, from Zwerling, 1976). They believed the college's own role ambiguity created an ambiguous role for them as well, that they were situated somewhere between high school teachers and college professors, and they decried having no defined role in higher education (London, 1980). They complained about the "student-centered ethos" that had "become one of the hallmarks of a community college" (O'Banion, 1972, p. 23), citing the difficulties they faced with colleagues who would accuse them of being elitists or not caring enough for students if their office doors were not always open to routine disruptions, or if they were too inclined to publish or conduct research (Sledge, 1987; Seidman,

1985). They were observed in formal interviews as exhibiting "a pronounced *inferiority complex*"—assumed to be perhaps a mixture of longing for the more traditional university role and sensing the threat that the role had become (Buttenwieser, 1987, as in McGrath and Spear, 1991). They were reported to be good candidates for frustration and burnout (McGrath and Spear, 1991).

Yet, the authors of *A Nation at Risk* listed numerous "tools at hand" that they believed were available for reforming the public elementary and secondary educational system. Among these tools was "the dedication, against all odds, that keeps teachers serving in schools and colleges, even as the rewards diminish" (National Commission on Excellence in Education, 1983, p. 15). And, as Page Smith, historian and educator, noted in *Killing the Spirit*, the great majority of students in higher education "are short-changed by the system. The principle exceptions would, of course, be those who attend small, private, one-denominational colleges and community colleges [our emphasis], where there is a strong tradition of placing the needs of students rather than the ambitions of professors at the centers of the institutions" (1990, p. 221). Both of these sources, and numerous others, document that the state of the current educational system defies simple explanation; the contributors to its current deterioration are many. But the majority of authors hold to the view that all evidence indicates that teachers have not given up, nor will they any time soon. A decade after *A Nation at Risk*, the educational reform movement has been pronounced "not working" (Bell, 1991) and the "love affair with higher education may at last be coming to an end" (Smith, 1990, jacket inset), but evidence still abounds that good teaching is neither dead nor dying in public schools, colleges, and universities (Roueche and Baker, 1986; Roueche and Baker, 1987).

Teaching and learning are at the heart of the study conducted for this book, and the teacher is the key—as multiple research efforts have endorsed—to the outcome of the teaching and learning experience. It is from this perspective that this chapter was written. While our focus is ultimately on faculty in courses and programs that directly serve the at-risk student, our discussion will begin within the larger, historical context. We will address what we know about the characteristics and teaching behaviors of faculty who have been identified by their colleagues and/or presidents as highly successful with all students, about the ways by which faculty are selected to teach courses and programs, and about the professional development activities in which they engage. Folded into these discussions are our featured programs' responses to the questions: "How are faculty selected for the program?" and "What professional development activities support their training?"

What We Know for Sure About Excellent Teachers

One thing we know for sure is that each of us can recall at least one teacher, and a good number more if we are fortunate, who made all the difference, who made such an impression that we can see her clearly even today, no matter how long ago we knew her, or can hear his voice, even if he has been dead for years. We remember that one thing or those many things he *did* that occurred at just the right time to change the course of our future or to simply help us over a very small hump. Findings from studies of teachers who make a significant difference in the lives of their students indicate that factors distinguishing effective faculty from others appear to be grounded as much in what they *do* as in what they think—in how they act, as in what they believe (Wilson, Gaff, et al., 1975). And, no matter what it was they did, much of what we remember is how they affected the way we felt about a subject or about a task or about ourselves.

From numerous studies on teaching excellence, a fairly discrete common core of teacher characteristics with which most would agree can be identified. It is not our intent to provide an extensive review of the research on excellent teachers, but it is important here to touch upon the broader characteristics of those who engage in excellent teaching. We preface this discussion with the notion that *excellent teachers can teach all students,* so we use the Teaching for Success model, as developed and described in *Access and Excellence* (Roueche and Baker, 1987, pp. 147–178), to provide a framework for this admittedly broad-brush synopsis of what we know about excellent teachers.

The Teaching for Success model is built upon 13 general teaching themes as identified in studies of excellent teachers: commitment, goal orientation, integrated perception, positive action, reward orientation, objectivity, active listening, rapport, empathy, individualized perception, teaching strategies, knowledge, and innovation.

Commitment. "Never doubt that a small group of thoughtful, committed people can change the world. Indeed, it's the only thing that ever has" (Margaret Mead). Excellent teachers are committed to the profession of teaching and take its responsibilities seriously—they are committed to sharing themselves and information with students, expecting great things of them, and teaching them responsible behavior.

Without a doubt, at-risk students, who are more likely to withdraw either from classroom interaction or from the institution with only slight provocation, will be dramatically affected by such faculty-student experiences. While research has provided many confusing and sometimes contradictory findings about the factors that contribute to retention and attrition, the centrality of faculty to student satisfaction and, thereby, persistence is unquestioned (Pascarella and Terenzini, 1979;

Terenzini and Pascarella, 1980; Pascarella and Wolfle, 1985; Toy, 1985). Astin's 1977 examination of the Cooperative Institutional Research Program's longitudinal information about more than 200,000 students at more than 300 institutions of all types concluded: "Student-faculty interaction has a stronger relationship to student satisfaction with the college experience than any other involvement variable, or indeed, any other student or institutional characteristic" (p. 223). Beal and Noel reported that all types of institutions, from a survey of 944 two- and four-year public and private colleges and universities, considered the "caring attitude of faculty and staff" to be the most important retention factor at their institution (1980, p. 19). Faculty and staff, in fact, are representatives of the institution; what they say about the college and what they do to show their support (or lack of) for its mission significantly affect what students believe about a college or about the quality of the college experience. Faculty become caretakers of a trust that students place in them to share factual and honest information about themselves, the institution, and the quality of the education in which they are investing, and "violation of this trust may have a devastating impact on high-risk students" (Toy, 1985, pp. 387–388).

The interaction appears even more significant when faculty are perceived as caring enough to go beyond the formalities of the classroom and the more formal teaching environment to entertain or socialize with their students (Pascarella and Terenzini, 1977; Tinto, 1987). Students report that a teacher's interest in discussing such topics as campus life and other intellectual pursuits of interest to the student are directly related to student reports of positive educational experiences (Theophilides and Terenzini, 1981; Tinto, 1987).

The notion that out-of-class interactions are so critical to student satisfaction in no way should diminish the importance and impact of in-class behaviors. In fact, it is the in-class interactions between students and faculty that are likely to be the most important precursors to contact outside of class (Shulman, 1985; Wittrock, 1985; Halpin, 1990). For example, faculty who actively encourage discussion and exploration in class are more likely to report more contact with students outside of class, viewing it not as a burden or a disruption of their other responsibilities, but as part of the teacher's role (Wilson, Wood, and Gaff, 1974; Feldman, 1976). And, teachers who spend time with students outside of class frequently find these same students enrolling time and again in their other classes and continuing the more informal relationships outside the classroom (Wilson and Gaff, 1975). Moreover, students who report frequent contact with faculty outside of class can describe, even four years after the fact, the intellectual outcomes more frequently than the personal/social outcomes of these experiences (Endo and Harpel, 1982).

Goal Orientation. "The great thing in life is to have a great aim and perseverance to attain it" (Goethe). Excellent teachers have set goals for themselves, goals that they have achieved and can point to with some pride. One thing we know for certain about the majority of community college students is that they have had difficulty in either envisioning or setting goals for themselves or in pursuing realistic goals. Excellent teachers are cognizant of their responsibility for proactively designing courses that help students define their own goals and map out paths to accomplish them.

Integrated Perception. "If students are to be motivated to learn, they must know why they are learning, how this learning connects with other learning, and where this learning relates to real life" (Parnell, 1985, p. 41). Excellent teachers have the ability to see the big picture—how the content and demands of their disciplines, other disciplines, and real-life experiences must fit together. They not only must understand it in order to give the verbal "picture" to their students, but they must understand it well enough to incorporate all of the pieces into their courses. In a three-year National Institute of Education study of literacy development, we discovered that the more graduate education faculty had completed, the more difficulty they had in relating to other aspects of their own discipline—much less being able to make their subject relevant or useful to learners; and few had identified the specific tasks that were required "in the real world" that were also required learning in their classes (Roueche and Comstock, 1981). We know that at-risk students have had a limited range of experiences; they come to college with a very narrow view of the world and their role in it. An integrated approach to teaching embraces a full range of visual and spoken images that help students remove the perceptual barriers that the classroom walls can create.

Positive Action. "When a resolute fellow steps up to that great bully, the world, and takes him boldly by the beard, he is often surprised to find that the beard comes off in his hand, that it was only tied on to scare off timid adventurers" (Oliver Wendell Holmes, Sr.). Excellent teachers encourage their students to try. "I tell my students that if they don't give it their best shot, they will never know how good they really are" (Kathie Whelchel, Anoka-Ramsey Community College, 1992 NISOD Excellence Award recipient). We know that at-risk students are frequently unwilling to "try" (Cross, 1976), that they identify with failure, that they need to experience success early on, and that they need to be rewarded for their successes (Roueche and Mink, 1982). And, as we are reminded in the film, *Dead Poets Society*, they need to experience the joy of learning from one who truly finds the task exhilarating.

Reward Orientation. "Unless the job means more than the pay, it will never pay more" (H. Bertram Lewis). Excellent teachers are spurred on by a "psychic income"—that bonus to one's paycheck that comes when a student demonstrates the excitement of learning something new (Futrell, 1984). They enjoy the "joy" of students being successful—teaching delights them! We witnessed the ultimate example of intrinsic motivation at the 1991 NISOD conference during the celebration and recognition of Excellence Awards recipients: Across a crowded auditorium of recipients and well-wishers, a teacher recognized a former pupil—and both were being honored for teaching excellence.

Objectivity. "If you can keep your head while all others about you are losing theirs, [you will become a man, my son]" (Kipling). All students, particularly those at risk, bring problems into the classroom; these problems may well be the catalysts for occasional behaviors that are trying or disruptive or confusing. Those teachers who are able to respond with patience, by providing some suggestions for alternative behaviors, without passing judgment on the student, transcend the problem and move swiftly toward some potential solution.

Active Listening. "The greatest compliment that was ever paid me was when one asked me what I thought, and attended my answer" (Henry David Thoreau). Earl Koile, an emeritus professor at The University of Texas and a psychologist in private practice, has remarked on occasion that as he was conducting research for several books on "listening," he was continually struck by the discovery that two professions most notably regarded as filled with "nonlisteners" are medicine and education! Excellent teachers are excellent listeners who create a classroom atmosphere in which students can feel comfortable with speaking out.

Rapport. "Laughter is not just a pleasure. It's a necessity" (Charles Schultz, creator of "Peanuts"). Research in the medical field has identified a strong correlation between a patient's *belief* that he can survive a critical illness and his subsequent survival. Research in organizational development points to the positive effects of hiring people who have a sense of humor; they are considered to be more flexible and able to resolve problems in a positive manner. While in education there has been little formal effort to correlate laughter, or having fun, with student performance, it is not too far off the mark to draw a critical relationship for ourselves—in everyday life, we are drawn more quickly and more tightly to pleasurable activities than to those not so pleasant. And we are more likely to be drawn to individuals who are more positive and open than to those who are not. A recent study of humor in the workplace expanded the findings to include the classroom and proposed that perhaps teachers who can laugh with their students would seem more approachable (Philbrick, 1989). Teachers who are willing to share their own foibles and experiences both inside and outside the classroom with their students are disarming, engaging, and nonthreatening.

Empathy. "Have patience. All things are difficult before they become easy" (Saadi). Excellent teachers share their own experiences with students, letting them in on the "secrets" of their own successes and failures, allowing them opportunities to learn that occasional feelings of frustration or awkwardness or sadness are quite common human responses to difficult situations. Klemp (1977) calls this highly developed ability "active empathy"—the ability to recognize, interpret, and act on the clues that others give.

Individualized Perception. "No longer can we afford to take an almost perverse delight in observing that some of the most creative achievers in society were misfits in the educational system" (Bruce Hartwick, Microtel Pacific Research). Excellent teachers understand the critical imperative of recognizing and responding to the individual differences of their students. They understand the familiar Rousseau admonition, "In order to teach French to Johnny, you must first know Johnny."

Teaching Strategies. "If faculty and students do not see themselves as having important business to do together, prospects for effective learning are diminished" (Boyer, 1987, p. 141). Excellent teachers are willing to make students active partners in the teaching/learning adventure; students may be the best sources of how they might learn best and what the course must provide to best serve their needs (McKeachie, 1978).

Knowledge. "Dare to know! Have the courage to use your own intelligence!" (Immanuel Kant) "I love the challenge of expecting the unexpected. My students never disappoint me; all my todays are very different. Every day is a learning experience for this teacher" (Irma Aguilar, Odessa College, Texas, 1992 NISOD Excellence Award recipient). Excellent teachers use their own classroom as learning laboratories; moreover, they remain actively involved in their own professional growth and development—they recognize the importance of lifelong learning.

Innovation. "If you have tried to do something and failed, you are vastly better off than if you tried to do nothing and succeeded" (Author Unknown). Excellent teachers actively seek out opportunities to investigate the rich collection of instructional strategies and technologies currently available to improve their teaching. They are considered to be instructional risk takers by many, but they bring creativity—what some have referred to as a rare phenomenon in today's college classroom (Boyer, 1987)—back into that arena.

Strategies for Identifying and Selecting Faculty

Salvage, Redirection or Custody? documented that instructors typically were assigned to remedial courses as a result of their status in the department; i.e, the higher the seniority or status, the more likely a faculty member would avoid such assignments in favor of more advanced courses. Since those instructors with more seniority tended not to take remedial assignments, it would follow that instructors in remedial classrooms tended to be less experienced than average. From the comments gathered from numerous remedial course instructors, the author concluded that they were unprepared for the specific courses they were teaching, that they did not understand nontraditional students and were convinced, by and large, that these students would not be successful. Sure enough, most were not. There were considerable obstacles to student success—teachers expressed low expectations of the students, and there was a lack of personal and professional commitment to teaching, primarily the result of the low regard that most of their colleagues held for the remedial courses. In fact, while teachers of advanced or specialized courses were firmly identified with higher education, this did not appear to be true of those who taught courses that were not considered "college level" (Roueche, 1968).

Low esteem accorded to instructors of remedial courses, in contrast to subject-matter specialists, was based at least partly on a lack of understanding of the complexity and difficulty of these teaching assignments. Unequivocally, the teacher was the key, the most important element in successful remedial programs; yet, in the late 1960s few junior college instructors had professional preparation in instructional processes. The incongruence of training, experience, and role expectations with the demands of the remedial student would inevitably take its toll both in student achievement and in instructor satisfaction. Roueche warned that selection and differential assignment of instructors had a major part to play in ensuring a good "fit" between the remedial instructor and the demands of that role.

By 1972 researchers were still finding that there was little commitment to the programs and the students they served. *Strategies for Change* concluded:

> Most community and junior college faculty are ill-prepared to handle the underachieving or low-aptitude student. Those selected for the job frequently enjoy low seniority and no tenure. Such assignments reflect the fact that teaching a remedial course is [still] a low-prestige assignment. The inexperienced faculty member, often fresh out of graduate school, has had little in the way of orientation or training in coping with the special needs of this group of students. Too few resources and inappropriate instructional materials conspire to defeat even the most conscientious instructor (Bushnell and Zagaris, 1972, p. 68).

Between 1968 and 1973 researchers discovered that much had changed in regard to the faculty selected to teach in successful remedial/developmental programs. While previously it had been the inexperienced instructor who was assigned to the developmental classroom, instructors in excellent (or model) programs now consisted almost totally of volunteers (Roueche and Kirk, 1973). Far from viewing their assignments as onerous, they took great pride in working with their students, they expressed positive expectations for them, and they related with them in an honest, caring way. Measuring their own teaching success in terms of their students' success in learning, the "new" developmental instructors were totally committed to the success of their students.

Unlike those of earlier times, these developmental instructors did not believe that student attrition and poor grades were indicative of a lack of motivation or ability; rather, they took responsibility for establishing a positive learning climate and ensuring that learning occurred. Put succinctly: "Hell, anybody can teach a bright student. That's no big deal! All those highly verbal students need are some directions, a timetable, and good books...My kicks come from working with those kids that traditional teachers gave up on a long time ago" (interview, Roueche and Kirk, 1973, p. 63). Instructors not only shared their learning objectives with students, but they also encouraged them to contribute their own objectives and activities to the curriculum. While they cared about their content, the "new" developmental instructors cared even more about their students. Having observed the difference that successful developmental programs could make in student learning, the authors recommended unequivocally that such programs should only be staffed by volunteers.

According to Cross's surveys of institutional changes in remedial or developmental services, restricting the teaching of remedial courses to only those faculty who expressed interest rose from 47 percent in 1970 to 56 percent in 1974 (1976, p. 237). In 1976 Cross was advocating the need to think critically about combining the skills of trained counselors with the skills of the faculty in developmental programs, in order to integrate the work of these two "educational specialists." She noted that in 1970 half of the community colleges had specialists in remediation on staff; yet by 1974, 61 percent of the remedial teachers had special training for working with underprepared students (1976, p. 238). These specialists were described as present or former teaching faculty from the fields of math and English; they had responsibilities for working on skill development and integrating the cognitive and social-emotional dimensions of the New Students; also, they had specialized training in counseling, remediation, and their own academic discipline (pp. 43–44).

Therefore, by 1977 many institutions understood that drafting teachers for developmental courses resulted in negative attitudes toward the instruction and toward the students (Roueche and Roueche, 1977; Roueche and Snow, 1977; Cross, 1976). Conversely, teachers who had volunteered expressed great interest in teaching these students, were more likely to seek a higher degree of preparedness for the task, provided highly relevant instruction, used motivational strategies, and possessed a caring attitude toward their students. Furthermore, they communicated honestly with them, discussed specific skill deficiencies as barriers to further academic progress, and assumed leadership and responsibility for overcoming these barriers.

However, the enthusiasm of committed remedial instructors should not obscure the uneasy fit they and their programs often had in their institutions. In 1982 Cohen and Brawer warned that community colleges were staffed primarily with regular faculty who had been at their jobs for years and were likely to hold views that had changed little over time.

Traditional faculty members remember their college in the 1950s and 1960s, when they had well-prepared students. They may feel nostalgic, perhaps even betrayed because the conditions under which they entered the colleges have changed so. At the same time, they may be pleased that the segregated compensatory education programs remove the poorer students from their own classes...Nonetheless, the teachers in the compensatory education programs run the risk of becoming pariahs, similar in that regard to occupational education instructors in the pre-1960s era (p. 237).

As late as 1983 Barshis and Guskey warned against a false sense, created apparently by "developmental education's advocacy literature," that there was a large supply of faculty available, eager and, moreover, qualified to teach in developmental programs. They concluded: "Sadly, such is not the case" (p. 90).

What We Know About the "Case"

Admittedly, the actual numbers of remedial/developmental instructors available and willing to teach has not been and probably cannot be determined; enrollment, institutional budgets (and/or commitment as reflected in the allocation of funds), and a variety of other institutional support decisions may be mitigating factors in the actual numbers of instructors employed. However, it is possible to draw some picture of institutional differences regarding employment trends of the remedial/developmental teaching population by describing the findings of two national surveys of all postsecondary institutions.

The National Center for Education Statistics reported that in 1989 the average number of instructors teaching remedial courses at all post-secondary institutions nationwide was approximately 15 per institution. However, when statistics were reported according to the institutional characteristics of private or public, the private schools employed an average of five, in dramatic contrast to public institutions, which reported an average of about 22. When statistics were reported for two- and four-year institutions, two-year institutions employed twice as many remedial instructors as four-year, 20 instructors compared to 10. Because reports from the two-year public colleges were not isolated for analysis, and our study looks specifically at that context, we chose to use the two-year college's average of 20 to further describe the training and assignment characteristics for remedial instructors. Of the 20 remedial instructors hired by two-year colleges, 12 had been hired specifically for the purpose of teaching remedial courses, five had degree credentials specific to remedial education, and about nine had been given specific training by the institution for their remedial assignment. Predom-inantly minority institutions were only slightly above non-minority col-leges in numbers of remedial instructors, 17 and 15 respectively. All other points of comparison, such as credentials and training, varied accordingly (National Center for Education Statistics, 1991a).

A recently completed study by the National Center for Devel-opmental Education at Appalachian State University sought to describe the state-of-the-art programs in developmental education. This study surveyed all postsecondary institutions, and preliminary data reported that of all full-time faculty who worked in developmental education, only 20 percent were working full-time in developmental education; in over one-half of the institutions, 100 percent of the developmental edu-cation faculty were teaching part-time; of all the institutions, only 7.1 percent had faculty teaching full-time in developmental education (Bonham and Claxton, 1992, p. 2).

What Some Award-Winners Say About Faculty Selection

Highland Community College selected its faculty for the first year of the Academic Information Monitoring System on the basis of their expressed interest in program involvement as determined by survey. At the beginning of the second year (1991–92), another survey was un-necessary—all of the incumbents elected to remain with the program.

Miami-Dade Community College's Black Student Opportunity Program (BSOP) requires that its instructors be regular classroom teach-ers at either Miami Southridge Senior High or Miami Northwestern

Senior High. They are to be subject matter teachers, especially in science, English, math, and social studies; they must recognize the students as BSOP participants and support BSOP's goals and objectives. [Of special note: While not featured in this study, there are other award-winning programs with similar focuses to BSOP that are staffed by college faculty; therefore, it is important to note here the particulars of the recruitment and staffing patterns that affect other such programs. The average Miami-Dade Community College faculty member has been at the college more than 15 years, and the faculty is overwhelmingly non-Hispanic White. A minority vita bank has been established to form a pool of qualified minority applicants; recruitment efforts are channeled through this program, and open positions are advertised in publications with large minority readership. Comprehensive listings of minority professional and civic organizations have been compiled, and a network has been established with graduate schools to help develop an interest in faculty positions at Miami-Dade. In 1987, with full approval of the board of trustees, President McCabe mandated that 50 percent of all new faculty and professional staff hires were to be minority.]

Middlesex Community College's Freshman Seminar and Cluster Courses require collaborative teaching among faculty, student services staff, and administration. When the Freshman Seminar was developed, five faculty volunteered to teach the course in addition to their full contractual workload for no additional compensation. They were considered among the best teaching faculty at the college, and each represented a different academic division. The instructors' shared belief in the concept of providing a support network for students was a central motivation, and their enthusiasm and commitment were such that a budget was later established to compensate them for their work. That enthusiasm spread throughout the college, and over 40 faculty and staff volunteered to teach Freshman Seminar during the recent fall semester. The budget has grown to compensate the increased numbers of instructors, and the feeling across the college is that the return has justified the funds expended. The instructors who volunteer are highly committed to the concept of the Freshman Seminar and are interested in teaching such an innovative course.

Division chairs request volunteers from the ranks of their best faculty for participation in the Cluster Courses. The results have been that over the last years close working partnerships have developed among faculty across discipline lines.

North Lake College faculty initially responded to a survey that sought their personal statements about definitions and indicators of student success and identified them by subject area. The vice president of student development selected faculty for the Advantage Program from their survey responses and subject area. A representation across the college was achieved by selecting faculty who could then serve as Advantage "liaisons" to their respective departments. Over the years a large pool of faculty have served as mentors and continue to remain available to work with the Advantage staff. Mentors are recruited, on a rotating basis, from faculty who have exhibited a genuine concern for and skill in working with students in the Advantage Program.

Richland College requires a master's degree with 18 graduate hours of specialization and teaching experience in a similar organization or equivalent experience in a high school for both full-time and part-time developmental positions. The only exception is for those individuals with extensive teaching experience and a bachelor's degree; however, no individual is considered for employment in the division without evidence of active teaching experience. All faculty who teach developmental courses are recruited and assigned by the division chair and program coordinators.

Santa Fe Community College's developmental faculty are selected by the head of the Developmental Studies program and area coordinators, based on their experience with at-risk students.

The University of Toledo Community and Technical College (ComTech) understands the importance of instructor interest and motivation in working with at-risk students, and there is a high level of involvement from all faculty in developmental education. Developmental faculty are defined as those who teach one or more developmental courses in a year. Since the remedial courses were first offered in the 1960s, developmental instructors have been selected from the English (Department of General Studies) and math (Department of Tech Science and Math) faculty who choose to teach some developmental courses each year and who have a commitment to curricular improvement. In contrast to the patterns of 15 or 20 years ago, faculty are tenure-track with university rank, given the unique relationship between ComTech and the University of Toledo.

Faculty select to teach developmental math and writing courses as they would any transfer-level course. Some faculty routinely choose multiple sections of developmental courses every quarter, while others select only one or two sections per year. But over the last several years, 100 percent of the math faculty and all but one of the writing faculty have chosen to teach developmental courses. By contrast, the reading and study skills faculty have been hired for their expertise in those areas and teach only those specific developmental courses. They, too, hold faculty rank in General Studies.

Part-Time Faculty

The increasing numbers of part-time faculty have raised a variety of concerns on community college campuses. In 1978 Tuckman reported a wide diversity in career aspirations among part-time faculty. Many were apparently satisfied with their teaching role at the college, but they did not hold much hope for advancement or opportunity there. They pointed primarily to the fact that the experience they were gaining was neither valued nor respected by the administration or their full-time colleagues at a level that would earn them any identity as a valuable full-time employee.

The report of the Commission on the Future of Community Colleges (1988) included two specific recommendations—in brief, that colleges should develop policies and programs for the selection, orientation, evaluation, and renewal of part-time faculty; and avoid the unrestrained expansion of part-time faculty and assure that the majority of credits awarded are earned in classes taught by full-time faculty. Some view the trend toward hiring increasing numbers of part-time faculty as de-professionalizing to full-time faculty (Cohen and Brawer, 1982), and others see it as an ebbing away of valuable time available for students outside of class, for important curriculum development and relationships with other faculty, and for opportunities and/or incentives for professional development (Richardson, 1992; Cross, 1990; Friedlander, 1980).

Professional Development

Early on, high school teachers formed the largest pool from which community college faculty were hired (Weddington, 1976), but faculty also were hired from colleges and universities and from business and industry. There was a mix of faculty who had little or no teaching experience with those who had years, a mix of faculty notions about the characteristics of community college students, and a mix of faculty attitudes toward the students. They combined to create an environment that demanded the design and implementation of professional development strategies focused on college mission, student population, and instructional methods. Some of the earliest recommendations included calls for graduate courses designed to train faculty for teaching in junior colleges, supported further by on-campus pre- and in-service programs to provide instruction in teaching strategies and to establish some common agreement about the junior/community college role and function (O'Banion, 1981). Yet, early on, development opportunities for faculty were limited to helping them understand the rules of the institution, rather than focusing on the improvement of teaching or understanding the student population.

Historically, there have been some obstacles to the notion of faculty development, defined here as systematic processes offered to groups of teachers in response to organizational needs and designed to promote growth, understanding, and improvement in the classroom (Gaff, 1983). Many of the earliest arguments are still heard today, and they are dangerous arguments! For example, there is the view that a teacher's performance is an individual and private matter, that it is a unique reflection of equally unique gifts and talents (Mauksch, 1980) and that these talents and gifts cannot be evaluated or scrutinized too closely (Miller, 1987). As Cross says, classrooms are still regarded by many "as the mystery boxes in education" (1987, p. 5). Moreover, there are those who believe that having a credential that says one has the knowledge says therefore that one has a license to teach and that teachers do not require support and training for improving their teaching (Pickett, 1984). While the arguments from faculty may be serious limitations to the implementation of professional development programs, and while many would point to the lack of serious evaluation of teaching effectiveness by which to determine if the effort was worth the investment of time and money, it has been discovered that ultimately the effectiveness of any program depends on administrative and institutional support (Lindquist, 1979). Yet, it is clear that faculty development has not been featured prominently in the budgets of the majority of American colleges and universities.

The idea of professional development is not new. In the early 1800s sabbatical leaves were related clearly to enhancing scholars' research capacities; in the 1960s they were strongly related to pursuing advanced graduate work (Eble and McKeachie, 1985). In the early 1970s it was obvious that professional development had expanded from acquiring knowledge or merely encouraging faculty to keep current in their fields to helping faculty adjust their instruction to the changing student clientele (O'Banion, 1981). A 1977 survey disclosed that 60 percent of U.S. institutions had programs for faculty development that aimed at instructional improvement (Centra, 1977). It is clear that significant progress was being made to that end (O'Banion, 1981; Eble and McKeachie, 1985). And, by 1988 the AACC Commission on the Future of Community Colleges recommended the following—in brief, make a commitment to the recruitment and retention of top quality faculty and to the professional development of these colleagues; increase the percentage of faculty members who are Black, Hispanic, and Asian; develop a faculty renewal plan, in consultation with the faculty; and set aside at least 2 percent of the instructional budget for professional development.

"For decades, community colleges have been known as teaching institutions, but in the past this phrase often meant institutions that don't conduct research. Now it is gradually moving toward its more accurate meaning—'institutions that cause learning'" (Cohen, 1973, p. 114). Over time there has been much evidence to support the notion that the most important objective of a staff development program is to provide information and training that can be transferred directly into classroom practice. Moreover, it should be an optimal mixture of teaching expertise and subject matter expertise (Cross, 1989). Indeed, "healthy staff development cannot occur where it cannot impact the instructional environment in significant ways" (Roueche, 1982, p. 28).

Time Is of the Essence: Effective Faculty Development Activities

The growing concerns about educational excellence make what happens in the classroom even more central to the community college mission. The faculty has become the institution's most valuable resource. While the 1960s and 1970s were decades of focus on the issues of access, the "1980s reforms set forth an agenda that must be accomplished by classroom teachers" (Cross, 1987, p. 2). Yet, simultaneously, reports indicated that between 1970 and 1983 faculty compensation, institutional support, and travel budgets were woefully deteriorating (Schuster and Bowen, 1985).

Added to the concerns about dwindling resources and increased responsibilities is the impending crisis of faculty turnover. It is expected that in the 1990s more than half of all college and university faculty will retire or otherwise leave the profession (Roueche, 1990); by 2000 between 30 and 50 percent of all community college faculty will retire (Jenrette, 1990). The challenges for developing these new faculty hark back to the earliest days of the community college, except, it can be argued, that today the stakes are even higher.

All faculty should be provided with the training and preparation they need to be excellent teachers. There are examples of highly effective faculty development programs across the country that are as varied as the faculties they serve. An extensive investigation of even a few of these programs would not be particularly useful for our purposes here, but there is some value to providing a broad overview of some of the more common approaches to effective faculty development. They can be easily arranged for discussion around the major components of any college: the student, so there is instructional development; the teacher, so there is personal development; and the institution, so there is institutional or organizational development (Gaff, 1975). However, there is no such easy arrangement in reality—each approach has some elements that would fit neatly into any other; they reflect, in effect, the complexities of the teaching enterprise.

We preface the discussion with this caveat: Professional development activities (e.g., regularly scheduled formal and informal interactive events, independent reading) should be continuous throughout the academic year for all faculty, beginning with a new faculty orientation to discuss college procedures, expectations, and students' characteristics. They should be integrated into the fabric of the institution (Eble and McKeachie, 1985) and evaluated for their timeliness and their value for maintaining currency in its programs. One-time activities have the potential to be catalysts for change, but by themselves—that is, without built-in institutional mechanisms (e.g., support)—they will not have long-lasting effects on either individuals or the institution.

Instructional Development. These activities focus upon teaching skills, such as planning, organizing, evaluating, motivating, using technology, and developing teaching strategies. They help faculty understand the range of experiences that students bring to the classroom, their possible motivations for being there, and their personality and learning differences (Eble and McKeachie, 1985; Brophy, 1987). They may involve faculty who have been recognized as master teachers to demonstrate teaching and evaluation techniques (Bloor, 1987), or faculty to serve as mentors for new teachers (Valek, 1987), or technology to provide demonstration videos for improving and expanding an individual teacher's repertoire of teaching strategies (Paoni, 1990).

The overarching and symbiotic relationships between objectives and outcomes of development activities are well demonstrated from the findings of a 1991 study of the variables associated with faculty attitudes toward at-risk students. Findings indicated that faculty who taught developmental courses were more sensitive to at-risk students than those who did not (moreover, that faculty in four-year parallel instruction held the next most favorable attitudes, and vocational/technical faculty held the least). Yet, more important, it was determined that faculty could be trained to develop favorable attitudes, particularly in relation to the effectiveness of instructional methods employed. "It was found that those teachers who indicated having received academic instruction and training for working with at-risk students felt their instructional modes were more effective in reaching those students than the instructors who indicated they had received no such training" (Tabb, 1991, p. 105). Interestingly, Tabb did note that while prior training had not appeared to affect faculty expectations of student success, it did affect their confidence level in their instructional methodologies. He speculated that while instructors may be unaware of their negative attitudes and effects of these attitudes on their students, one could argue that they were likely to feel more capable of success with these students as a result of more confidence in their teaching strategies. Implications for professional development were obvious.

Personal Development. These activities seek to help faculty develop their interpersonal skills and their abilities to relate to students; they focus primarily on the affective domain in the teaching arena. While there are few data available that describe the effects of the "fully functioning" adult teacher on a student's learning experiences, "it is unlikely an immature faculty can lead students toward their own integration and self-development" (Cohen, 1973, p. 108).

Institutional or Organizational Development. These activities are designed to help faculty and the institution create an effective teaching and learning climate, where teachers and administrators work together to offer the most appropriate and cutting-edge education for their students. For example, they may include special opportunities for innovation—developing interdisciplinary courses and programs (Wranosky and Mitchell, 1987; Greening, 1987; Collins and Stanley, 1991; Recktenwald and Schmidt, 1992) and team-teaching (Ortego, 1991)—or opportunities to participate in training or retraining experiences off-campus.

For professional development efforts to be effective, there must be "something in it for faculty"—that is, there must be mechanisms by which faculty are motivated by, involved in, and enthusiastic about the effort. While the explanations for how motivation enhances learning and achievement may be difficult to understand scientifically, we do know that it is important. We know that if two people of the same ability have the same opportunity and conditions under which to achieve a goal, the motivated person will surpass the less-motivated person in performance and outcome (Wlodkowski, 1985). Extrinsic motivators, such as better pay or institutional recognition for teaching excellence, are perceived as significant rewards for performance, but as Cross notes, "college faculty members are more likely than people who have chosen other careers to respond to intrinsic motivators" (1989, p. 17). They appreciate the opportunity to discover new ways of doing things—that is, of teaching—that will eventually lead to improving the ways they can help students learn.

> Intrinsic motivation, [then], will be bolstered if experiences lead people to feel more self-determination and confidence. Intrinsic motivation and the rewards that such motivation produces are perceived as pleasurable psychological states (Roueche, Baker, and Rose, 1989, p. 195).

What Some Award-Winners Say About Professional Development Activities

Highland Community College includes mentoring by the dean and project director among its professional development activities for program staff and faculty, as well as college-funded opportunities for travel and additional study.

Miami-Dade Community College allocates funds annually to staff development; approximately 25 percent of the funds are earmarked for minority affairs. Many of the activities are designed to heighten staff awareness and to identify strategies that support minority student needs. Recently, topics have included cross-cultural communication, retention of Black athletes, and cultural influences on learning styles.

External consultants frequently meet with faculty or administrative planning groups to provide needed expertise to help assess ongoing efforts or to assist in the development of new programming. Consultants have been retained by the college to develop strategies to enhance inter-ethnic understanding and to expand teaching alternatives that will enhance the learning potential of minority students and non-native English speakers.

A graduate course developed jointly by Miami-Dade teaching faculty and faculty from the University of Miami School of Education was implemented in January 1989. Titled "Teaching and Learning in Higher Education," much of the course is devoted to cultural factors that affect learning styles and preferences, and their implication for the instructor and his/her repertoire of teaching strategies. All faculty new to Miami-Dade are required to take this course prior to receiving tenure, and experienced faculty are encouraged to enroll as well.

Middlesex Community College holds a faculty and staff training day each June for all Freshman Seminar instructors, both new and returning. During that day, teams of faculty or faculty and staff present instructional strategies and concepts to the group. For example, a faculty member from the health careers division and the director of student activities have led a session on how to encourage group participation in a classroom setting. Another faculty member from the biology department and a counselor have led a session on assisting students in goal setting. A member of the English department gives a presentation annually on teaching students to write descriptive and thoughtful journal entries. An administrator and counselor lead a session on perceptions of the community college, with all members of the group participating. The training session is both didactic and participatory, and faculty and staff are exposed to a teaching style that is much different from any they have experienced.

Richland College assigns mentors to all new full-time faculty for the first year of employment. Additionally, program coordinators and professional support staff provide assistance for all new faculty.

Orientation, professional development, and other support services are provided by the division chair and other college personnel. An evening/weekend office provides similar support for part-time faculty. Faculty attend professional conferences and are encouraged to share their expertise at state and national conferences.

Santa Barbara City College is required by the state and federal grants supporting the math and English components of TAP to involve faculty in such staff development activities as workshops, reading, curriculum development, and identification of techniques successful with underrepresented ethnic minority and high-risk students. In recent years, the staff development program has focused on approaches for meeting the educational needs of underrepresented and high-risk students.

The University of Toledo Community and Technical College's **(ComTech)** faculty development fund supports travel and seminars, as well as guests on campus, for the purpose of enhancing all professional capabilities of its faculty. Each of the grants provides some travel dollars for conference attendance. The college is proud of TREE, the Center for Teaching Resources to Encourage Excellence, the vehicle for faculty and staff in-service. Faculty may also participate in the TIPS program, a teaching improvement program disseminated from the University of Kentucky and targeted to college faculty.

Other programs that do not require funding include a faculty mentoring program for every untenured faculty member, faculty training for supplemental instruction (SI)/volunteer tutoring, computer seminars, and collegewide seminars on writing across the curriculum, critical thinking, and questioning in the classroom.

Conclusion

You can define good teaching any way you like. Simply take any outcome, process, or quality that seems desirable, and then define good teaching as whatever something called a teacher does to bring it about efficiently. Even a cursory fishing in the literature will net such definitions by the dozen. Good teaching has been defined as what the 'teacher' does to produce inspired pupils, excited pupils, interested pupils, creative pupils... (Broudy, as cited in Lewis, 1975, p. 19).

Excellent teaching and excellent teachers are really at the "heart of the matter" in community colleges. These award-winning programs have focused on selecting teachers who expressed interest in the courses and the students, who agreed to work collaboratively, and who were experienced in the classroom. The programs support professional development for teaching improvement and meeting the needs of at-risk students.

It is not possible to spend too much money or time seeking out and hiring the very best faculty; moreover, once hired, it is not possible to spend too much time or money orienting them to this special environment and developing their teaching and interpersonal skills. In business, Peters and Waterman (1982) contend that excellent companies are characterized by an ability to incorporate change in their institutions. In education, "excellence characterizes a school or college that sets high expectations and goals for all learners" (Pickett, 1984, p. 31). We contend that learners sit on both sides of the teacher's desk.

In recommendations from *A Nation at Risk*, the authors include the following as one of seven in the category of "teaching": "Persons preparing to teach should be required to meet high educational standards, to demonstrate an aptitude for teaching, and to demonstrate competence in an academic discipline. Colleges and universities offering teacher preparation programs should be judged by how well their graduates meet these criteria" (National Commission on Excellence in Education, 1983, p. 30). If community colleges want to continue to regard themselves as teaching institutions, and good ones at that, then they, too, should be judged for their abilities to select and train excellent teachers.

The Door Opens with Identification, Orientation, and Involvement:

Who Am I? and What Am I Doing Here?

I shall be telling this with a sigh
Somewhere ages and ages hence;
Two roads diverged in a wood, and I—
I took the one less traveled by,
And that has made all the difference.
> **—Robert Frost,**
> **"The Road Not**
> **Taken"**

In the mid-1960s, a developmental writing teacher, just completing her first year of teaching at a downtown community college, remarked to her colleagues: "I find it amazing that so many of my students will work so hard to make it when there is so little in their past to give them the confidence to try; I also find it remarkable that they finally achieve so much in spite of what at first appear to be overwhelming academic and personal odds; but, what I find most unbelievable is that they take the chance and even come at all!" Although more than a quarter of a century later these remarks might well be made with the same amount of incredulity by contemporary developmental teachers, increased attention to the growing numbers of at-risk students at all levels of education has expanded what we know about *who* they are and *why* (for what purposes) they come to college. Moreover, we have expanded our knowledge about belief systems and circumstances that affect their decision to try, and we know more about the complexity of the patterns of their attendance and their leaving. But we have only just begun to use that information to make informed decisions about *what* to do with them.

Expanding the Bird's-Eye View of the At-Risk Student

Some [students], whether because their previous education has been scanted in deference to no doubt well-meant social experimentation or for other reasons unknown to me, arrive seriously underprepared in English, foreign language, history or mathematics, and not infrequently in all those subjects. The Committee on Admissions and Financial Aids, rightly impressed by these individuals' *motivation* and *promise* [our italics], simply has to gamble on their ability, once in college, to make up for lost time; and the gamble pays off in a gratifyingly large percentage of cases. Neverthless, the diversion of effort into essentially remedial learning and the resultant foreclosing or at least postponement of other curricular possibilities imposes a tax one can't help feeling sorry to see levied against the progress of undergraduates. Its cost is further compounded by the fact that it can easily extend beyond the baccalaureate, continuing to be a burden to students pursuing professional studies at the graduate level (Ford, 1984, p. 32).

This statement reflects the immensity of the problem of underpreparedness in higher education. Franklin L. Ford served as dean of the faculty of arts and sciences at Harvard from 1962 to 1970; the students of which he spoke were Harvard undergraduates. Of course, the students he described are not the at-risk students that we describe, nor are the problems that he observed as severe as we believe them to be currently, but his comments do succinctly address the pervasiveness of the problem and its cost to institutions and individuals. In 1982 this commentary by Richard Lanham, director of the UCLA Writing Program, on the academic times at the University of California at Los Angeles, appeared in *The UCLA Monthly*:

> From 40 to 60 percent of approximately 4,000 entering UCLA freshmen—the top 12 percent of all California high school students—currently fail the English proficiency examination.

> Basic skills are the university's business right now because our students don't possess them. College students read and write like high school sophomores, law students (if you are lucky) like freshmen, and a high school principal crows with glee when his graduating seniors read at ninth-grade level (1982).

In 1985 Astin, a professor at that same institution, wrote with dismay that while UCLA accepted only those applicants who graduate in the top one-eighth of their high school senior class, more than half were required to take Subject A—a noncredit remedial course in English composition, "unflatteringly referred to as bonehead English" (1985, p. 107). Astin went on to say that some college faculty offer a common, but unrealistic and unproductive, response to the literacy problem—simply raise the standards of admission. Yet, he continued, institutions cannot afford to lose the body count (an economic loss with enrollment-driven funding and the steady decreases in college-age populations into the 1990s), nor will those for whom doors to higher education have so recently been opened—minority and low-income groups—be willing to accept their closing. The traditional efforts to educate underprepared students have been viewed essentially as the sink-or-swim philosophy (admit them but provide no special support or direction) or the philosophy that by admitting them, the institution has committed to help them achieve their educational goals (1985).

Complicating all philosophies about the institution's responsibilities to underprepared students is the continuing controversy created by the question posed after the first national study of remedial programs: Is it even possible to accomplish literacy development in college remedial courses, in one or two semesters, what 12 years [or less for many] could not achieve? (Roueche, 1968, pp. 47–48). Further complicating the issue of institutional responsibility, as Astin observed from his research, is another basic and quite subtle problem—the faculty's widespread belief "that underprepared students are simply not capable of profiting from higher education" (1985, p. 108).

Yet, Rossman and others, in their study of the City University of New York's (CUNY) 1970 decision to implement an open-admissions policy (when any graduate of a city high school was eligible to attend any one of the CUNY campuses) found that at the time of entry to college, the open-admissions students were substantially behind in verbal and mathematical skills as compared to the regularly admitted students; by the end of the first year, however, the open admissions students had improved substantially, reaching at least the levels demonstrated at the time of admittance by the students who had been regularly admitted (Rossman, 1975). Astin (1985) concluded from a review of that study that not only are underprepared students educable, but with adequate time and resources, they can reach a developmental point where they can perform college-level work.

Both Astin and Roueche agree that too little research has been conducted on the issue of whether underprepared students are educable at the college level. However, there are important and closely related recent studies of the military's experience with "cast-off youth"—cast off from school and work—that provide ample evidence that many who have been labeled as too limited in basic reading and mathematics skills to be "trainable" are indeed trainable in significant numbers. One recent study focused on the outcomes of Project 100,000, a mid-1960s social experiment by the military. Up to 100,000 personnel per year who did not meet minimum skill standards for recruitment (on the

Armed Forces Qualification Test, which measures reading and mathematics abilities) were accepted for military service, entering a special training program to be educated, socialized, and trained (Sticht, Armstrong, Hickey, and Caylor, 1987). The armed forces, as the nation's largest employers of young adults and the nation's largest testing and vocational training institution, was in fact enlisted in the War on Poverty; in support of the experiment, former Secretary of Defense Robert McNamara both warned and forecasted:

> Poverty in America affects national security too, by its appalling waste of talent. In the technological revolution that is seeping over the second half of our century, the prime national resource becomes more and more the potential of the human brain (McNamara, 1968, p. 130).

But critics of the military's use of "lower-aptitude personnel" warned of dire consequences—disciplinary problems, a "degrading" of the military services by the poor conduct and performance of these "new standard" recruits, and a waste of education, training, and post-military benefits. Sticht, et al., (1986) found far and away the majority performed satisfactorily (80 percent of these "cast-offs" completed their tour of duty, and more than 90 percent were rated above average in their service), did not cause excessive disciplinary problems, and did benefit from training and educational offerings of the military (8,000 made lifetime careers of the military, more than two-thirds took advantage of the G.I. Bill). Moreover, the military services unknowingly accepted even more men (almost 360,000) than were involved in Project 100,000 due to a mistake in the scoring of the Armed Services Vocational Aptitude Battery (ASVAB) (Eitelberg, 1988, pp. 73–74). When studies were conducted to determine how well the "PI's, potentially ineligibles" had performed (see Ramsberger and Means, 1987; Sticht, 1989b), the conclusion, as drawn by the Department of Defense's director of accession policy, was: "...a quarter-of-a-million people who did not meet the enlistment standards and should not have been able to do the job did in fact do it pretty well" (Sellman, 1987, p. 420).

A critical observation and stinging accusation surfaced from these findings: "The question is, does it make a difference in terms of performance if the military knows or does not know that people are low-aptitude?" (Sticht, Armstrong, Hickey, and Caylor, 1987, p. 65). As Astin commented: "What evidence does exist...suggests that the noneducability of underprepared students is a myth" (1985, p. 108); or as Roueche observed, "They simply have not been taught" (1984, p. 24).

Some of What We Know About the At-Risk Student's Decision to Try

Difficulties Perceiving Alternatives to Present Situations

Historically, humankind's beliefs about free choice reflect perceived juxtapositions of choice to current cultural and/or religious notions of fate and divine will. Many of the world's best-known literary works of fiction and social consciousness—for example, from Homeric epics, to *Oedipus Rex*, to Shakespeare's *Hamlet* and *MacBeth*, to Dreiser's *An American Tragedy*, or Wharton's *The House of Mirth*, to Sartre's *Being and Nothingness*—abound with those reflections, with remarkable examples of the individual struggling against all odds, approaching goal achievement, and having it snatched away by a force, or a fate, that is omnipresent and omniscient; of a social class unquestioningly accepting a pathetically harsh role in life without so much as a thought of another path or option; of the individual being driven by his own emotions and feelings that can be neither controlled nor changed, inexorably leading him to a place or position that he cannot avoid (see Greene, 1990, pp. 37–48, for a rich discussion of these themes).

> Perhaps strangely, given the presumed existence of open roads in our free society, there have been countless renderings of worlds in which there could be no interventions, no seizing of alternative possibility. We have been repeatedly made to feel an inexorability that informs the workings of environment, heredity, and history as well (Greene, 1990, p. 38).

In contemporary society, that "inexorability" has been described aptly. Among those who describe it well is Tessa Tagle, president of the Miami-Dade Community College Medical Center Campus. In painting a picture of poverty's life-stifling grasp on her own college neighborhood, she describes an inability to "seize an alternative possibility," which intensifies a learned tunnel vision that narrowly defines life choices, or at least reduces the options dramatically:

> They are the people who are always there—generation after generation...many of our poor still do not make the thoughtful connection between education and a better quality of life from within those neighborhoods where the motivation to want, to be, to do has ceased—not because of some cultural, racial, or other characteristic measure, but because of repeated broken promises, severed funding, or fragmented or politicized social services which have encouraged dependency (1991, p. 2).

In addition, President Raul Cardenas at South Mountain Community College (Arizona) describes this lack of thoughtful connection in a dramatic story about community perceptions. He recalled that when Paradise Valley Community College (Arizona), set in an affluent community, invited high school seniors and their parents to a "get to know your college" meeting, 3,000 invitations were mailed, and 1,000 people participated. Yet, while the invitations to seniors and their parents in the less affluent South Mountain service area numbered 8,000, those who participated numbered but 10!

> People in the community must be brought to understand, by example and by experience, that the college can be a factor for success in their lives. Changing the minds of this poulation, creating confidence or even a willingness to consider that the college can make a difference, is slow and tedious (Cardenas, in Gillett-Karam, Roueche, and Roueche, 1991, p. 198)

It is the limited belief in or vision of options, the ceasing of motivation, the depency on something outside themselves, that eventually drive one to an ultimate resignation: "The resignation may be due, of course, to helplessness, to the feeling of powerlessness due to discrimination or exclusion, or to the inability to 'read' the socio-economic situation" (1991, p. 42).

Learned Helplessness

Many at-risk students bring a sense of helplessness and uncontrollable failure with them to the classroom. The concepts of locus of control (Rotter, 1966) and attribution (Weiner, 1979) have come to the attention of learning and developmental theorists in the wake of considerable research suggesting that students' degrees of involvement in learning tasks are influenced by their perceptions of internal and external factors that control their behavior (Astin, 1985, p. 155). If students believe that "others" or "influences"—such as teachers, or poverty, or ability—control what happens to them, then they will assume a "why try?" attitude (Roueche and Mink, 1982). In her two surveys of developmental services, Cross documented that a major reason for student failure, as identified by the majority of respondents, was the student's "unwillingness to try" (1976).

In experiments with animals (Seligman, 1975) and with college students (Hiroto, 1974), the subjects *learned* to be helpless after being placed repeatedly in painful or traumatic situations that they could not control or alter, and they came to expect that any response to avoid the pain or trauma in future similar situations would be futile as well. Seligman noted that a single experience would not create such a lasting belief pattern, that eventually the experience would lose its effect; however, recurring experiences in which the subjects had no control produced significant behavior changes, including impaired motivation to respond, impaired ability to learn new behavior, and emotional disturbance (Roueche and Mink, 1982). Students who had experienced such situations generalized their attitudes, perceptions, and behaviors to all remotely similar future situations.

Moreover, Seligman discovered that when people or animals believe that what they do has no relationship to or is independent of responses or outcomes, they find it difficult to do anything at all to help themselves—they have learned helplessness very well. For example, when dogs believed that they were inescapably trapped in a painful situation, they would continue to accept the pain and attempt no escape, even when an escape path was obvious and even when the experimenter was coaxing them to safety and away from the painful situation. On the other hand, if animals and people discover that they can control a painful or traumatic situation by escaping it, they can control their fear; in addition, they can accept trauma and discomfort longer if they believe that they can control it or escape from it if they wished. However, if they feel they have no control, they simply become depressed and passive, slow down intellectually, and become socially unresponsive.

The effects of uncontrollable circumstances on an individual's belief system are powerful. Laboratory research on these phenomena, corroborated by research in personality theory, indicate that a belief that one can control outcomes is an important component of a healthy personality. Rotter's locus of control variable is expressed on a continuum from externality (control over outcomes is totally beyond one's individual control) to internality (control over outcomes is totally within one's individual control). Rotter hypothesized that a person's locus of control, his internality or externality, or at points along the continuum, is a result of a pattern of his past behaviors and experiences. This pattern, this mixture of both pleasurable and painful circumstances, forms a generalized expectation for future experiences. Verifications of Rotter's theory have generally shown that internal individuals have higher self-concepts, are generally better adjusted, more independent, more successful, more realistic in their aspirations, more open to new learning, more creative and flexible, and more self-reliant, and they show more interest in intellectual activity and achievement. External individuals believe that no matter how hard they try, they will fail for reasons that they cannot control; they believe that they cannot control what happens in the course, that the teachers "give" grades, that trying will not result in better grades. Many educators are beginning to realize that what has been identified as lack of motivation in students may well be students' belief that they are not in control of what happens, rendering all of their efforts futile (Roueche and Mink, 1982).

Inability to Set Realistic Goals

Another characteristic of the at-risk student, as identified by developmental educators in Cross's surveys, is the inability to set realistic goals. This behavior is also associated with individuals who can be described as failure-identifiers who are failure-threatened (1974). Atkinson and Feather's (1966) theory of achievement and motivation suggests that achievement-oriented persons will work hard at tasks for which their chances of success are 50-50; these individuals are not challenged by tasks that are too easy, and they do not choose tasks in which they have very slight chances for success. Using past experience to predict future behavior, they sometimes will choose to be risk-takers, but they are confirmed realists in the majority of their choices.

The failure-threatened personality will choose at all costs to avoid failure; he will either accept the difficult task that he knows he cannot complete and therefore does not threaten him, or he will choose the easiest task because he knows he can accomplish it. Some developmental educators have even described the unwillingness of their students to leave a task that they have accomplished repeatedly to take on the next task at a new level of difficulty (Cross, 1974). Some colleges have explained that in preregistration counseling sessions in which both at-risk students and more traditional students are advised against enrolling for courses identified as too difficult in light of their academic test results or high school grades, the at-risk student will more likely choose to enroll in the face of imminent academic disaster than will the more traditional student. At-risk students will choose these courses over others that are more realistic in spite of the advice, appearing not to be threatened by tasks that they already know are too difficult for them to complete. Some of these fear-of-failure theories may also address some of the reasons that the at-risk student would choose, according to Cross (1974), to apply at an open-door community college that would accept them in any case, or a highly selective college from which they would expect rejection, rather than a college whose entrance requirements were less clearly drawn and from which they might be rejected.

Limited Perceptions of Pay-Offs for Getting an Education

In 1988 Bill Honig, California's superintendent of education, remarked: "In a free country, where you have free choice, you have to choose from an educated perspective. Our teachers never make the most important point about education: It helps you lead a better life" (Magnet, 1988, p. 94). Because experience remains the best teacher, driving that point home or making it credible requires moving from words to actions; students must experience the evidence, or at least have the opportunity to witness a small glimmer of that "better life." William Rukeyser, a California education official, after describing the newly formed California Partnership Academies in 48 public high schools statewide (partnerships between selected secondary schools and high-tech businesses that created internships for dropout-prone but promising ninth graders), observed: "One of the big things lacking for kids from lower socioeconomic groups is real-life examples of how education pays off...A kid from a privileged suburb sees the direct connection between having an MBA and a BMW every day. But for others, it's an abstract concept that doing well in school pays off, literally" (Molnar, 1992, p. 39).

Helping At-Risk Students Make the Decision to Try

As John Dewey once observed, there must be a "place where the formed disposition and the immediate situation touch and intersect" (1934, p. 266). Efforts must be made to keep history from repeating itself—to inform the welfare mother that she is not compelled to have more children and remain in the system forever, the divorced older woman that she need not face the rest of her life without job skills and on limited funds, the high school dropout that he is not trapped by his poor decision in a life of low-paying jobs or unemployment, and the potential (no matter how youthful) school dropout who has no role models to provide incentives for graduation that there is another path to take. Dewey concluded sadly that most people who are caught in what appear to be desperate or dead-end circumstances are unable to "imagine" their way out of the events of the past and propel themselves into another kind of future—they cannot re-evaluate the importance of their past experiences on present circumstances, nor imagine what would be possible if they decided to consider different options for their lives. They cannot learn from their past mistakes and use that learning to help shape new circumstances. As the philosopher Mary Warnock wrote: "There is always *more* to experience and *more in* what we experience than we can predict" (1978, p. 202). More importantly, she continued that "it is the main purpose of education to give people the opportunity of not ever being, in this sense, bored: of not ever succumbing to a sense of futility, or to the belief that they have come to an end of what is worth having" (p. 203).

Yet, it is not enough that these individuals see the wall that is standing in the way of something they want, then decide their predicaments or situations should not be tolerated; they must be guided into the idea that the change is possible (Greene, 1990). They must, as Freire (1970) emphasized, be brought to understand that the situations in which they live do not have to continue, that their own deliberate action is capable of effecting change. Of singular importance is the effort that the individual invests in making a change. It must be that individual's decision to take the change on as a project: "There is a continuity, then, between existing opportunities, the lived situation of the individual...the interest of the individual, and the grasping of the second chance" (Greene, 1990, p. 44).

For many years, critics and supporters alike have expressed their amazement that while most colleges and universities were tightening registration requirements and raising enrollment standards, community colleges were actively recruiting the very students that these other institutions were writing out of their enrollment policies. Early on, most recruitment strategies were designed to appeal to the potential returning adult student, many of them women, the GED recipients, and potential students for specially funded job training and literacy development programs. Others addressed the traditional college-age student, as linkages with high schools encouraged co-enrollment and summer bridge programs. Since 1971 recruitment of at-risk students has been on the increase; the Davis, et al., (1975) study of that year recorded that 66 percent of all colleges studied were involved in some kind of recruitment efforts; in 1976 Cross recorded that in her 1970 survey, 64 percent of the community colleges were recruiting nontraditional students, up to 82 percent by 1974. In 1977 Roueche and Snow documented that 89 percent of community colleges were recruiting nontraditional students through local newspapers. Recruitment methods most frequently cited were radio and television advertisements; solicitation of local agencies; career days and campus open houses; shopping mall booths; local fair exhibits; personal telephone calls; use of mobile vans' visits to high schools, military bases, and homes; direct mail; and special projects directed to appeal to particular groups—older students, returning women, and so on. Many colleges used teams of faculty and students to visit with potential students, assuming that current students would be the more effective salespeople of the idea of going to college (Roueche and Snow, 1977).

Recruitment efforts are currently being designed to appeal to younger students in the lower grades in public schools, as data indicate dropout rates at earlier and earlier ages (National Center for Education Statistics, 1992). A "new" medical school at the Medical Center Campus at Miami-Dade Community College, designed for youngsters between the ages of 11 and 14, is implemented in the summers to interest and further encourage young students to consider medicine as a vocation and to tackle the overwhelming likelihood that the majority of them will drop out at 14, 15, and 16 years of age (Tagle, 1991, p. 2; Gillett-Karam, Roueche, and Roueche, 1991). South Mountain

Community College's Achieving College Education Program identifies the lower quartile of high school students in its service area, visits them in teams to interest them in South Mountain, invites them to the college at the end of their sophomore year, and begins a summer bridge program that increases in intensity and scope annually until the students are taking college courses prior to high school graduation and then enrolling in South Mountain (Gillett-Karam, Roueche, and Roueche, 1991). Santa Fe Community College's "Magic of Education" programs were created to help influence local children to stay in school. This joint program between the college and the Santa Fe Public School system encourages students in grades 6–12 to stay in school and to continue their education after high school. Career fairs, among other activities, provide students with information about vocational training, career options, and preparing for college. Such efforts encourage and lead potential students to "see the wall" and to identify possible steps by which to take it down.

Responding to the At-Risk Students' Decision to Try

Equity and Excellence

Cross (1984) observed that the "overwhelming purpose of education is...making winners out of ordinary people. Yet, historically, in most of the periods emphasizing excellence, education has reverted to *selecting* [our emphasis] winners rather than *creating* [our emphasis] them." Sticht identified an impressive example of the selection versus creation phenomenon. After analyzing Project 100,000 data, he reported that, contrary to expectations, skill development training for potentially ineligible men appeared to have been successful; by all evaluative criteria, these men had performed satisfactorily as a group. He expressed amazement that, in light of the data analysis, the project still had serious critics and many openly pronounced it an absolute failure. Yet, he was most surprised by the military's final response, observing that in view of the project's positive outcomes, "It might have been expected that the policy of excluding hundreds of thousands of young adults from military service might have been reversed. But it was not. Instead, standards were immediately raised, and a request for more millions of dollars to recruit higher quality personnel was made by the military and accepted by Congress" (Sticht, 1989a, p. 2279).

Robert McCabe, president of Miami-Dade Community College, observed:

Many who are concerned with improving the quality of postsecondary education offer a simplistic solution to the problem, and that is to reverse the gains in access and limit admission to those demonstrating high ability on completion of high school. While raising admission criteria might be appropriate for certain universities, such a policy applied to all higher education would have a devastating, negative impact on this country. The American economy needs more, rather than fewer, well-educated individuals (1982, p. 1).

Astin observed: "The more I consider the twin issues of excellence and equity, the more I am convinced that there is something inherently contradictory about a higher education system where quality and opportunity are in conflict rather than in harmony" (1985, p. 100). In surveying leading educators about their views on the relationship between excellence and equity, Astin not surprisingly discovered the yin and yang of a continuing controversial issue, the clashes of theory and practice, the conflict of design and implementation. On the one hand, "It's nice to have an educational system that functions in a way that's reasonably congruent with the constitution of its country" (Chickering); and "I think it is a false populism to play one against the other...Only a simple-minded understanding of democracy leaves out the possibility for excellence" (Katz) (in Astin, 1985, p. 101). Yet, on the other, "...I feel that equity, as I have defined it, costs so much...that for the foreseeable future, equity is unattainable with quality" (Bowen); and the simultaneous pursuit of excellence and equity is seen as difficult:

> ...as we provide opportunities for the so-called disadvantaged to reach some level of performance at a given set of institutions, society keeps changing the rules of the game, so it's no longer 'Did you get into college?' or 'Did you graduate?' but 'Where did you graduate from?'.... It's a vanishing Holy Grail. It's the way this society is constructed (Edgerton) (both in Astin, 1985, p. 102).

While the arguments are serious and convincing, they must be resolved in some fashion to address the overwhelming demands of meeting the needs of the at-risk student; in the words of the Carnegie Commission on Higher Education: "What the American nation now needs from higher education can be summed up in two words: quality and equality" (1968, p. 53).

Orientation

Quality and equality are those intangibles that some might see as essential to "leveling the playing field." One of those levelers might well be orientation—a critical entryway into the college. The at-risk student, perhaps even more than the traditional student, requires a careful orientation into what is essentially a new world. In a 1989 study that used 1980 U.S. Census data to determine the extent to which community college students were *first-generation* college students, Willett discovered that 80 percent came from families where the parents or grandparents did not hold college degrees (1989). In light of the increasing diversity among their student populations, it is curious that there is so little evidence that community colleges value, much less require, strong orientation programs. Several of the colleges housing award-winning programs featured in our study required orientation. De Anza College, "unlike most community colleges in California" (Mekis, 1990, p. 32), requires an "orientation to college" course when students arrive on campus. Some four-year institutions also require orientation to their programs. However, there are concerns that orientation at four-year institutions is not designed to provide for the special needs of transfer students (Richardson and Bender, 1987; Jacobi, 1988), nor are orientations typically held for students who enter these institutions in the spring or summer of the academic year (Mekis, 1990).

One orientation that we know well is at The University of Texas at Austin. This particular orientation is mentioned here not because it is unique, but because it is so revealing about long-held perceptions of differences in student "needs." All students entering the MBA program—a highly selective graduate business program—are required to attend orientation activities prior to the beginning of classes. The fact that these students have already been identified as "eager beavers," are academically well-prepared, and are savvy about college and university environments does not deter the university from making this demand, and attendance is taken daily. One reward for successful completion of the orientation is the opportunity to take advantage of early registration.

What do these graduate business students learn in orientation? In addition to the traditional information about the college and the university, program options and requirements, potential markets for later job searches, and so forth, they are provided with some rather untraditional data—they are provided with copies of the results of students evaluations of all MBA faculty (the faculty are named in the reports). Moreover, they hear their future professors and currently enrolled MBA students talk about stress—how to deal with and manage the anxieties and worries of graduate school; about time management—how to arrange personal schedules for important combinations of work and leisure time; and so on. All university expectations and almost everything that one would need to know to be successful at the university are quite clear by the orientation's last session.

Astin recommends offering similar orientation sessions for all students, informing students about the importance of being highly involved with the institution and informing them about the signs of low involvement—boredom with classes, academic difficulty, minimal contact with other students. Tinto (1975) stated that among the most serious problems with which at-risk students must contend are those created by family background (social status, values, expectations), individual attitudes (sex, race, ability), and precollege schooling (GPA, academic and social attainments). These factors interact with the student's goal commitments (as seen in commitments to academic performance and development) and institutional commitment (as seen in interaction with peer groups and faculty) (Tinto, 1975). Cope and Hannah's (1975) review of research on student goal and institutional commitment led to the conclusion that, of all the personal attributes they studied, "personal commitment to either an academic or occupational goal is the single most important determinant of persistence in college" (p. 19). Every institution should get students to commit to goals early on, perhaps beginning with such questions as "Why are you here?" and "What do you want to achieve during your time with us?" (Noel, et al., 1986).

Various researchers have identified critical activities for orientation sessions for all students. Counseling and advising to identify student interests and goals typically headed the list. Others included evaluating the student's academic standing and identifying appropriate remedial sessions/classes, and reviewing established institutional early-warning systems (Roueche and Baker, 1987); scheduling opportunities for peer associations and peer counseling (Reyes, 1986); touring campus and classroom layout, meeting with departments and former students who will serve as support groups, meeting with faculty and potential mentors, and incorporating social occasions (such as picnics) into the orientation design (Vallejo, 1988, personal interview, as discussed in Drew, 1990).

Astin recommends that initial orientation should be followed with orientation courses held during the first term after enrollment, which would provide continued and in-depth familiarity with the college and an arena where students' life goals and relationships with the college experience could be discussed (1985). Another suggestion was that the college seminar course should be collectively taught by interdisciplinary faculty, working closely with counseling services and students' faculty mentors and meeting weekly to include

- Extracurricular activities and clubs; college culture; how to make new friends
- Library orientation
- Test-taking and study skills

- Academic regulations—grade point averages, probation, course withdrawals, remedial assistance
- Selecting a major (take a career exploration exercise to assist in determining a career choice)
- Stress management
- Understanding the transitional period into college life
- Commitment to a college career and how to finance it
- Understanding oneself and others; self-reflective exercises; keeping a journal that the faculty mentor can review, thus discovering potential problems
- Basic writing skills and vocabulary building
- AIDS information; everything students want to know, but are afraid to ask
- Leadership training
- Successfully completing the "freshman experience"
- A fantastic celebration at course completion; student commitment to the freshman year (Vallejo, 1988, as discussed in Drew, 1990)

While students need information about the college and about what is expected of them, it is surprising how many institutions fail to provide adequate information or provide it in a format that is useful or available to the student. Too frequently, the information that is provided is too formal to be useful to the student, and in fact may not offer so much as a glimpse of the informal character of the social and intellectual communities on campus—those communities that may have more to do with a student's deciding to stay or leave than any or all other factors combined (Tinto, 1987, p. 146). Moreover, they infrequently give the student information that she needs to establish personal contact with individuals on campus that can help her with advising, counseling, financial aid, and so on; yet, this makes establishing those nonthreatening contacts overly dependent on the student's ability and willingness to seek important information that she needs.

It is the establishment of early contacts for new students—with other students, with faculty, and with staff—not just the dispensing of information, that sets apart the most effective orientation programs from those less so (Tinto, 1987). It is that foundation, the creation of a system whereby important social and intellectual relationships are established, that helps new students make the transition into the world of college (Pascarella, Terenzini, and Wolfle, 1985, from Tinto, 1987). Tinto lists a variety of techniques for orientation:

- Bringing upperclass students, faculty, and staff to meet with new students in informal situations in order to discuss the sorts of hurdles they are likely to face during their college careers
- Creating mentoring and tutoring programs with more experienced students and faculty that extend throughout the year

- Creating a mentoring system that provides informal advising and opportunities for making friends and identifying important role models
- Using orientation as the beginning stage of an institutional retention assessment program through assessment of student needs and concerns
- Creating an important linchpin around which institutional services can be provided in an integrated and systematic manner
- Using data from admissions and past student cohorts to produce estimates of "dropout proneness" for different student groups, to trigger "early-warning systems" in an integrated manner, and to target students for special interventions (abstracted from Tinto, 1987, pp. 147–48)

A 1990 issue of *Innovation Abstracts* featured "Hunting for Orientation Ideas," a description of an orientation program that required all new faculty and staff to participate in a "scavenger hunt" for important information and documents. The subcommittee in charge of the hunt identified the targets, based on the following criteria: importance of site to the hunters; importance of site for campus geographical orientation; and importance of site for students. The participants were to return with "treasures"—documents or stickers that indicated they had reached the destinations successfully. The hunt was to last approximately 70 minutes, and a map was provided for the sake of efficiency; a group leader was provided with the map and a list of scavenger hunt clues. Responses to what was first considered a risky orientation proved both enjoyable and useful. Numerous colleges responding to the article recounted their adaptations of this orientation for their incoming students. They included

- Bring back a "buck" (college-created) from the financial aid office.
- Bring back a bookmark from the library's service center.
- Bring back the number of living plants in the counseling office.
- Bring back a balloon from the child care center.
- Bring back a flyer from the computer learning center.
- Bring back the office number for disabled student services.
- Bring back the name of the statue in front of the gymnasium.
- Bring back a picture of the receptionist for the vice president of academic affairs (provided by the college).
- Bring back an appointment sheet from the medical center.

Participants, rather than thinking the hunt childish or a waste of time, remarked that they felt more at home and more familiar with their surroundings, that they learned more about the college in a very short period of time, and that they believed that it made the college "less concrete and more heart" (Forman, 1990).

Student Involvement with the College

"Students learn by becoming involved" (Astin, 1985, p. 133).

What I mean by involvement is neither mysterious nor esoteric. Quite simply, student involvement refers to the amount of physical and psychological energy that the student devotes to the academic experience. A highly involved student is one who, for example, devotes considerable energy to studying, spends a lot of time on campus, participates actively in student organizations, and interacts frequently with faculty members and other students (p. 134).

Research consistently indicates that half of the students attending community colleges and four-year institutions do not meet with faculty members outside of class, many have had but few individual contacts with their instructors, and many students may be seriously affected by the consequences of this limited interaction (Pace, 1989; Baird, 1990; Friedlander and MacDougall, 1992). While Astin observes that one of the major barriers of minority students' success in college is their previous academic experiences (1982), and while Zwerling believes that "a student's past and background, in effect, become his or her destiny" (1980, p. 55)—in other words, that the decision to remain in college will be most negatively affected by past academic performance, low aspirations, and low socioeconomic status, Tinto claims that the decision to remain in college or to withdraw is "more a function of what occurs *after entry* [our emphasis] than what precedes it" (1987, p. 6).

Tinto disagrees with those researchers who minimize the importance of social contact for community college student persistence and who discourage colleges from creating significant social communities on campus: "...there are reasons to suspect that social and intellectual contact beyond the classroom may be as important, if not more important, to persistence in commuting colleges as it is in residential ones" (Tinto, 1987, p. 75). Moreover, he suggests that the methodology of the quantitative research, which produced the findings with which he disagrees, may have masked important factors in a student's decision to leave the college; perhaps the social interaction is so low on community college campuses that significant relationships between contact and departure cannot be measured for the general population or for special subgroups within that population.

Pascarella and Terenzini, in *How College Affects Students* (1991), note that numerous research findings have documented the importance of residency programs to keeping students in school, and that community colleges, almost by definition commuter institutions, must find mechanisms by which they can offset the absence of such programs. They must discover ways to encourage and promote "fit" between the institution and the student, to provide in some other fashion the complementary features that a residency program would provide—the relationships that develop from active and physical association with the institution. In the case of disadvantaged students, researchers have assigned particular importance to residential programs for retaining these students who are torn between the institution and community responsibilities, between college and families (Muehl and Muehl, 1972; Chickering, 1974).

These researchers and others point to the importance of external "pulls" on the student who lives at home and in a community where value orientations do not support the goals of a college education (Roth, 1985; Weidman, 1985, both as discussed in Astin, 1985). Disadvantaged or at-risk students may discover that they must "at least partially reject membership in communities that have been part of their upbringing" (Tinto, 1987, p. 61). As a case in point, a study of De Anza College's minority transfer program yielded several critical perceptions held by staff members; among them was the notion that students sacrifice cultural background and ethnic identity when getting an education: "When you are from a different cultural background than the majority, you have to play their game to get to where you want to go. You have to compromise a lot of what you're comfortable with, in order to succeed in school"; "I think a lot of us grow up feeling un-okay about ourselves because we're brought into a system that we're supposed to fit into rather than be a part of. It's like we've got to fit, we've got to change, we've got to mold ourselves..." (Mekis, 1990, p. 98). Yet, as Tinto suggests, persistence may be "aided by the existence of a supportive subculture in one's home community, as well as within the college" (1987, p. 210). However, there is a real cost to this supportive subculture in the college; Pascarella and Terenzini (1991) warn in their recommendations for future funding policies that community colleges' disproportionate numbers of disadvantaged and "high-risk" students will increase significantly the costs of providing for such "supportive subcultures"— increased demands for the support services and intervention strategies required for their academic success are simply more costly. De Anza College's forecast for the future of A STARTING POINT is an instructive example, indeed (see Chapter 3).

Assessment

The controversy surrounding comprehensive basic skills assessment for all students became especially heated in the late 1960s and early 1970s. Arguments were that assessment would lead to "unfair tracking" of students into courses that identified them as academically "needy" and that minority students would be unfairly identified because their performances on traditional standardized tests were predictably low (given the alleged cultural biases inherent in these testing procedures). However, in the early 1970s, when it became clear that the greatest numbers of students in developmental programs were majority, not minority, students, as well as the fact that developmental students cut across all gender, age, and academic levels, the idea of assessment became less controversial. As assessment has expanded to include a variety of procedures, and as outcome data have indicated that test scores are still the best indicators of potential academic difficulty, the controversy has abated.

Moreover, the controversial nature of assessment is mellowing somewhat as increasing calls for educational accountability nationwide are providing impetus to institutional efforts to evaluate instruction, both in general and in basic skills. Florida was one of the first states to mandate minimum competency skills testing, beginning at the high school level and, in 1984, extending to college. The College-Level Academic Skills Test (CLAST) was specially constructed to measure 117 computational and communication competencies through math, reading, and writing subtests, as well as one essay requirement. Normed for college sophomores, all parts of the CLAST must be passed by any student wishing to receive an associate degree or enroll in upper-division classes at a four-year institution in Florida.

While the intent of the testing program was to guarantee individual skill levels, at the institutional level the program has been used as a measure of institutional success (although there are serious questions about the validity of using aggregated scores as measures of institutional success) (Rogers and Steinhoff, 1991). In a study of Florida colleges, the purpose of which was to investigate attitudes of faculty toward the CLAST as well as concerns of senior administrators related to competency testing, use of test results, and strategies intended to improve student performance, the researchers found that institutions used aggregate test results as a starting point for "informal self-assessment," measuring curricula against the targeted competencies and making indicated changes. The testing program had added urgency to questions of how best to provide academic support for at-risk students.

Other statewide mandates are playing an increasing part in shaping the evaluation processes of postsecondary education and, in particular, of developmental education, and in exerting focused attention on the at-risk student. The Texas Academic Skills Program (TASP) was created in 1987 as an early assessment and academic support program for all students entering Texas public institutions of higher education. It includes mandatory testing, advising, placement, remedial education, and the evaluation of results and effectiveness of remediation at the college and state levels. Since fall 1989 state law has required students to take the TASP Test—a basic skills examination to determine students' levels of reading, writing, and mathematics—and to ascertain whether the skills they demonstrate are adequate for "college success," as defined by higher education faculty (also see Placement for further requirements). Students are required to satisfactorily complete all three sections of the TASP Test before taking any upper-level courses beyond 60 semester credit hours. (Students who completed any college-level work prior to fall 1989 are exempt from the TASP requirements.)

The current state and national focus on the assessment issue comes as a result of a myriad of concerns about underpreparedness and at-riskness and, moreover, about elementary, secondary, and higher education's inability or unwillingness to affect or address these problems. Assessment at individual colleges and universities, as research data indicate historically, is not a new idea; however, as some researchers observe: "Much of the good work being done in community college preregistration assessment is overshadowed by the nightmare of poor and often destructive practices that pass for assessment" (Barshis and Guskey, 1983, p. 87). Barshis and Guskey trace poor assessment practices to the following causes: low priority for assessment; poor institutional leadership; declining resources for testing and counseling; a "body count" approach to recruitment and registration (usually including a mass registration in larger community colleges); an unwillingness by academic departments to be involved in the testing process; unclear or faulty prerequisite structure for entry-level courses; part-time students, late registrants, and advisees of ill-informed faculty "falling into the cracks of any comprehensive assessment effort"; inconsistency in programming; and inadequate acquisition of valuable information about student deficiencies, attitudes, and so on (1983, pp. 87–88). Finally, they point to the questionable links between the specific objectives of developmental courses and services and the skill levels being assessed.

In *Salvage, Redirection or Custody?*, Roueche (1968) reported that the most common criterion used for placing students in remedial programs was test scores. At the same time, available research indicated that there was little, if any, correlation between the placement test scores and subsequent grades or success in remedial programs (Schenz, 1964; Powell, 1966). Test scores were rarely used to determine if students had made progress or were ready to enter college-level courses; rather, the grades they earned in the remedial classes were used to determine their eligibility. One of the final recommendations of this first study of remedial programs was that colleges should "seriously reconsider the practice of using only aptitude and achievement test scores for the purpose of placing students in remedial programs" as research indicated that they had validity only when "used in *conjunction* with other predictors." Further, it was recommended that if test scores were to be used for placement purposes, the scores should determine student achievement in the remedial program and readiness to enter regular college courses (Roueche, 1968, p. 48).

A 1971 study determined that approximately 50 percent of all colleges provided some form of assessment of student learning difficulty (Davis, et al., 1975). In 1976 Cross reported that her surveys of remedial or developmental services indicated diagnostic testing had increased from only 40 percent of the colleges responding in 1970 to 82 percent of those responding in 1974. In 1977 Roueche and Snow documented that 83 percent of community colleges, from a study of 300 two- and four-year colleges, used diagnostic testing or assessment. When data from 1,452 institutions of higher education were reported in a 1984 study, all respondents favored mandatory pre-assessment although there were significant differences among the groups, among the assessment practices, and among the skill areas of reading, writing, and mathematics; on the average, four-year institutions were more inclined than community colleges to implement mandatory assessment (Roueche, Baker, and Roueche, 1984). Also, in 1991 the National Center for Education Statistics documented that in fall 1989 about 90 percent of institutions providing remedial courses used placement tests to select participants for such courses—specifically, 94 percent used placement tests for remedial writing, 93 percent for mathematics, and 88 percent for reading (1991a). In 1992 a study of developmental education in selected two- and four-year institutions, funded by the Exxon Education Foundation, determined that 96 percent of those surveyed had assessment and placement procedures in place, and 75 percent had mandatory assessment. These researchers, as well, reported that the four-year institutions were more likely than two-year institutions to implement mandatory assessment (Bonham and Claxton, 1992).

In *Access and Excellence* (Roueche and Baker, 1987), serious skill deficiencies of incoming students were identified as one of the most critical problems facing Miami-Dade Community College, a college that enrolls a more diverse student population than any other community college in the nation. Beginning in spring 1979 and fully implemented by fall 1981, assessment testing (using the Comparative Guidance and Placement Test) was and currently is required of all first-time-in-college students carrying nine hours, students who have earned 15 or more credits, and students planning to enroll in a mathematics or English course—in effect, assessment is mandatory for all students. Non-native speakers of English are allowed to take a different test, but they must show adequate proficiency in English prior to enrolling in any college-level courses, which requires that they take intensive training in English (Roueche and Baker, 1987, pp. 47–48).

In 1987 a council report to the American Association of Community Colleges Board of Directors, "Access, Assessment, and Developmental Education in the Community College," noted "that access through the open-door community college without comprehensive assessment and developmental programming was counterproductive to the basic purpose of providing opportunity toward the achievement of student aspirations" ("Access, Assessment, ..." 1987, p. 38). Assessment was defined as "a systematic process by which students' abilities and interests are determined" (p. 39). It proposed, in particular, that *effective* assessment programs should be broader in scope than pre-enrollment tests of ability in the traditional basic skills of mathematics, reading, or writing, and that they include measurement of self-concept, study skills, motivation, educational readiness, educational goals, and past achievement.

Placement

In the 1960s and 1970s, there was serious controversy over the issues of mandatory assessment, but not nearly as serious as that created by the issues of mandatory placement. Current research findings attest to the reality that, while issues of mandatory assessment are advancing to some resolution, issues surrounding mandatory placement are still unresolved in the majority of institutions of higher education.

In 1977 Roueche and Snow addressed the question of mandatory placement:

> Should we require students to take some remedial courses if we deem them necessary? This is a touchy issue; however, *our data support such a practice* [our emphasis]....We must exercise care in requiring developmental courses. We must be careful, too, that these programs are not merely another systematic attempt to segregate minorities into a lower-quality educational track. We can and should demonstrate that these courses are meeting the objectives for which they have been established....We do not improve quality by mandatory attendance; instead, we may encourage frustration and deterioration. However, some colleges with mandatory courses for some students do seem to provide an opportunity for students to feel good about learning—and students spread the word (p. 85).

Interestingly, Sticht (1989a) spoke to that potential "frustration and deterioration" following his review of the Project 100,000 data. After expressing his great surprise that the military would choose to raise recruitment standards at tremendous expense rather than initiate other similar projects—thus providing the military with a sizable pool of "new standard" recruits—Sticht noted that one implication of the military's experience with lower-aptitude personnel is that similar attitudes may be held by civilian organizations:

> If we declare large numbers of the citizenry "functional illiterate," we may cause needless abandonment of many youth and adults, and the proliferation of programs of "second chance" and "remedial" education that are not genuinely needed. The assignment to such programs of millions of youth and adults might undermine their self concepts, and contribute to a reduction in their motivation to seek work, and to pursue programs of education and training that contribute to genuine needs. This may account, in part, for the fact that many eligible adults do not pursue adult literacy education, and over half of those that do quit before completing their objectives (referenced to Sticht, 1988; taken from Sticht, 1989a, p. 2279).

Sticht's negative perception of remedial efforts is obvious. He may well mirror a larger general sense of concern about the ineffectiveness and the inhumanity of remedial programs that in turn strengthen any general aversion to mandatory placement.

So what have the last two decades of addressing the placement issue produced? Cross's 1970 and 1974 surveys of developmental services recorded that from 1970 to 1974, the practice of requiring remedial courses for certain students fell from 79 percent to 59 percent of the institutions surveyed (Cross, 1976). The 1977 national survey of developmental/remedial education programs documented that remedial/developmental courses were mandatory in 28.8 percent of responding institutions and not mandatory in 61.2 percent (no response 10.1 percent). In addition, developmental courses were optional in 74.8 percent and not optional in 8.6 percent of responding institutions (16.5 percent no response) (Roueche and Snow, 1977, pp. 137–138). The 1984 national survey reported that responding community colleges mandated reading (40 percent), writing (46 percent), and math (42 percent) remedial courses; four-year institutions, on average, were slightly more inclined to mandate enrollment (Roueche, Baker, and Roueche, 1984).

The National Center for Education Statistics's survey of college-level remediation reported that in fall 1989:

- At least 50 percent of those institutions offering remedial courses usually required students needing remediation to take remedial courses.
- Remedial courses were voluntary at only 2 to 3 percent of responding institutions.

- At the remainder of the responding institutions, remedial courses were recommended but not required.
- Remedial writing was required by 68 percent of the institutions, remedial mathematics was required by 63 percent, and remedial reading by 54 percent.
- Requiring remedial courses was more common at four-year colleges than two-year colleges—for example, 74 percent of four-year colleges and 51 percent of two-year colleges required remediation in mathematics, 80 percent of four-year colleges and 57 percent of two-year colleges required remediation in writing, and 65 percent of four-year colleges and 45 percent of two-year colleges required remediation in reading. In contrast, recommending but not requiring remedial courses occurred more frequently in two-year than four-year colleges—for example, taking remedial mathematics courses was recommended by 48 percent of two-year colleges and 23 percent of four-year colleges (1991a, p. 8).

The Southern Regional Education Board's study of practices for remedial studies in all institutions of higher education in SREB states concluded that the majority of all responding institutions had mandatory course requirements in reading (61 percent), writing (72 percent), and mathematics (71 percent). However, the data indicated significant variations by institutional type and subject area: for example, institutions with mandatory course requirements ranged from 90 percent for four-year to 61 percent for two-year institutions; mandatory course requirements for liberal arts/comprehensive institutions ranged from 66 percent for reading to 87 percent for writing (Abraham, 1992, p. 12).

The Appalachian State University's National Center for Developmental Education's 1992 study of developmental education practices in two- and four-year institutions documented that 50 percent of the responding institutions reported mandatory placement; moreover, four-year institutions were more likely than were two-year to implement mandatory placement (Bonham and Claxton, 1992).

How important is mandatory placement to the success of at-risk students? From various descriptions of exemplary developmental programs, a reasonably consistent pattern of thorough assessment leading to appropriate placement was discovered (Roueche and Snow, 1977; Beal and Noel, 1980). The 1984 study of college responses to low-achieving students documented that one characteristic of succcessful programs was mandatory placement (Roueche, Baker, and Roueche, 1984). In response to the overwhelming problem of significant academic skill deficiencies among its incoming students, Miami-Dade Community College instituted mandatory developmental courses. College officials observed that because the lack or the low level of skills with which a student enters the college could well extend the time it will take to get into regular college-level work and complete a degree plan, the college's requiring skill development courses prior to entering college-level work could add months or years to the college experience. However, they agree that student skills at the time of admission are not the focus of their concern; rather, they choose to focus on the skills the student possesses when he completes his work (Roueche and Baker, 1987). A study to investigate responses to Florida's CLAST determined that "to be most effective, participation in academic support programs should be mandatory, closely monitored, and tied directly to specific credit courses" (Rogers and Steinhoff, 1991, p. 37).

While the term *mandatory* did not appear in the language of the 1987 council report to the AACC Board of Directors, the message of the report strongly implied that "access" and "skill development" are the two sides of the "educational quality" coin, that development is a critical outcome of the assessment process.

> Community colleges that allow or advise underprepared students to enter classes for which they are not prepared may be closing the door to student success and blocking the road to achievement of both institutional and student educational goals. Assessment is a vital component for effective teaching and learning. An effective assessment program will promote educational quality, access, and the efficient use of institutional resources ("Access, Assessment, ...," 1987, p. 39).

Simultaneous Enrollment in Regular Courses

A familiar medical analogy can describe what's wrong with simultaneous enrollment in remedial and college-level courses. If a runner is diagnosed with a serious heart problem and undertakes corrective measures for that problem in the morning, he should not be allowed to run the 50- or 100-yard dash in the afternoon. The corrective measures should be completed satisfactorily prior to his receiving permission to participate in a race. A common alternative position to absolute restriction is allowing this same individual to take part in some less strenuous activities for a variety of social and avocational reasons, but restricting him from engaging in those activities that would have serious and potentially life-threatening consequences. In practice, however, institutions are allowed to respond to similar skill problems by any means they devise. For example, in Texas, students required by state law to take the TASP Test and further required to complete any remediation courses that test results indicate are necessary, are required to enroll for remediation in *one area each semester only, even if two or three areas of deficiency have been identified* [our emphasis] (Hanson and Kerker, 1991).

The NCES national survey (1991a) reported that some institutions allowed students to take any regular academic courses along with their remedial courses, others limited students in remedial courses to some regular courses (for example, a student in remedial mathematics may not be allowed to take any regular mathematics courses but would be allowed to enroll in regular English or history), and others did not allow them to take any regular academic courses until they had completed their remedial coursework satisfactorily. It specifically reported

- About two-thirds of institutions allowed students to take some regular academic courses while taking remedial courses
- The remaining one-third of the institutions allowed students to take any regular academic course while taking remedial courses
- Almost no institutions (1 to 2 percent) entirely prohibited students who were enrolled in remedial courses from taking regular academic courses (pp. 9–10)

Two-year colleges were more likely to allow students enrolled in remedial courses to simultaneously enroll in *some* regular academic courses than they were to allow simultaneous enrollment in *any* regular courses—for example, 69 percent allowed some regular academic courses for students enrolled in remedial reading, and 31 percent allowed any regular academic courses; 72 percent allowed some regular academic courses for students enrolled in remedial writing, and 27 percent allowed any; 71 percent allowed some regular academic courses for students enrolled in remedial math, and 27 percent allowed any (1991a, see Table 9, p. 32).

The SREB survey reported that when asked whether simultaneous enrollment in remedial and regular college courses was *not permitted, permitted with restrictions,* or *permitted without restrictions,* about three-fifths of the responding institutions *permitted with restrictions* and one-fifth *permitted without restrictions* (Abraham, 1992, p. 14).

As part of the Systems for Success model, Miami-Dade Community College restricts those students identified as needing remedial instruction from particular coursework and from too burdensome a course load; students are further required to successfully complete the developmental work before moving on to any courses required, for example, for the associate degree. The success of Miami-Dade's students on the CLAST, institutionally and when compared to all other "rising juniors" at Florida community colleges and four-year institutions, has been cited to further support the contention that the developmental courses are effective: "...about 30 percent of the students who are successful on the CLAST are students who had deficiencies when they entered Miami-Dade" (Roueche and Baker, 1987, p. 73).

Transfer

The American Association of Community Colleges's declaration that 1990 was "The Year of the Transfer" (Bender, 1991, p. 27) focused renewed attention on the college transfer function. Many researchers and critics express continuing concern that the transfer function is losing ground (Cohen and Brawer, 1982), that fewer numbers of community college students are transferring to four-year institutions as increasing numbers of students are enrolling in vocational courses and terminal degree programs—although Astin reports that while the transfer students are accounting for a smaller proportion of community college enrollments, the transfer population is still substantial when viewed from a national perspective (1983, p. 123). In addition, critics warn that meeting the needs of increasing numbers of at-risk students spread institutional resources too thin and place all college programs in jeopardy (Richardson and Bender, 1987); and that attending a community college reduces considerably the likelihood of transfer and, in the event of transfer, for performing as well as those native to the four-year institution (Brint and Karabel, 1989). In fact, transfer and graduation from a four-year institution have become major indicators of success for the at-risk student.

Increasing numbers of students enrolling at community colleges have the potential of swelling the numbers of students moving into four-year institutions—in 1989 *The Chronicle of Higher Education Almanac* recorded that approximately 45 percent of all students in public higher education were enrolled in community colleges ("The Nation," p. 5). Yet researchers and other educators have charged that community colleges do not collect data to document adequately how many students transfer or how well they perform after transfer (Clagett and Huntington, 1992). It has been suggested that problems with collection and dissemination of transfer data may well be created and perpetuated as a result of colleges either misunderstanding or being confused by the basic concept of accountability—even in the face of continuing public questions and concerns—and as a result of the "fear of knowing" what the numbers would divulge about the college's performance. Yet, collecting and disseminating consistent data would provide important information for colleges with which to support their level of accountability, help them defend themselves from criticism, and serve as standards for institutional self-assessment (Brawer, 1991).

Numerous studies, based primarily on the National Longitudinal Study of the High School Class of 1972 (see Adelman, 1992b), have shown that students initially enrolling in a community college are less likely to complete the bachelor's degree than those who begin in a four-year institution (Pascarella and Terenzini, 1991, pp. 372–373). The difference (about 15 percent or more) is unchanged even after controlling for socioeconomic status, educational aspirations, and other background variables. Brint and Karabel's *The Diverted Dream* (1989) cites these studies to support one of their major criticisms of the community college.

Walleri, in his review of *How College Affects Students* (1991), and Adelman, in his report *The Way We Are* (1992b), note that several factors can be identified as affecting community college entrants' poor transfer rates, including the attrition within individual community colleges prior to graduation. Walleri cited these Mt. Hood Community College (Oregon) statistics: Of students aspiring to earn bachelor's degrees, only 35 percent were in attendance after two years, and only 24 percent had made significant academic progress (p. 9). Attrition from the institution included many students who transferred prior to graduation from the college. He further wondered if the new AA block-transfer program with the Oregon state system would affect the current attrition rates and result in more students entering one of the state system colleges at the junior level. "Continued refinement in the analysis of attrition will certainly help to explain the phenomenon, but only an improvement in persistence and transfer is likely to deflect the criticisms increasingly being leveled at commuinty colleges" (Walleri, 1991, p. 9).

Some current research findings indicate that community college students who transfer tend to do as well as or even better than those who began at the four-year college. In Oregon and Washington, for example, it has been determined that as many as 40 percent of the bachelor's degrees awarded at public four-year institutions are earned by students who first attended community colleges (Walleri, 1991, p. 9). A recent study by the University of Michigan documented that "successful community college students who transfer to a four-year college for their junior and senior years have just as good a chance of completing a baccalaureate program as those who begin at a four-year institution" (Reinhard, 1992, p. 6). The researchers in the Michigan study looked only at these students after they transferred, not at all community college students prior to transfer. The researchers tracked 422 students who graduated from high school in 1980, entered a community college, and transferred to a four-year institution within four years, and compared them to 1,899 students who began at four-year colleges. By 1986, 69 percent of both groups had graduated or were about to graduate from a four-year college. An important conclusion drawn from the findings was that successful transfers from community colleges and students who began their college careers at four-year colleges "shared many academic and social characteristics...they were considered more advantaged than those who did not transfer" (p. 6). The study continued by identifying some of those advantages: the students were more studious, more ambitious, more successful academically, more likely to attend full-time and take more courses (particularly math and science), and less likely to have worked full-time while in the community college.

The Michigan researchers, Lee, Mackie, and Marks, drew several key conclusions from this study: community colleges do not appear to act as "transformational" institutions; increasing the number of successful transfers is "a major responsibility" of the community college; colleges should strengthen guidance programs to do more than direct "attention to accumulating a good academic record in community college...but also to assist students who wish to transfer in selecting the advantageous academic 'target' environments"; and community colleges appear to actively resist improving the transfer function (Reinhard, 1992, p. 6). Yet, their overarching conclusion remained that a community college education does not create barriers for those who eventually transfer to a four-year institution.

Moreover, Pascarella and Terenzini noted from their survey of research findings that students who have attended a community college do not appear to be affected adversely by their training and experience when their level of educational attainment is taken into account. However, they note:

> Taken as a body of evidence, the studies reviewed...suggest that the "cooling-out" function of the two-year colleges may have negative implications for occupational status *largely* because initial attendance at these institutions tends to inhibit educational attainment. Such a disadvantage is not immutable, however. Those two-year college students motivated to complete and capable of completing bachelor's degrees in the same period of time as their peers from four-year institutions do not appear to be seriously disadvantaged in competing for jobs of equal occupational status. In short, when educational attainment is held constant, any residual occupational status disadvantages attributable to initial attendance at a two-year college become quite small and perhaps trivial (1991, p. 441).

Bender, reporting on the findings of his study, *Spotlight on the Transfer Function: A National Study of State Policies and Practices*, declared his surprise at the discovery of an "interesting, subtle reality." Reading the legislative language in resolutions and bills regarding articulation and transfer that were before the legislatures of 13 states during 1989, he found that both the statements and the messages in these documents were typically focused on student interest. However, he noted that, strangely, in most institutional policies that are written from voluntary organizational activities or through coordinating boards or task forces, it was "not unusual to find that the institution's interest is the focus of the between-the-lines language" (1990, p. 24). Moreover, he expressed his surprise at colleagues, even in states with such legislation pending, who essentially blamed students for any difficulties they might experience with transfer to a four-year institution: "...*they* do not look carefully at requirements for credits and curriculums to transfer...*if they have done their homework* prior to enrolling in courses at...community college" (1990, p. 24).

Bender outlined three problem areas with transfer that have nothing at all to do with what some regarded as the "student's fault": upper-division institutions are changing their requirements and not communicating these changes with two-year colleges; access for minorities to the baccalaureate is complicated by the competition created when four-year institutions and community colleges attempt to work with middle and senior high schools, but not in collaboration with each other; the largest percentage increase in transfer is in the applied associate degree area, not the academic area as most would believe, and few states have institutions with applied baccalaureate degrees, such as in engineering technology (Bender, 1991). Donovan, et al., contend: "Currently, neither faculty nor counselors at two-year colleges typically know precisely what courses count toward matriculation at even the major receiver institutions" (1987, p. 7).

Bender's research on improving the transfer function led to several questions—one directed at how an institution can achieve the flexibility to accommodate the varied and diverse interests and needs of its students and still provide a curricular structure that is transfer-oriented, and another directed at providing a curricular structure that does not require separate academic and vocational tracks. As Astin reported, different "tracks" lead to very different life options, and students in the lower tracks often perceive "dropping out" as their only option (Astin, 1982, p. 27). Yet, Bender found it ironic that some would advocate separately administered academic colleges within a college (Astin, 1988; Rendon and Amaury, 1988) when perhaps the "blurred academic and vocational boundaries that characterize the community college at least leave the student's options open to all possibilities" (1990, p. 25).

A 1986 study of organizational determinants of Hispanic and non-Hispanic student transfers from three selected two-year California colleges in the Bay Area noted that the colleges' reputations for good transfer records, perceived individual differences in colleges' student capability, and historical relationships within an esablished network between particular two- and four-year institutions appeared to drive the transfer process (Turner, 1992). Turner noted: "If institutionalized linkages between two- and four-year colleges exist systemwide, and if low-transfer [poor transfer records] community colleges have a high concentration of minorities, these linkages may have a differential effect on the transfer of minority and majority students" (p. 32). Moreover, she concluded that the theory behind the California Master Plan for Higher Education—that is, that all transfer courses at a community college transfer to all four-year colleges—may not be borne out in practice, and that community colleges may not be "stepping stones" to all four-year colleges as the plan proposes (p. 31).

A 1988 survey of community college transfer students who had been admitted to a major research university sought to collect data on demographic or personal characteristics, previous academic experiences and preparation, and items measuring perceptions of faculty/student interactions and experiences with academic advising assistance (Hughes and Graham, 1992). Of the 348 transfer students attending the university's orientation sessions, 267 students responded. The data were compared to the first semester's grade reports for each student. Among the findings was the observation that community college transfer students "may not have accurate perceptions of the academic expectations of a large research-oriented institution...over 40 percent of the transfer students did not achieve satisfactory academic performance or dropped out..." (p. 42). The only variable that indicated a statistical association with academic success in the critical first semester was class attendance at the community college; students missing five or more classes per session at the community college did not perform satisfactorily at the university. However, researchers suggested some possible explanations for students' unsatisfactory progress: community college students may not feel confident about their ability to succeed at a major university; they may find the culture and the related support services too different from their experiences at the community college; their earlier behaviors of seeking advisement or faculty assistance may not translate to other environments; or perhaps these behaviors are not associated with academic performance at all. The researchers advised that results of their study indicate that colleges should design programs that assist transfer students in making the transition to a larger and more competitive academic environment and encourage them to define realistic expectations of their performance during that critical first semester.

In fall 1992 it appeared that a California legislative initiative would help make 1992, not 1990, as AACC had declared, the more likely year of the "transfer." Heralded as a plan to strengthen and improve the relationships between two- and four-year institutions and provide some models for a brighter "transfer" future, the proposal required the University of California and the California State University systems "to establish policies whereby qualified freshman applicants would be admitted but redirected voluntarily to California's Community College (CCC) System" (Rodriquez, 1992, p. 1) to one of 107 community colleges identified to participate (p. 5). Students accepted at one of these university campuses who would volunteer to take their lower-division work at a community college would be guaranteed admittance, after completing the first two years of work, with junior-level standing in the program at the campus where they were originally accepted. The interdependence created by linking the three systems was hailed as a potential major victory for higher education in the state and dictated the role of transfer in particular. Furthermore, proponents believed that the economic impact of substantial savings to a state budget in crisis would be significant. The CCC indicated that such a requirement would be "a big plus for the state's community colleges. Even though we educate the most students [1.5 million], in the past we have consistently not been afforded [adequate] budget support. It's a giant step forward in establishing relationships" (p. 5). Legislators and college and university officials observed that if the proposal were enacted into law, it would be some time before the major questions—for example, the effects on all college and state budgets, minority and majority student enrollment, and regular community college transfers—could be answered. Not yet enacted into law and perhaps more realistically considered a dormant plan, in view of the state's budget woes, the initiative has served to put Californians in particular on notice that the issue of transfer will continue to draw serious attention. In the meantime, individual community colleges are to continue pursuing their own arrangements with four-year institutions.

So how do at-risk students get from outside to a program or classroom inside the college? What efforts are made prior to college enrollment that affect what potential students ultimately decide to do? We asked the award-winning programs to respond to these questions: "By what criteria are students identified for program admission (e.g., test scores, recruitment)? Once enrolled, how are they oriented to this program?"

Transfer-Oriented Programs: A STARTING POINT, QUEST, and TAP

The following three award-winning programs were designed and implemented to address the low transfer rates of underrepresented students from community colleges to baccalaureate-granting institutions: A STARTING POINT at **De Anza College**, QUEST at **Illinois Central College**, and TAP at **Santa Barbara City College** (see Chapter 3 for program goals and objectives).

Participants in **De Anza College**'s A STARTING POINT (ASP) are predominantly self-selected; the program is voluntary, and the students are those "whose personal goals are the same as those of the program"

(Mekis, 1990). The only criteria for selection are a desire to transfer and ethnic identification as noted on the general college application. [Because of the labor-intensive methods employed, limited facilities, and human resources, recruitment is capped at 100 entering freshmen students annually. Once that "magic number" is reached, recruitment ends, and additional students are placed on an interest list and referred elsewhere on campus.]

Recruitment activities occur only during six weeks in July and August. The original outreach and recruitment goal was to increase the number of underrepresented students gaining access to the college by 20 percent. Although the goal of 20 percent was on the original proposal, it was never an emphasis of the ASP staff nor was it "held over their heads" at any time by the dean of counseling or the vice president of student services. (The increase in targeted students transferring successfully is to the complete satisfaction of the college president, vice president of student services, dean of counseling, and the faculty senate—who demonstrated support by allocating an additional two-and-one-half full-time permanent positions to ASP.)

Participants are required to attend two separate orientation programs. The initial orientation is a two-hour seminar to introduce potential participants to ASP, its staff, the range of services offered, and the program expectations. The second orientation, COUNSELING 100X: Orientation to College, is a one-unit, four-day, 24-hour class with a focus exclusively on transfer-related and college survival information, an overview of De Anza's instructional and student services programs and the systems of higher education in California (the CSU's, the UCs, and the independent colleges). Representatives from each of the three systems, as well as ASP alumni, participate. Participants are exposed to a variety of student services, local and national internship opportunities, and scholarship programs, as well as to the notion of seeking advanced degrees beyond the baccalaureate. Also, each day concludes in a small group format to permit activities designed to encourage and enhance verbalization, introspection, positive peer feedback, and positive self-image.

Students are required to sign an agreement in order to participate in the program. They must also provide high school transcripts and SAT or ACT test scores (if taken), and complete De Anza's English and math placement tests. Furthermore, the students are encouraged to:

- Stay in contact with ASP staff and keep them informed of address changes
- Keep all appointments with ASP staff
- Authorize ASP staff to contact instructors and obtain academic performance reviews
- Inform ASP staff when, and if, they experience difficulty that may affect school performance

- Notify A STARTING POINT staff of changes in educational plans
- Set up an exit interview when educational goals are completed or when the student leaves for any other reason (from Mekis, 1990, p. 22)

Each student is required to see her counselor regularly, is encouraged to consider seeking a degree beyond the baccalaureate, and is expected to meet with a representative from at least one college in which she is interested for potential transfer.

The ASP staff and program provides

- Counseling and individual academic performance reviews
- Math and English study groups
- Faculty mentors (role models)
- Skills assessment
- Contact with four-year college representatives
- Information on available scholarships, financial aid, and study abroad programs, and local and national internships
- Emotional and psychological support
- Faith in the student's ability to succeed (from Mekis, 1990, pp. 22–23)

One of the students in the program, when asked if ASP had helped him succeed, responded:

> Yeah, let me put it this way: what they did for me helped me to do better [academically] and if I had not done as well, I might not have gotten as far as I am. They helped me to apply for scholarships, and it was not just the money, but the feeling that good things can happen to me—that if I try and apply for something, it can happen. Just realizing this opens up a lot of possibilities out there...things that I wouldn't have considered before. One of the things...[the director of the program] likes to do is encourage students to reach beyond what they perceive they can do—the idea of pushing yourself, and looking for new experiences. I think that's what helped me to challenge things that I might not have challenged before (from Mekis, 1990, p. 87).

The staff of QUEST at **Illinois Central College** (with a student population of almost 400 in the QUEST program and a college population of 13,000–14,000) actively recruits at all 35 high schools in the ICC district at least once each calendar year. To be admitted to QUEST the student must

- Rank in the upper one-half of high school graduating class
- Apply for admission to the college and send a high school transcript to the admissions office
- Participate in group registration held in May for fall semester

- Attend a special orientation for QUESTers in mid-August (Friday before classes begin on Monday)
- Enroll in classes designated for QUEST students
- Be enrolled in an associate of arts and science (transfer) degree program

Most QUEST students arrive at ICC with mediocre academic backgrounds and know little of their abilities or of their potential for becoming "learners."

A major program goal is that QUEST will have ethnic and skill-level diversity in its student population; specifically, the aim is for 15 percent of the QUESTers to be members of typically underrepresented minority groups. Both high school graduates and GED students are accepted into QUEST, and approximately 15 percent typically have ranked in the lower one-half of their high school graduating classes. Most QUESTers are first-generation college students with critical need for financial support.

To be accepted into QUEST, students must agree to complete any remedial work that assessment scores indicate is necessary for success prior to enrolling in related college-level courses; many will require one year or more to meet these requirements. During this time, QUEST staff supports students' efforts—for example, helping them identify tutors and the critically important sources of financial aid.

QUESTers must attend a full-day orientation. In addition to providing all the important information about the college students will need to know, orientation staff have set a goal that by the end of the day students will know 40 new people and will know where all of their classes will be. The orientation day includes a visit from the president, who has breakfast with the group and shakes the hand of each student; a scavenger hunt—students become familiar with the campus as they gather important information and documents from various services and areas; and a lunch on the college patio with college faculty and the QUEST staff. Orientation activities are designed to increase the opportunities for bonding between staff and students and create a sense of student connectedness to the college. Activities include competitions—the staff competes among itself to collect the most student signatures and to gather the most student responses to such questions as, "If I gave you $10,000, would you eat a cockroach?" Former QUESTers share their experiences with "hang in there; I did it and so can you." Other activities that continue into the semester encourage "the community of learning." For example, students share experiences with faculty—cultural events, field trips, and other out-of-classroom activities. Free tickets to college and community concerts, plays, and lectures are provided to QUEST students and the faculty who accompany them. An overnight trip to Chicago is a highlight of the semester: on a recent trip, one-third of the QUESTers had never been to Chicago, yet it is only two and a half hours away; the itinerary included visits to museums and Chinatown. Another program goal is that, prior to graduation, each QUESTer will develop one skill that requires using and developing his or her body; skiing lessons, for example, are arranged at a nearby mountain resort (the director commented that the experience of watching inner-city students learn to ski is unforgettable). The students build confidence in their abilities to try and then accomplish tasks that they had never considered before. According to the director, the early bonding and continuing opportunities for developing strong staff-student-college relationships provide multiple opportunities for staff to break through the "barrier of silence" that accompanies so many at-risk students to the college.

Because of QUEST's status as a transfer program, staff work formally and, perhaps most important, informally with four-year institutions to smooth QUESTers' transfer efforts, to identify important sources of financial aid for them, and frequently to obtain full scholarship funding for future educational support.

Santa Barbara City College's Tranfer Achievement Program (TAP) is intended to serve underrepresented minority students recruited into the program through high school and community outreach activities and from faculty and student services staff referrals. SBCC views minority achievement as a preparation problem rather than a racial problem and directs resources toward early identification of needed prerequisite skills.

Students considering enrollment in TAP are required to participate in a 30-minute group orientation session. At the conclusion of this session, students are asked to complete an application to join TAP and sign a contract agreeing to complete needed transfer-related activities identified on the Transfer Task Inventory. Students who enroll in TAP are required to schedule a 30-minute appointment with a TAP counselor to develop an individual educational plan and to identify the activities on the Transfer Task Inventory they need to complete in order to prepare for transfer to a four-year college or university.

Aggressive outreach is supported by referrals from local high schools, college faculty, counselors, staff, and a computer-supported database. To help overcome the disparity between the number of underrepresented students at the college and those actually applying for transfer, the TAP recruiting program begins at the junior and senior high school levels. TAP counselors, in collaboration with the SBCC high school relations officer, coordinate and conduct high school recruitment and outreach activities, including orientation tours of the college campus, luncheons with college faculty and administrators, and presentations by TAP counselors to high school students in English as a Second Language (ESL) and other classes.

Promotional materials are distributed to prospective and current students in such programs as Cal-SOAP (which provides postsecondary support and motivation to students from backgrounds underrepresented in colleges and universities), Academic Outreach (a component of the University of California's effort to identify, inform, and prepare minority and low-income students for university eligibility), and MESA (secondary school's Math, Engineering, and Science Achievement program). Personal contacts with students in the seventh and eighth grades focus on providing them with exposure to a college-going culture while conveying high levels of enthusiasm for postsecondary education.

In order to identify, contact, and encourage a greater number of underrepresented students to persist in school, efforts are being made to broaden community liaisons, particularly with local civic groups and the Hispanic Leadership Council. Future efforts will include the development of an advisory board, which will include representatives from secondary schools, local community leaders, business representatives, and university personnel.

On-campus recruiting efforts are aimed at closing the gap between participation rates in transfer course curriculum of Whites and people of color. Outreach activities are directed toward the early identification of minority students placed in basic skills courses as well as those students who have declared majors in which minority participation has been historically minuscule, namely math and sciences. Students from various campus organizations such as the Black Student Union, Educational Opportunity Program (assists low-income students), and United Minority Engineers club are involved in TAP recruiting activities. Recruiting potentially eligible students is additionally facilitated by referrals from college faculty, TAP counselors, and basic skills assessment staff. Students are also invited to participate in TAP through direct mail, personal and phone contact, and classroom visits.

The college offers orientation sessions designed to introduce incoming students to the programs and services available at the college. Initial services include the assessment of basic skills in math, English, and reading, and creating plans that will enable a student to progress through the proper courses that meet transfer requirements. Further, students must meet with TAP advisers to discuss needs and resources and to examine the various options available to them. They receive copies of articulation agreements of general education requirements and lower-division major prerequisites of the UC and CSU systems. Four-year school representaives meet with TAP students to provide transfer information and pre-admission counseling. These activities are supported by the SBCC Transfer Center, which also coordinates

College Day and provides access to college catalogs and four-year campus publications. The four-year schools also host overnight trips where TAP students are housed at the host campus and experience university life. A career counselor explores interests, abilities, values, and career paths with the students. Other resources available to the students include the UC publication, "Answers for Transfers," campus videos, and university-sponsored workshops held at SBCC. (The components of Academic Planning and Progress and Academic and Transfer Application/Transition are included in Chapter 6.)

What the Other Award-Winners Say About the Intake Processes: Identification and Orientation

Students at **William Rainey Harper College** who are prospective, current, and former athletes are eligible to receive advising and support for the Academic Advising program. Student athletes are informed about the program via large information meetings, as well as individual meetings with the athletic academic coordinator. Assessment tests are required for all students who enroll as full-time students at the college, and those students who place into remedial courses are required to pass each with at least a grade of "C."

Students are admitted to **Highland Community College**'s Student Support Services if they meet any of three criteria: economic need, first-generation college student, and/or physical disability. Of the students meeting the initial criteria, those with academic need are selected for participation. Academic need is determined by one of the following criteria: initial academic assessment via ACT or ASSET test scores, referral by instructors and/or financial aid office, or referral by area high schools or state agencies. Participants are oriented to the program through a series of interviews/advisement sessions with the project director and counselor. These interviews serve to provide needs assessment data as well as generate academic advice for the participants. Participants also receive on-going orientation information, monthly schedules of activities, and notification of special project services.

Students are selected into **Miami-Dade Community College**'s Black Student Opportunity Program by the following criteria:
- Mid-range stanine scores on the Stanford 4, 5, 6
- Teacher, administrator, counselor recommendations
- Parental permission
- Recruitment via ninth grade classes in feeder schools

Once the students are selected, the director and high school campus-based coordinators meet with the students and their parents regarding program requirements, history, scholarship/financial aid components, courses that are to be taken, and other information critical to participation. Orientation sessions are conducted intermittently to discuss important strategies, such as test taking, decision making, goal setting, communicating, financing a college education, and becoming ready for college/university life.

Middlesex Community College's Retention Committee agreed that both Freshman Seminar and Course Clusters should not be geared to developmental students only, given that all community college students have a need for experiences and programs that foster their connection with the college. These two programs, however, have been developed for students who are enrolled in the largest academic programs: liberal arts, liberal studies, and business. Unlike a program such as nursing, where faculty and students build a solid connection and support network, these large programs have and develop little, if any, sense of community.

The Freshman Seminar is required for all entering students in these three academic programs; although, due to space restrictions, the requirement in the business program has been delayed. The Clusters are an optional package of courses offered to students in these programs during registration. Faculty advisers meet with incoming students in small groups at registration and explain the Cluster concept. Some of the Clusters are geared for students whose placement scores are at a developmental level; others are for those who have demonstrated satisfactory college-level skills. Since the Cluster courses are offered at prime times during the day and are preselected for students, they are appealing as a registration option.

Approximately one-half of the entering students have placement scores in reading below the twelfth grade level, and about one-third have scores below the ninth grade level. The college's attrition rate approximates the national average among community colleges. The college has taken some significant steps to address the problems of students with skill deficiencies: There is mandatory placement in reading, writing, and mathematics courses; and pre- and co-requisites are in place for all college courses based on reading, writing, and math skills.

There are five methods of referral into **North Lake College**'s Advantage Program:
- High-risk students are identified by two or more of these variables: reading assessment test score below college level; reading score below college level and enrolled in six or more hours at the 100 or 200 level; enrolled in developmental math or having assessment scores indicating computational skills below college

level; younger than age 20 or older than age 40; enrolled in a telecourse; enrolled in a self-paced course; dropped or failed more than 25 percent of hours attempted in the last 12 months; registered during late registration
- Counseling referrals—students who have a grade point average below 2.0
- Faculty referrals
- Self referrals
- Suspended student referrals

Each student is sent a letter of introduction to the program during the first week of the semester. Students are encouraged to make an appointment or stop by to meet with a mentor. Mentors are simultaneously given their lists of students to follow for the semester. Students are contacted by telephone and given additional information about the services available through the Advantage Program. Self-referred students are seen by the mentor or Advantage staff person on duty. Orientation to the Advantage Program is best conducted when the student visits the Advantage Center, but information is given to the student through each telephone and written contact.

Students are assessed in **Richland College**'s testing center prior to placement in developmental studies courses and programs. This assessment to determine reading (by standardized test), writing (diagnostic writing), and math ("in-house" math test) competence identifies the specific level at which students should be placed in developmental courses. Once assessment results are available, students are advised by counselors and faculty regarding courses and programs. Cut-off scores as defined by faculty in the individual teaching areas are used to place students at the appropriate levels. ESL students are tested (standardized test) and are placed in ESL, developmental, or college-level courses based on the scores from that assessment.

Once students have entered the appropriate developmental courses, they complete diagnostic tests to determine beginning work. Students enrolling in developmental math are given placement tests only if either the student or the instructor requests testing (that is, if there is some question about inappropriate placement).

Methods of identification of students vary among programs at **Santa Fe Community College,** but all identification is based upon an intrusive counseling and orientation program that reflects the college's belief that it cannot be a passive institution, waiting for students to seek advisement and counseling. Intrusive counseling is a proactive approach, requiring the counselor to establish contact with students and address student needs before they become insurmountable problems. The intrusive counseling program operates through the following mechanisms.

1. Preregistration advisement to assure that students:
   - Are at the right institution, both socially and academically
   - Are at the proper entry level
   - Are in the right program of study, given their interests and needs
   - Have adequate financial resources to complete the semester and/or program
2. Appropriate preregistration referral for course placement evaluation, career planning, or other services.
3. Establishment of an advisement file for each student, which is continuously updated with test scores, transcripts, personal data, and student contact records.
4. Regular student contact with advisers initiated by advisers, appropriate referrals for assistance, and record of contact on student contact form.
5. Implementation of an "early alert system" through which guidance services counselors receive information from faculty and staff on students who are experiencing difficulties; counselors initiate contact.

Santa Fe Challenge. Students are identified at the time of initial intake, during the admissions and advisement process based on educational conferences and enrollment plans; further, they are selected on the basis of financial need as well as their potential for success. Advisers recommend candidates for acceptance in the program. Prior to registration, participants receive both the standard orientation to the college and an additional orientation to the Challenge Program. At these sessions students are able to complete the admissions procedures, take the Course Placement Evaluation, be advised, hear about support services, meet other new students, go on a campus tour, and register for classes.

Tuition and required fees are paid for Challenge Program participants for the first year of their enrollment. A college staff member becomes a mentor for the student, regularly assisting with student progress and success. The Challenge Program then encourages its participants to undertake service projects that will help other students and the college in general. They are encouraged to "give back a little" to the campus community and other students by participating in and assisting with a minimum of two SFCC events (e.g., College Night, Career Day, Educational Options Fair, Sixth Grade Visits).

During the second week of classes, a special "welcome" reception is held for all Challenge participants and their mentors—college faculty and staff members. At this social occasion, students have the opportunity to meet other Challenge students and to visit with their mentors. The mentor's role is to encourage and listen, to guide and inspire the student to succeed and grow educationally by meeting on a monthly basis with the student and keeping careful records of all contacts. The mentor provides academic support, career/personal counseling, transfer/articulation counseling, and assistance with service projects.

Santa Fe Student Success. Definitions of success generally fall into four categories in this model. The first category is personal enrichment, an approach to education that many use intermittently throughout life. The transfer goal defines the second category, applicable to those who wish to complete two years at SFCC before enrolling at a four-year institution. The third category includes degree- or certificate-attainment goals, and the fourth category defines success as improving specific job skills. All four categories are clearly different in their requirements for support, and making this distinction before undertaking the advisement process allows the college staff to treat students appropriately.

In general, students identified in the second and third groups require more advisement and registration attention, while those in categories one and four—the personal enrichment and the skills upgrading groups—can often take the "express" route directly to course selection and registration. For groups two and three, the next step is a formal advisement session in which the students and their advisers become acquainted and explore such issues as previous academic records, military experience, other time commitments, as well as support needs such as financial aid and child care. These data assist the advisers in making appropriate recommendations to students, further enhancing the likelihood that the students will achieve success.

Most students must take the Course Placement Evaluation (CPE) to determine which math and English courses are appropriate for their skill development needs; other students may be encouraged to take tutoring in their weak subjects, as well as to attend workshops designed to help them make the most of the college experience. If financial aid is required, procedures and referrals are discussed. The student then completes the "educational planning form," enabling him or her to select courses and register.

Santa Fe Community College's Assessment/Course Placement Evaluation. This program was designed initially to assess incoming students on a voluntary/recommended basis; however, for the last four years, all students (with few exceptions) have been required to take the CPE. CPE measures the reading, writing, and mathematics proficiency of incoming students. It determines the levels at which students should begin their coursework in English and math and which prerequisites students must meet. CPE is not used to compare students with one another, nor does it give grade-level equivalencies.

Santa Fe Orientation Model. Orientation to SFCC has been implemented since the college opened in 1983. Orientation begins the moment a prospective student inquires about SFCC. New student intake provides students with information needed for a smooth transition to college and the elements necessary to succeed there. It requires two college success courses, as well, for all new degree-seeking students. This extended program reflects a broad range of offerings tailored to the needs of individual students and delivered to all students as an ongoing series of interventions; it is not a "one-shot" experience.

Santa Fe Developmental Studies. SFCC has a mandatory assessment and placement policy to ensure that students have the basic skills needed to succeed in their college-level courses. In addition to testing for placement in English and math courses, many students are required to take Course Placement Evaluation to establish that they meet the prerequisites for selected courses. Students must take the CPE if they are planning to take a math, English, science, or business class; register for more than seven credit hours; or pursue a degree or certificate. Students who have taken the ACT or the SAT within the past five years may use these scores in lieu of taking the CPE. "We don't want to deny admission to anyone. That's what our 'open door' admission policy means. At the same time, we want to be sure students are placed in the right level of classes to increase their chances for success" (Anita Shields, director of admissions and records).

Suffolk Community College begins its efforts to retain students at the moment they make their first contact with the college. Before any personal contact occurs, SCC introduces students to the campus through literature, brochures, catalogs, and other items, which help to create a campus image. Recognizing that students need to feel connected, be a part of, and be integrated into campus life, the dean of instruction observed: "Students are less likely to commit academic suicide the greater their campus involvement."

Students' involvement with campus begins with an orientation (conducted by the director of student activities, dean of students, and the office of instruction), with Freshman Seminar classes, and with Universal Testing. The Freshman Seminar classes develop the skills students need for success: time management, note taking, reading, testing, and resources. This course is required for graduation for all full-time day students.

Students with academic deficiencies are identified through the Universal Testing Program, which was instituted in 1987 on the Eastern Campus. Earlier, students were tested in reading, math, and English without mandatory placement. The results of the tests were used by the counselors to attempt to convince students that they should enroll in skill development courses. However, since Universal Testing has been instituted, all matriculated students have been tested; these test scores, in combination with other standardized test scores and the students' high school records, have been used to institute mandatory placement in developmental courses when designated cut-off scores on assessment tests have not been achieved. While in the developmental program, students may enroll in no more than 14 credit hours and make changes in courses only after written approval by the office of instruction or counseling.

Students are identified for participation in **The University of Toledo Community and Technical College**'s (**ComTech**) developmental education program through mandatory placement testing. Students are required to complete tests in reading, writing, and mathematics. Specifically, the college has been using College Board tests: the Degrees of Reading Power, a holistic measure of reading achievement; the Diagnostic Test of Language Skills, a measure of language usage; the Diagnostic Test of Math Skills, measures in arithmetic and algebra; and a faculty-developed measure in the area of business math. However, the college is in the process of changing to the ACT-developed ASSET testing program. Students who meet established criteria (cut-off scores) are required to enroll in courses designed to provide prerequisite skills. Successful completion of the developmental courses are mandatory prerequisites for all programs. All developmental education courses are graded on a Pass/No Credit basis.

In addition, students may choose to enroll in developmental coursework. Frequently, nontraditional students lack the confidence to enroll in college-level work and will choose developmental coursework initially. The admissions staff strongly supports developmental education's efforts to provide this important initiation to college work, and they encourage students who lack confidence for negotiating college work to contact the developmental instructors. Other population groups are recruited into developmental education, including what the university calls "conference" students. These are students who have selected another college as the entry point for enrollment in the university but whose ACT scores, high school GPA, class rank, or other indicators suggest that they could profit from developmental coursework. The developmental program also provides the reading and study skills preparation for athletes through a special curriculum called PASS. Similarly, the developmental unit provides the curriculum for the summer bridge program associated with TRIO programs. With the financial support of a learning disabilities tutor via a developmental education grant, recruitment and referrals are made by the Office of the Physically and Mentally Challenged (disabled). Radio ads for the University of Toledo highlight ComTech's "award-winning developmental education program" as "a place to start if you are underprepared but motivated to attend college."

All students who enroll through the traditional routing of placement test deficiency are assigned an adviser. The developmetal education adviser's primary role is to provide support to PREM (premajor) students—those students whose scores on mandatory placement tests indicated that they are underprepared for transfer-level coursework in at least two of the three traditional areas of study: reading, writing, and mathematics. The adviser's responsibility lies with scheduling students' classes so that they take required courses during the first quarter if possible. The adviser has the additional responsibility, if necessary, of providing convincing evidence to PREM students that mandated prerequisite courses will indeed further their chances for success in college.

One designated adviser coordinates the Student Retention Project—a project that encourages faculty to refer students who, in the first two or three weeks of the term, are absent for more than three classes. During the fourth week, these faculty refer students who are failing. In each case, an adviser contacts the student to determine the nature of the problem. Often the problem is simply that the student dropped a class and added another, or he may have been placed on another shift at work. Closer to the mid-term point, students who are not passing are referred to the Student Retention Project and subsequently to the Learning Assistance Center, where they find appropriate help.

The goal of the Student Retention Project is to provide feedback to the instructor within a 24-hour turnaround time. This strategy works to get students back to class. The advisory committee is working on new strategies that will improve the students' GPAs as well.

Orientation during the summer and early fall provides advisers with increased opportunities to advise both traditional and adult students in a less hurried atmosphere. Students and parents come during the Summer Advising, Orientation, and Registration program. Students (entering freshmen, readmitted students, continuing students, transfer students) sign a program agreement during orientation that, in addition to listing test scores and prerequisite coursework, stipulates the following:

> The Community and Technical College of the University of Toledo and the above named student hereby agree that the course requirements listed below must be satisfactorily completed in order for the student to be considered eligible for acceptance into the intended Major.

The Agreement remains in effect until all of the prerequisite coursework has been completed. However, the student may enroll in intended major courses where the prerequisites for such courses have been met.

Upon completion of the required courses, the student will be assigned to an academic adviser in student's Major Program of Studies.

Monitoring student preparatory work is a linchpin of ComTech's developmental education effort. Cases in point are the following generalizations about courses offered within the Tech science and math department:

- There are *no* nondevelopmental courses that do not require a prerequisite course or waiver by placement test/transfer credit.
- All nondevelopmental math courses have specified *math* prerequisites.
- All science courses have a *reading* prerequisite.
- Some science courses carry both a *reading* and *math* prerequisite.

ComTech's commitment to providing academically underprepared students with prerequisite skills to undertake and successfully complete a college education is clearly articulated in an excerpt from its developmental education mission statement:

The mission...is accomplished through advising, carefully sequenced preparatory coursework, and individual learning assistance. The goal of the DE program is to serve, with excellence, metropolitan and regional students who wish to pursue a college degree but find themselves, *for whatever reason* [our emphasis], not ready for college. It will be their first choice because of its reputation as an excellent program capable of meeting the needs of the academically underprepared.

Conclusion

Virtually all students experience some level of apprehension and difficulty making the decision to go to college and then actually going there. For some, the stress and the isolation that they feel will pose such serious problems that they will be unable to overcome them (Cutrona, 1982). The stresses that they feel may force them to withdraw from the institution, or worse, to do so poorly in their studies that they will eventually fail and/or withdraw. As Tinto observed: "...individuals in college are rarely provided with formal rituals and ceremonies whereby...connectedness is ensured" (1987, p. 98).

In most situations, new students are left to make their own way through the maze of institutional life. They, like the many generations of students before them, have to learn the ropes of college life largely on their own. For them, daily personal contacts with other members of the college, in both the formal and informal domains of institutional life, are the only vehicles by which incorporation occurs. Not all individuals, especially those recently removed from the familiar confines of the family...are either able or willing to make the needed personal contacts on their own. As a result, not all new students come to be incorporated into the life of the institution. Without external assistance, many will leave...(Tinto, 1987, pp. 98–99).

If they decide to come at all, the difficulties that at-risk students face are multiplied exponentially when intake processes break down. The processes described in this chapter reflect the diversity of the students, but essentially they reflect an insistence that students will not go unnoticed or fall through the cracks of the system. As Ernest Boyer observed in remarks to a large gathering of community college presidents and their administrative teams:

Reinhold Neibuhr put it precisely when he said: 'Man cannot be whole unless he be committed. He cannot find himself unless he find a purpose beyond himself.' I have to tell you that in the work we do in the schools, especially in the high schools, I'm impressed that one of the most fundamental pathologies among the young people in our culture is their sense of disconnectedness—their feeling that they do not belong, they do not fit, and there is no defined purpose in their lives. How can one go dead at such an early age? I've been in high schools where it seems to me that *many students drop out because no one noticed that they had dropped in* [our emphasis] (Boyer, 1992, p. 4).

Instructional Strategies:

Identifying Some Realities of "How" to Get There

I see a need to become advocates for education that encourages autonomy and individuality... We now need to help students become collaborative learning entrepreneurs, confident in their own abilities and judgments. One of the critical needs of the community college today and tomorrow is to build, or rebuild, students' confidence that they can indeed learn... I see a need to become advocates for the kinds of education that emphasize the processes of learning, for a time when our store of information is expanding so rapidly that the real need is to learn how to learn... Shifting from content to process is exceedingly challenging for those of us who have spent a lifetime being content-oriented.
—**Paul Gallagher**
May 21, 1990

everal years ago, while wandering through a carnival shooting gallery, we observed a player, armed with a modified pellet gun, firing at a succession of metal "critters" moving along on a mechanized track. Some of the critters would fall flat after a "hit"; others would slide by untouched after a "miss"; some appeared to be stunned by a "near miss," leaning at a slight angle momentarily and then regaining equilibrium and continuing along the track out of firing range; and others were "surprises" that popped up just at the moment they came into the line of fire, the element of surprise disrupting the player's concentration and firing rhythm. After his allotted firing time, the player put down his gun and expressed his amazement that what appeared, at first blush, to be a fairly straightforward, even elementary, activity could have put his coordination and response-time skills to such a test and, essentially, lead him to wonder if he was losing his touch.

As we reviewed introductory material for our question about instructional strategies, we were reminded of this gallery game and remarked how much it paralleled what we have experienced in institutional practice. Practitioners have been compelled to take repeated aim at a virtual parade of academic needs that at-risk students have brought to the classroom. Even a cursory review of instructional strategies that have been developed over the last 30 or 40 years, primarily to meet the increasing demands made on a traditional educational system, documents some successful "hits"—the strategies that appear to improve student performance (for example, those that implement students' active learning experiences). Others have been "near misses"—they appeared to work momentarily, holding out great promise, and then proved less effective over time (for example, textbook-programmed instruction). And still others have been "misses"—they are the strategies on which custom appears to have a stranglehold, and even with solid evidence that they are generally ineffective, they persist (for example, the lecture method).

Perhaps it has not always been so much the fault of the strategies as our inability as players to implement them well. For example, some of the "near misses"—perhaps programmed instruction is the best-known of those—have made more historical contributions to the body of knowledge about how we learn than to the body of information about teaching techniques. Moreover, perhaps the "misses" have simply been in the hands of too many unimaginative or less talented players. Or, perhaps we have been too simplistic in our thinking and have believed that "single shots" are the answer to eliminating problems with multiple causes.

In choosing to continue as players, practitioners look to design more "hits" and fewer "misses." If current literature is any indication, these practitioners—if they choose to investigate—have an expanded field of available sources, many focusing essentially on discovering more about *how* we learn, and many others focusing on applying what we know to *how* to accomplish it. Cognitive scientists argue that what they are discovering is useful to practitioners, but rarely are they consulted or their findings read. Practitioners report that they are so busy "doing" what they do that there is little time left for learning about, then designing and implementing, new and improved approaches.

Complicating these issues is the unfortunate reality that we have built few avenues along which these various disciplines can, or do, travel together. Yet, the "how" discoveries and applications have tremendous implications for the improvement of instructional designs. Also, contemporary rediscoveries of decades-old but curiously "modern" strategies combine to produce fascinating material for the improvement of teaching and learning. The vastness of the instructional strategies terrain can be overwhelming, and descriptions of the multitude of innovations would take us far beyond the limited scope of this discussion. However, we include here some of the basic notions that are dominating discussions about contemporary instructional designs.

Some of What We Have Learned About Learning

The Dual Nature of Cognition

One of the hallmark achievements of cognitive science is the confirmation of the dual nature of cognition: all human intellectual activities, such as thinking, communicating, problem solving, and learning require both *processes* and *knowledge* (Sticht and McDonald, 1989, p. 24).

Research in the cognitive science field has demonstrated that possessing a body of knowledge about a subject improves one's ability to comprehend what is being said about that subject or to comprehend what has been written about it. For example, prior experiences with a subject (e.g., through field trips and videos), expand the base of knowledge that in turn improves comprehension of what is being read, said, or seen.

The dual nature of cognition makes the teaching of *process* without a *knowledge* base on which it can operate futile (Gardner, 1985). Cognitive psychologists have discovered that what a reader knows about what she is reading greatly influences her ability to understand and learn from text—"you gotta' know somethun' to learn somethun'" (as quoted in Sticht and McDonald, 1989, p. 31). For example, in one study of young adults in a remedial reading program, students who lacked knowledge about what they were reading had to have an eleventh-grade "general reading" ability to comprehend the material with 70 percent accuracy; yet, the students who had a significant amount of knowledge about what they were reading had to have only a sixth-grade "general reading" ability to comprehend with 70 percent accuracy (Sticht, et al., 1986). Increased knowledge gives individuals "the edge on learning more and more efficiently" (Sticht and McDonald, 1989, p. 31).

Reading specialists tell us that the more "world information" (Chall, 1983) we have, the better we can process new information in any medium. The more "world information" one possesses, the more structures he can create to "restructure" or fine-tune the information that he has stored (Rumelhart, 1980). Students with more limited worldviews and more limited experiences are at a decided disadvantage when processing information from any medium. As Adelman observed:

The more 'world information' you possess, for example, the more you can laugh at the allusive banter of late night television hosts such as Arsenio Hall or David Letterman, or a deft film script such as Steve Martin's *L.A. Story*. This is not a new story.

Humor is a product of empowerment, and enriches the life of any society. When we laugh together, we are less likely to confront each other in anger. People who know nothing from Shakespeare laugh less at a showing of *L.A. Story* than people who do. Comparatively and figuratively speaking, the space of their lives is a smidgen smaller. The point remains the same even when one changes the movie and its allusions. And it remains the same if one changes the culture and the language of the movie and its allusions (1992a, p. 8).

Functional Context Education

Visiting a Canadian college several years ago, we observed the first day of class in an introductory air conditioning/heating repair course. The instructor, a delightful Scotsman, welcomed the students and distributed a packet of materials—course text, handouts, schedules for audiotutorial support sessions, and so on. Then he walked over to one of the 20 or more air conditioning and heating units (many name brands, some gas and some electric) that were situated around the room and patted it gingerly. He looked out at the students and said: "I am here to help you; also, the materials you have just been provided on electrical circuits and gas conduits, among others, and the supplemental tutoring sessions should help see you through this course." He gestured toward the units. "All of these air conditioning and heating units are here to help you, too; they are all broken, and your job is to fix each one of them. So, there you have it! Get on with it now—and, by the way, attempt to avoid blowing up or electrocuting yourself or anyone else!" And with that, class began.

Research in cognitive development has revealed that both children and adults have difficulty learning and applying new knowledge and information processing skills when education and training occur out of context (Sticht, et al., 1986). Sticht noted that early principles similar to what later came to be called "functional context education" appeared more than 40 years ago. These principles predated a considerable body of literature currently referred to as contemporary cognitive science (including artificial intelligence):

△ Relating new instruction to old
△ Making curriculum sensible by justifying topics and applying theory
△ Focusing on purpose by providing immediate and explicit objectives
△ Assisting learning by creating a hands-on environment
△ Supporting topics only as needed and (where appropriate) using actual equipment

△ Limiting memorization by associating topics with practical applications

△ Organizing units of study into meaningful subunits organized around a whole (Sticht, 1989a, pp. 2283–2284)

That is, instruction should build new knowledge on old; should be meaningful to the learner (he should know what is to be learned and why); and should be facilitated by limiting rote memorization, including more "whole-to-part" organization of learning units, and utilizing more practical applications.

Yet, in basic skills courses, reading is often taught as a process, and the content being read is not considered important to that process; mathematics is taught as abstract subject matter, and the subject is not linked to any practical uses; history is presented as a series of topics, and it is not related to potential solutions for social and political problems; and so on.

> The decontextualization of subject matter from functional contexts results in such beliefs that 'first you learn to read, and then you read to learn.' This is the widespread belief that causes schools to teach reading in the primary grades as content-free processes, with the idea that once this 'basic skill' is learned, it can then be applied to learn the 'real stuff,' that is, the content knowledge areas of the curriculum at the higher grades...the decontextualization of education leads to the belief that literacy 'levels' must first reach a certain 'height' before one can learn vocational and other technical knowledge. The 'basic skills' are thought of as something that one must first get and then apply (Sticht and McDonald, 1989, p. 13).

> Instruction should be organized around the use of the information that is being presented. Basic skills should be taught within the context of important context. Students can be taught arithmetic while they are learning about consumer issues, science or other important topics. Reading can be taught while learning social studies, mathematics, and other content areas. In general, integration of content and skill learning should be encouraged...This would be a change in thinking for many schools of education (Sticht and McDonald, 1989, p. 34).

Learning to Learn

Computer scientists, in their designs of artificial intelligence, have provided us with the concept of an "architecture" of a human cognitive system, based on the metaphor of the mind as a computer (as discussed in Sticht and McDonald, 1989). Cognitive scientists refer to the mind as having long-term and short-term memory databases. The short-term or "working" memory has limited capacity and draws upon the long-term memory for information required for participating in some temporary and short-term activities—e.g., comprehending, decision making, communicating, and so on. Findings from studies of the limited capacity of working memory is that this capacity can be expanded if some of the mental processes it attempts to store are automated—for example, if the decoding aspect of reading becomes automatic (performed without consciously attending to it), then the process of reading and comprehending can be accomplished more efficiently. And, in mathematics, for example, if the small amount of space in the working memory is filled with having to remember how to add, subtract, multiply, and divide when one is trying to comprehend the check for a restaurant meal, mistakes are more likely and time expended is increased. If, however, one has automatized calculations, such as the multiplication tables, then these calculations can occur simultaneously while the working memory space is available for the processes of searching and comprehending what is written on the ticket (Sticht and McDonald, 1989).

Students can be taught to determine the relative importance of information they are learning and, therefore, where on the memory continuum they need to store that information. Students who "forgot" on Tuesday everything they needed to know for a test on Monday did not learn the material; they only held it in the short-term portion of memory, then forgot it as they moved "new tenants, or information, into the rental space" (Weinstein, 1992). If they determined that the test information was not important long-term, or if they decided not to invest the time in learning it (a decision with which the instructor may not agree), they would do nothing to move it to long-term memory. Therefore, students should learn how to identify important material and then how to apply learning strategies for making that material memorable and meaningful. The term *metacurriculum* refers to a learning-to-learn curriculum that is implemented at the same time as the regular course content. Instructors can model the strategies by overtly discussing them in their teaching: when using an analogy, for example, the process can be identified and an explanation can be made for why it is helpful for generating meaning. In addition, instructors can share the strategies of students who were successful on course tests.

These learning-to-learn strategies have a number of characteristics in common:
- They are goal-directed activities—the learner must know what her goals are for studying or learning
- The studying and learning strategies must be selected with some level of conscious thought and active selection process

• Studying and learning strategies require effort and time

Perhaps it is the last characteristic that is most difficult for students to internalize. Time is one of the two most critical conditions for learning material so well that it is stored in long-term memory, or for developing any skill; the other is active engagement. Time provides the opportunity for practice, for putting polish on the skill; therefore, too little practice limits results. It is that condition that makes quick-fix reading or writing or study skills programs ineffective.

Some of the following strategies are included in the metacurriculum:

- Creating analogies—looking for similarities or resemblances between two or more things, usually between something you already know and something you are trying to learn
- Applying new knowledge—using new knowledge with different task materials in different contexts, as in creating sample questions and answering them
- Transforming the new information—putting the new information into your own words (paraphrasing), or summarizing it in your own words
- Comparing and contrasting—looking for similarities and differences between new information you are trying to learn and existing knowledge (Weinstein, 1992)

The Social Nature of Learning

A review of findings from learning and memory retention studies indicate that we retain 10 percent of what we read, 20 percent of what we hear, 30 percent of what we see, 50 percent of what we see and hear, 70 percent of what we say, and 90 percent of what we do and say (Roueche and Roueche, 1989). Among the major recommendations of the National Institute of Education's *Involvement in Learning* was: "Faculty should make greater use of active modes of teaching and require that students take greater responsibility for their learning" (National Institute of Education, 1984, p. 127). Socrates's quintessential teaching strategy—to teach is to ask—prevails; but it should prevail interactively. Students should not only answer the questions, but they should raise them and actively seek the answers.

Cooperative learning.

...despite the known fact that social situations are often highly effective learning experiences, the traditional classroom is not a very social place. Beginning with their earliest school experiences, children are cautioned to do their own work, to keep their eyes on their own paper, and not to talk to their neighbors.

Rarely do we permit, let alone encourage, social problem solving (Cross, 1976, p. 124).

Research on the effectiveness of cooperative learning in helping students master new ideas has suggested that many students learning in pairs, and in larger but manageable groups, can learn and retain new information better than they can alone (Sticht and McDonald, 1989; Cross and Angelo, 1988). In her development of metacurriculum, Weinstein emphasized the importance of a student's teaching information to someone else—using some form of cooperative teaching, peer tutoring, or group work to help consolidate and integrate new knowledge (Weinstein, 1992).

Research also reveals that socially organized, task-oriented activities (both in-class and out-of-class), in which students can talk about what they have learned, is critical to improved skill development and application (from Sticht and McDonald, 1989, p. 13). For example, studies of students in music appreciation and history courses have determined that their answering questions embedded in videodiscs and their working in pairs with these discs improved their long- and short-term memory and increased their interest in the continuing interaction with the technology (Ullom, 1989; Light, 1990). Frequently mixing classes of native speakers with foreign-born speakers, particularly in social settings, improves the language development of both groups (Friedlander and MacDougall, 1992). In addition, tandem or partnership testing provides opportunities for students, usually in groups of two, to play both student and teacher roles, to improve their ability to support their own statements, and to develop their collaborative skills (Roth, 1986; Lester, 1987).

Lecturing.

Lecturing is an unnatural act, an act for which providence did not design humans. It is perfectly all right, now and then, for a human to be possessed by the urge to speak, and to speak while others remain silent. But to do this regularly, one hour and 15 minutes at a time...for one person to drone on while others sit in silence?...I do not believe that this is what the Creator... designed humans to do (Patricia Nelson Limerick, from Smith, 1990, p. 210).

In 1973 Roueche and Kirk identified common elements of successful programs for at-risk students; while they determined that no single instructional method was common to all of these programs, lecturing was identified as singularly inappropriate. Unfortunately for students, most lectures have none of the spontaneity "which alone justifies the lecture as a form of teaching" (Smith, 1990, p. 212). Too many professors are afraid to show excitement or enthusiasm about their subject for fear of appearing too unscientific or unobjective, appealing to students' emotions rather than their intellect. There is a part of academe, as a former community college colleague expressed it, that truly believes "learning is grim and serious business," and they prove it with dull lectures.

However, there is evidence that practitioners have taken new directions with lecture to make lecturing more useful and palatable to students:

- *Orchestrating:* preparing mini-lectures of 5- to 15-minute presentations; giving mini-lectures only on student demand; creating that demand by giving students handouts with questions covering important content or asking students to identify questions they do not think they could answer on a test
- *Using the element of surprise:* breaking the lecture by pausing and throwing out a problem that requires a written response
- *Using student reporters:* requiring individual students to review the last lecture in writing and report to the class for a two-minute update prior to the new lecture
- *Piquing curiosity:* confronting students with gaps in their pictures of the world to stimulate curiosity about what is to come
- *Team teaching:* involving students in watching two instructors draw from each other, bringing multiple perspectives to one or more disciplines
- *Acting out:* applying dramatic skills to bring an idea or an individual "to life" (abstracted from Roueche and Roueche, 1989)

Using Technology

As Naisbitt observed: "The gee-whiz futurists are always wrong because they believe technological innovation travels in a straight line. It doesn't. It weaves and bobs and lurches and sputters" (1982, p. 41). Such is the picture painted of some of the most visible and powerful changes in instruction—the application of the computer to improving learning, teaching, and instructional management (O'Banion, 1989). As Terrel Bell observed: "We simply must recognize how outdated our current teaching practices are" and "be more aggressive in bringing to the vast American education enterprise all that can be provided through optimum use of technology in teaching and learning" (1991).

Since the 1960s there has been an emerging shift in focus from teaching to learning. Early on, in the practice of the 1960s, the focus on learning turned out to be "merely *independent* study of the same materials...dominated by the behaviorists' model of reinforcement and repetition" (Anandam, 1989, p. 109); and the implementation of CAI, or computer-assisted instruction, meant "responding" to computers more than actually "using" them (Shaw, 1989). Later on, in the '80s, the focus on learning included many of the insights derived from cognitive psychology and proposed "to use technology for *individualizing* the learning environment (Anandam, 1989, p. 109). Today, in practice, there is ample evidence to suggest that we have come to a place with technology where "what a student learns is no longer separate from how he or she learns...; [t]echnology now demands integration of method and content" (Shaw, 1989, p. 33). Students, learning through technology, are not only learning new content, but they are learning the new technology. Moreover, the new technology is introducing new programs and areas of study to the college curriculum, as well as introducing avenues and intersections by which to cross, and blur, disciplinary and department lines.

Contemporary Issues Regarding the Concept of Individualized Instruction

The widespread adoption by the late 1970s of individualized instruction and the intense focus on the centrality of the concept of mastery learning to new teaching strategies signalled major changes in instructional methods. Individualized education methods, derived from Bloom's concept of mastery learning (Bloom, 1971), begin with five basic principles (predated by the principles of functional context education and since recommended in part by the NIE's Study Group on the Conditions of Excellence in American Higher Education), all recognized as "essential ingredients for effective learning":

- The student must be active rather than passive
- The goals of learning must be clear and must be made explicit to the student
- Very closely related to the need for course objectives is the desirability of small lesson units (frequently referred to as learning modules) dealing with a single concept
- Effective learning requires feedback and evaluation
- Recognizing the enormous individual differences in rates of learning (not only do individuals differ from one another, but most of us differ from time to time and from task to task in our own learning efficiency), all approaches to individualized instruction feature self-pacing—permitting the learner to control, to a greater or lesser degree, the pace of the presentation (Cross, 1976, pp. 52-54)

Neither theory nor practice suggests that individualized instruction requires less of the teacher; indeed, it requires more than does traditional instruction. "Ideally, the instructor is constantly observing and adapting to the progress of the learner—a task calling for considerably higher-level teaching skills than the more traditional task of presenting information to a group of students and hoping that a majority are attending to the presentation and understanding what is said" (Cross, 1976, p. 54). And, in fact, that *was* the *ideal*, but history records that the interpretations of these principles have created documentable disarray and disjointedness in classroom instructional practices.

Over the last decade or so, in particular, it has been difficult to say anything about individualized instruction with great certainty. The uncertainty arises from the model on which Bloom has based his mastery learning concept—the ideal relationship between a student and a tutor. There is still very little known about how this ideal model is transformed into practice:

> (mastery learning)...fails to identify the classroom's collective properties which give rise both to management and time allocation problems. It also fails to acknowledge that classroom properties are instructional conditions equal in importance to individual student characteristics, and classrooms are part of a larger school environment which imposes constraints of its own. The tutorial model narrows attention to the learning of individual students and is unlikely to consider the instructional activities of teachers as being concerned with alternative allocation of time, materials, and tasks and dependent on the composition of a diverse collectivity and the constraints of time and administrative policy within which they operate. Tutors need not cope with diverse interests and capacities or the problems that diversity generates, and it is difficult to understand how classrooms can work with a model designed to fit a radically different case (Barr and Dreeban, 1978, pp. 125–126).

These researchers were not attacking the premises of mastery learning, but rather they were identifying some of the major problems with its implementation: they recognized, as did researchers in a three-year study of literacy development (conducted for the National Institute of Education) that there were "no clear procedures for implementing these designs in existing school organizations, nor any agreement on criteria for determining whether or not they have been implemented" (Roueche and Comstock, 1981, p. II-115). In 1981, in the final report of this study, researchers observed, as had Cross in 1976, that there was a continuing tension between behaviorists and humanists; and while it had abated somewhat over the last two decades, in practice the accommodations each group made to the other's propositions and the resulting blurred distinctions produced conflicting reports about the individualization of instruction. For example, during the course of the larger study of *all* curriculum areas of the colleges, a detailed investigation of remedial reading courses uncovered two distinctions made in the reading programs—(1) distinctions between individualized instruction through "prescriptive techniques" (utilizing reading machines, programmed texts, and students working in almost total isolation), and (2) individualized instruction through "personalized techniques" (the students in self-directed activities, oral interaction between students and instructor). The former could be linked with behavioral theory and the latter with cognitive field theory. As the researchers observed: "The notion of individualized pacing and the relaxing of total time constraints [were] absent in these formulations (though they [were] so vaguely formulated that one cannot say that such individualization [was] strictly excluded)." They saw, in practice, that "any number of pedagogical systems that were touted as 'individualized' by their creators" bore "little resemblance to the 'mastery learning' scheme" (Roueche and Comstock, 1981, p. II-116).

In the late 1970s, when prescriptive programs were far more common in community colleges than were personalized programs (Aron, 1978, p. 233), it was apparent that we were struggling to accommodate the new ideas of individualization within the confines of more traditional schedules and models. We became familiar with such brand names as Personalized System of Instruction (PSI), Computer-Assisted Instruction (CAI), Computer-Managed Instruction (CMI), Programmed Instruction, and Audio-Tutorial Systems—all basically behavioristic approaches to instruction (Cross, 1976, p. 50). However, these singular instructional applications have provided practitioners with important insights about the appropriateness of *systems* of instruction, and applications are proliferating in practice. Yet, as Cross and others have warned, we should beware of looking to systems to help us rid ourselves of the "many 'inefficiencies' of the classroom" for fear that "we may inadvertently be discarding the unidentifiable 'something' in the academic environment that stimulates great and even lesser minds to unusual accomplishments and cognitive satisfactions" (Cross, 1976, p. 110).

Institutional Instructional Strategies

Support Services. Frequently, counseling, tutoring, learning laboratories, and other learning-support areas that are available outside of the formal classroom setting are criticized as being too costly in the face of their returns. Yet their roles in the institution provide bridges between the fairly traditional instructional gaps in most colleges (Roueche and Snow, 1977). Cohen admonishes classroom instructors to get more involved with support services, to help coordinate support services with instruction. Barshis and Guskey argue that too often these services "rely upon student initiative for their use" (1983, p. 94), and they encourage a more directive approach to guiding and/or requiring students to participate in those services that their performance indicates they need.

National and regional surveys over the last decade indicate that institutions of higher education are assigning increasing importance to the role of support services. In 1977 Roueche and Snow found that almost 80 percent of the two-year colleges in their study had a learning assistance center, approximately 62 percent used peer tutors, and 64 percent used counselors primarily on a full-time basis. *College Responses to Low-Achieving Students* documented that about 60 percent of all institutions assigned counselors to developmental programs, but only about 17 percent used peer counselors, and less than half had an organized learning assistance center (Roueche, Baker, and Roueche, 1984). In the Southern Regional Education Board's 1989 survey, institutions were asked to identify the academic support services they provided students who needed remediation: 87 percent used counseling/tutoring centers, 86 percent used assistance labs/learning centers, 82 percent used peer tutoring, 64 percent used faculty tutoring, additional diagnostic testing services were used by 61 percent, and 14 percent used other approaches (Abraham, 1992, p. 16). The National Center for Education Statistics's 1989 survey documented that 98 percent of the responding institutions offered at least one support service, such as peer tutoring and counseling (National Center for Education Statistics, 1991a).

Credit. A critical index of institutional support for at-risk programs is the allocation of credit.

> Initially, at least, the major 'reward' that education has to offer these students is college credit. Ultimately, all students may come to appreciate the personal satisfaction of learning; until then, New Students, more than other students, need the immediate and tangible reward of credit. The defense of no credit for remedial education is made on the grounds that to grant credit for below-college-level work is to lower standards and to cheapen college degrees. But we may be protecting standards that do not exist. We already know that what is senior-level performance in one institution is below the level of acceptable freshman performance in another; furthermore, it is highly unlikely that A and B students have been or will be hurt by the granting of credit for remedial courses. While college credit for below-college-level work may threaten institutional egos, it should not threaten the egos of *educators* whose task it is to help students learn. In any event, the trend is toward credit, and most of the recent literature advocates granting credit for remedial or developmental

courses. In 1970, less than one third of the community colleges were granting degree credit for remedial courses; by 1974, 53 percent were granting degree credit and 42 percent were granting nondegree credit (Cross, 1976, p. 44).

Roueche and Snow, in their 1977 national survey, found that over half of the community colleges and nearly 40 percent of the senior colleges granted degree credit for developmental courses. They observed: "For colleges that are not offering degree credit, we would advocate doing so; laws permit it, students want it, and our data recommend it" (p. 98).

Findings from a national survey of institutions of higher education, as reported in *College Responses to Low-Achieving Students* (Roueche, Baker, and Roueche, 1984), describe the following policies about the awarding of credit for remedial/developmental courses:

- More than 60 percent of all respondents offered transcript credit for basic skills instruction; approximately 20 percent did not.
- The awarding of transcript credit was relatively consistent across all institutional types and for all three of the basic skills areas.
- Community colleges tended to award institutional credit to a higher degree than all other institutions.
- Doctoral degree-granting universities and liberal arts colleges tended to endorse this process to a lesser degree.
- All institutions, except community colleges, tended to award credit for writing more often than for reading or mathematics.
- Doctoral degree-granting institutions and liberal arts colleges were less likely to award credit for reading instruction than all other institutional groups.
- All groups of institutions awarded degree credit: averaging 40 percent in reading, 44 percent in writing, and 40 percent in mathematics. Writing credits were most often awarded by all institutional groups, with the exception of community colleges (p. 45).

The National Center for Education Statistics reported that in fall 1989, approximately 20 percent of those institutions of higher education across the nation responding to its survey awarded degree credit for remedial courses. About two-thirds awarded institutional credit; this credit did not count toward degree completion but did count in determining full-time status. One-tenth awarded no credit for remedial courses (1991a).

In the 1988–89 Southern Regional Education Board survey, responses from its regional institutions of higher education indicated that "reforms during the 1980s have all but eliminated the controversy over the awarding of degree credit for remedial studies" (Abraham,

1991, p. 12). The survey sought information about *types* of credit awarded by institutions for each subject area, including: *degree credit* that counts toward GPA and an academic degree; *institutional credit* that counts toward status as a part-time or full-time student, but not toward the degree; *elective credit* that counts toward elective requirements; and *no credit* (p. 12).

- Only about 2 percent of the public and 5 percent of the private institutions that responded still award degree credit for remedial courses.
- Institutional credit is the most frequently awarded type of credit by both public and private institutions. However, public institutions are almost twice as likely to offer institutional credit as private institutions. Private institutions are about as likely to award elective credit as they are institutional credit for remedial courses.
- The decision to offer institutional credit is primarily a response to requirements for financial aid eligibility.
- Surprisingly, a higher proportion of the liberal arts/comprehensive institutions (public or private) award degree credit in writing and mathematics than do two-year colleges. Conversely, the percentage of two-year colleges that do not award any credit for remedial courses (about 16 percent over all subjects) is greater than for either the liberal arts/comprehensive colleges or doctoral/research universities (p. 12).

What Some of the Award-Winners Say About Instructional Strategies That Are Critical to Retention

We asked our award-winning programs to respond to this question about instruction: "What instructional strategies implemented in the program have proven critical to retention?"

Because **De Anza College**'s A STARTING POINT does not have an instructional component per se, the program director did not respond to this question. However, in her responses to our question regarding faculty selection, she mentioned that A STARTING POINT originally introduced the concept of supplemental instruction to the Tutorial Center, which ultimately instituted it and made it available campuswide. Also, the program maintains a high interest in increasing faculty interaction and faculty involvement with various aspects of program services.

William Rainey Harper College's Athletic Academic Advising program does not have an instructional component; however, some strategies being considered are seminars relating to transferring to four-year universities, drug abuse, time management, and sexual assault. In addition, the director noted that the staff's attention to student progress has been critical to improved retention for all students involved in the program. She noted that each student may be affected differently by the program—some may have needed information and obtained it, others needed the monitoring system and profited by it, and still others may have needed the knowledge that support was available and that they could go to someone for help.

Highland Community College's Student Support Services does not have an instructional component. However, the director observed that program participants consider the integration of advisement, individualized instruction, and academic progress monitoring to be pivotal in improving retention of at-risk students.

Illinois Central College aims to provide all students with a curriculum that will develop 15 basic competencies by the time each earns his or her degree; some of the competencies are skills, some are knowledge, and some involve growth in attitudes and values. QUEST attempts to help students develop these competencies by providing a range of skills and knowledge, integrating their learning into a more coherent curriculum, providing more active modes of teaching that involve the students, and creating a sense of group belonging and social integration.

In an attempt to provide greater breadth, the QUEST curriculum has 46 hours of general education courses, rather than the 35 normally required for the ICC transfer student. Moreover, many of these courses are prescribed for the QUEST student in contrast to the cafeteria-style curriculum of the other ICC transfer students. The curriculum is also more integrated through interdisciplinary courses and team teaching. To achieve these competencies, some exciting courses were revamped, and some new courses were created, especially interdisciplinary courses that were team taught. One new course, for example, "Survey of the Social Sciences," is taught by five faculty from the disciplines of geography, sociology, history, economics, and political science. Together, these faculty show the relationship between the disciplines as well as covering the subject matter. The other innovative courses offered are "Effects of Technological Change," "Chemistry and Society," "Theatre and Literature," and "Art and Music."

Prescribed courses also result in a more coherent curriculum and *greater integration of learning*. This integration is achieved through more interdisciplinary courses and team teaching. In addition, the competencies are consciously reinforced across the curriculum. Instructors meet weekly to coordinate their courses and to plan the connections they choose to make between them. Some faculty are given release time to guest lecture in different kinds of courses.

There is a greater emphasis on *active modes of teaching and learning.* The teaching methods planned for the program are calculated to engage the student's active participation: small group work, study groups, independent study, tests that call upon the student to connect pieces of information and generalize from them rather than merely repeat memorized information. More "open-ended" kinds of assignments are offered, assignments whose outcomes are less predictable and whose means and direction are left to the student. Through such active modes, the students will not only learn more fully, but will also grow in critical thinking skills, flexibility, leadership, and intellectual curiosity.

The program addresses the social aspect of the student and attempts to support learning activities that occur outside the classroom, as well as within. This creates *a sense of belonging to a group, a collegiality among students and faculty, and is termed the community of learning.* To foster this sense of community of learning, students not only share common experiences within the same classes, but they participate with the faculty in a number of cultural events, field trips, and other activities outside the classroom (see Chapter 5 for additional information). The QUEST lounge is a "common place" containing student mail slots; it also serves as a place for in-between class gatherings, study group meetings, and meetings between students and faculty.

Because **Miami-Dade Community College**'s Black Student Opportunity Program is implemented initially at the high school level, it relies on the instructional strategies that are used by teachers in their regular high school classrooms to be effective with the BSOP students as well. The director indicated that if the number of BSOP students increases to a level where efforts to develop a team-teaching concept for the program would be economically feasible, he would attempt to design such a strategy and seek to implement it in BSOP. At the high school level, these students currently are developing strong informational and basic skills by enrolling in appropriate college/university preparatory courses. They are being exposed to additional social, personal, cultural, and academic growth experiences.

The most successful instructional strategy in **Middlesex Community College**'s Freshman Seminar and Course Clusters has been the emphasis on collaboration; in Freshman Seminar, the most successful strategy has been the team-teaching approach. The goal in both these programs is to involve students in the college community and in the learning process. That involvement cannot occur completely until there is a strong collaborative community among faculty and staff. These two programs provide a framework for networking and support.

In Freshman Seminar, communication and interaction are emphasized, through written journals, group exercises, and a group project that is directed toward community services or an educational project. The journals, which are submitted weekly, are a means by which students can express themselves on a variety of topics, and the instructors write lengthy comments in reply. Group projects have taken many forms, such as a series of letters written to incoming freshmen that was compiled by one class; a video project on services at the college; a volunteer effort for the homeless; and a video project on drunk driving. Emphasis is always on interaction and collaboration. The Freshman Seminar course carries one credit and meets twice a week for one hour for the first two months of the semester.

Examples of the Cluster groups in the Course Cluster model, which was offered in 1989 through 1991, are:

Introduction to Psychology
English Composition
Environmental Studies
Freshman Seminar

Basic Writing
Reading Strategies
Fundamentals of Mathematics
Freshman Seminar

Introduction to Business
Accounting
English Composition
Freshman Seminar

North Lake College's Advantage Program does not include an instructional component in the sense of classroom instruction or lecture strategies. The purpose of the mentor-student relationship, however, is to offer students the opportunity to have a resource person to answer questions, assist in solving problems, and provide consistent/ periodic encouragement.

In addition, student success seminars are held for groups on a regular basis. Seminar topics have included time management, stress management, and test-taking strategies. Two videos, "Where There's a Will, There's an A" and "Math is a Four-Letter Word," have been used as resources.

Richland College's developmental studies program is most challenged by the measurement of student success. Program review is continuous, and new instructional strategies are studied and often implemented in the program. No data are currently available to demonstrate how different instructional strategies affect retention; however, different approaches to delivery of instruction are reviewed regularly.

Teaching strategies include individualized instruction, where instructors develop plans for each student in the class to address his/her individual needs. Individualized instruction is most frequently implemented in reading and writing classes for disabled students and for adult students with head injuries. Self-paced individualized instruction is implemented in developmental math. Course content is outlined, and students complete the course at their own pace. Students who complete a required percentage of the work but not the entire course are permitted to re-enter the course and to attempt completion during the next semester. Computer-assisted instruction is also implemented in reading and writing classes. All of the reading students use CAI as reading lab work, and the response has been tremendous. CAI is used to a lesser extent in writing, but a review of the college's writing program (including developmental and ESL writing) could result in more CAI for writing students.

Traditional enrollment in developmental reading, writing, and ESL courses is 17 students per course, and maximum enrollment for developmental math is 25. Keeping the classes small is considered an important retention strategy.

Vital instructional elements that have been the keys to the success of **Santa Barbara City College**'s Transfer Achievement Program are the math support groups and a multidisciplinary English program. The math study groups are designed to help SBCC underrepresented students transfer successfully. The groups are modeled on the Treisman project at UC Berkeley (helping underrepresented students in math-related majors pass calculus), adapted to the different needs and objectives of SBCC students. Two classes were chosen for the initial study group projects: elementary algebra (Math 100) and intermediate algebra (Math 107). Three part-time UC Santa Barbara students served as group facilitators. Facilitators, themselves members of underrepresented ethnic minorities, had advanced calculus backgrounds and had some experience in tutoring. Basic to the concept of the study group is cooperative learning, sharing of experiences, and swapping strategies. Taking a lesson from the Treisman project, the math study groups were not remedial in orientation, but rather were designed to expose students to challenging and creative exercises and assignments that would complement the course curriculum (see Chapter 7 for complete description of study groups).

The English Division has initiated a Multicultural English Transfer (MET) program designed to assist underrepresented students in preparing to tranfer to four-year schools. The program offers a multicultural classroom environment and a multicultural and multidisciplinary curriculum; it was implemented on a pilot basis in spring 1991.

Student course selection is monitored by counselors through TAP's Academic Planning and Progress component. By providing students with academic advising early and continuously throughout their enrollment at SBCC, this counseling initiative increases the likelihood that students will take the courses directly related to their transfer goals. Individual educational plans are developed with a counselor on a semester basis to map the academic courses required for transfer. Active intervention on the part of the counselors—not waiting until students come to them with problems or questions, but rather identifying potential problems through computer tracking and inviting students in for counseling and assistance—has been a critical instruction and retention strategy.

The Transfer Application/Transition component provides additional counseling and support to assist students in making the final move into four-year environments. For example, many students find the summer after graduation from SBCC to be a critical time—there may be pressures to go to work and contribute toward the family's income rather than diverting earnings toward school. Preliminary experiences with the TAP pilot confirmed current research findings that a large percentage of underrepresented students who are accepted into four-year institutions do not complete the transfer process because they fail to enroll. The project attempts to work toward continued counseling in order to prevent this failure.

Santa Fe Community College's developmental studies program uses a variety of services, adaptive equipment, and learning materials to assist students with differing learning styles and special needs. The reading, writing, math, learning strategies, and human development courses are taught with both traditional and self-paced formats, supported by tutoring and CAI.

Within the developmental division, any SFCC student can have up to two hours of *free* tutoring per credit course each semester (two semesters maximum for any one course). In the developmental writing center, students can receive help with writing assignments; the center is open during posted hours three days a week, but tutors are available by appointment throughout the week. Students can also receive free word-processing instruction. Flexible scheduling provides some options for course completion through such strategies as short courses, contract courses, and open-entry/open-exit courses.

General strategies employed by **the University of Toledo**'s **(ComTech)** Developmental Skills Education Program have helped to increase retention through the following strategies:

- Students take mandatory placement tests in the areas of reading, writing, and mathematics. Students meet established test criteria in order to pass a developmental course or courses. The developmental courses are mandatory prerequisites for all programs.
- All developmental education courses are graded on a pass/no credit basis.
- The faculty in the two academic departments in which the courses are taught (General Studies, and Technical Science and Mathematics) teach both developmental and nondevelopmental courses.

Instructional strategies for specific courses include

Reading

- The reading coordinator meets biweekly with all instructors to facilitate uniformity of instruction as well as to provide a forum for exchanging teaching ideas.
- The four-credit-hour course has a built-in lab component for practicing strategies, yielding a six-hour-per-week clock requirement. Labs are taught by part-time instructors.
- A mandated co-requisite is a four-credit introductory sociology course to facilitate transfer of learning.
- Grades in sociology are tracked to aid in evaluation of student outcomes.
- A holistic approach is used in which the ability to see relationships between ideas is stressed, through such strategies as:
  △ Recognizing organizational patterns
  △ Comparison-contrast charting
  △ Mapping
- The ability to read critically and comprehend beyond a literal level is also emphasized. Instructional strategies used to enhance students' abilities in this area are:
  △ Distinguishing fact from fiction
  △ Recognizing connotative language
  △ Recognizing basic argument structure
  △ Summarizing

Study Skills

- The course is required of students who are identified as deficient in two or more of the mandatory testing areas (reading, writing, and math); it is optional for others.

- The supplementary workbook is a collaborative writing effort of full- and part-time faculty.
- Leadership is provided by the reading/study skills coordinator, who has release time annually.
- The course topics include:
  △ Listening/lecture note-taking skills
  △ Time management
  △ Taking responsibility for one's own learning and knowing where to get help; good decision-making skills
  △ Stress management/handling test anxiety
  △ Test preparation/test-taking skills
  △ Effectively accessing library information

Mathematics

- A developmental mathematics coordinator helps to ensure consistency of instruction.
- Input from all developmental mathematics instructors, full- and part-time, at a quarterly meeting helps to shape the curriculum.
- Algebra is offered in two different time formats to accommodate students. One course covers the material in one quarter for those students with the appropriate algebra background, and the other course is offered over two quarters for students with no algebra or a weak algebra background.
- The study of success rates of developmental mathematics students in subsequent nondevelopmental mathematics courses has been used to evaluate and revise the curriculum.
- A database has been established to facilitate longitudinal tracking of developmental mathematics students.
- Pre/post-testing in all courses identifies areas that need attention.
- The basic mathematics curriculum is updated regularly to include many concepts espoused by the National Council of Teachers of Mathematics in its *Standards*, as well as other current practices involving the adult learner.

Writing

- Many "Basic Writing" sections are taught in the computer lab with students using word processing to compose their paragraphs and essays.
- An English curricular coordinator helps to ensure consistency of instruction.
- Policy requires that a sample of assignments in developmental writing classes taught by part-timers be evaluated by full-time

faculty; this ensures maintenance of standards and consistency of holistic evaluation.

- The study of success rates of developmental writing students in subsequent transfer-level composition courses has been used as one means of evaluating the developmental curriculum.

Program staff and faculty agree that the Developmental Education Program will continue to be an excellent program through its research to understand the needs of its students and the application of that research to curriculum design and instructional delivery.

Conclusion

For the last 25 years, a new interest in human cognition and its development has swept across a variety of scientific disciplines; findings from studies in anthropology, sociology, psychology, computer sciences, philosophy, linguistics, and others reveal fascinating information about the mind, how it works, and how it can be developed. It is curious that while research has been conducted actively for several decades, cognitive scientists have not developed strategies for sharing information among themselves or providing "translations" of their findings into applications useful to educators. Moreover, it is odd that, unlike medical schools that require a formal and solid grounding in the medical sciences, schools of education do not require a solid grounding in the cognitive sciences that "underpin education" (Sticht and McDonald, 1989, p. 14).

It may be simplistic to draw too strong a link between the problems that at-risk students have introduced into higher education and renewed interests in instructional innovations across the higher education landscape. As Cross and others have noted, the "instructional revolution" appears to cross higher education institutional lines. But hindsight has provided us with the perspectives to identify some dramatic relationships. These problems have created much controversy, both in the field and in the literature, over the proper "instructional system" or pedagogy for teaching developmental reading, or writing, or math, or for teaching in general. Yet, as hard as we have tried to make that discovery, our efforts, combined with the diversity we face, have brought us to this reality, best posited by Cross in 1976:

> It now seems clear that we are not going to improve instruction by finding *the* method or methods that are good for all people. The research on teaching effectiveness has been inconclusive and disappointing because, I suspect, we were asking the wrong questions. When we ask whether discussion is better than lecture, whether television is as good as a live teacher, whether pro-

grammed instruction is an improvement over more traditional methods, we find that for that mythical statistical *average* student it seems to make little difference how we teach. But when we look at the data student by student, it is clear that some students improve, some remain unaffected, and a few actually regress under various teaching conditions. The very process of averaging the pluses, the minuses, and the non-changers wipes out the message that different methods work for different students. Psychologists are now asking the more sophisticated interaction questions about learning styles—which methods work for which students? (p. 112)

Perhaps what we have learned is that we do not *do* as well as we *know;* and, even more likely, perhaps we have learned that we do not yet *know* enough to design the most effective instructional strategies. Moreover, too often what we believe, or what we might call educational theory, can be and has been pragmatically altered as it is put into practice. For example, as we have observed, the term "individualized instruction" is used often to legitimize strikingly different practices.

Regardless, the conversations and the controversies about instructional improvements will continue. However, we cannot escape two realities with which it is difficult to quarrel. The first reality reminds us that intertwining of process and knowledge is critical to teaching and learning: "Pedagogy cannot be specified independently of content... and content cannot be specified independently of function or purpose. In other words...one cannot talk about *how* to teach without first talking about *what* is being taught...and one cannot talk about what is being taught without talking about *why* it is being taught" (Roueche and Comstock, 1981, pp. II-117–118).

The second reality reminds us that we had best take our own advice and "learn to learn." George Leonard, more than two decades ago, expressed it well: "Anyone who tries to draw the future in hard lines and vivid hues is a fool. The future will never sit still for a portrait. It will come around a corner we never noticed and take us by surprise" (1968, p. 139). Essentially, he set out to describe "education's most powerful ally"—the sheer joy of learning. It is that joy, in fact, that must be at the heart of our designs, whether that joy is produced by humans, machines, or both.

Program Evaluation:

The Proof of the Pudding

Thomas Paine once observed: "A long habit of not thinking a thing wrong gives it the superficial appearance of being right." Long-held beliefs die hard deaths, if they ever die at all. They appear almost insulated from close inspection by their longevity. Their challengers call their defenders to arms. And, while examples of these "long habits" are abundant in our society, perhaps in few arenas are they more entrenched and unquestioned than in higher education.

Perhaps no institution knows better than community colleges the frustration of being caught in the web of "long habits." Astin observes that community colleges, more openly in some states than in others, have been consigned to "the bottom of the academic pecking order" because they lose out on all of what have been generally agreed-upon indices of "quality"—specifically, their students are less well-prepared, they have fewer Ph.D.s on their faculties, they have smaller libraries, and they have lower expenditures per student than their four-year counterparts. The image problem costs them status and prestige that in turn costs them money. He argues, however, that using these criteria as judges of educational quality is both unreasonable and illogical, that "they reflect something about what an institution *has* but very little about what it *does*" (Astin, 1983, p. 134). Yet these arguments have created little change in the long-lived

I think sometimes I would want to stay the way I was, in isolation, unaware, because it's scary to think there are so many important decisions I will be faced with, knowing that I will have to follow through with what I decide, no matter what the consequences.
—Peggy DeA.,
1973
(from Zwerling, 1976)

perceptions that "institutional hierarchy is a valid reflection of relative levels of educational quality" (Astin, 1983, p. 134).

One approach Astin recommends for debunking the traditional notions of academic quality and challenging the validity of what he observes are spurious indexes for measuring quality is measuring the *value* that an institution *adds* to a student's educational experience. Over a decade ago, the Commission on Higher Education of Minorities recommended that all institutions of higher education should revise their traditional testing and grading procedures to reflect an institutional *value-added* mission. That is, institutions should be responsible for enhancing students' cognitive and personal development; an array of pre-admission, formative, and exit assessment tests would provide accurate indications and evidence of an *institution's actual contributions to student outcomes*. In 1988 "10 'Radical' Suggestions for School Reform" included: "Develop in each [public] school a pretest and a post-test to measure to the school's own satisfaction its effect on student performance…The good schools would be those that show the steepest curve of improvement, not necessarily those whose students earn the highest average scores" (Wiggins, 1988, p. 28).

> If institutions were judged by how much they added to their students' cognitive functioning rather than by how well they functioned at the time of admissions, there would be no reason why community colleges could not achieve a level of quality comparable to that of any other kind of institution. The more selective research universities, on the other hand, could not continue to argue that their programs were of high quality simply because their entering students were better prepared. In this regard, it is not surprising that some of the most vigorous resistance to the commission's value-added recommendations has come from people associated with elite institutions (Astin, 1983, pp. 137–138).

While there is little evidence currently that the *value-added* notion has spawned serious challenges to the long-held notions about educational status and quality, some of the challenges to "superficial appearances" are being translated into legislative and institutional assessment initiatives across the country.

Emerging "Incentives" for Effective Evaluation: Wolf in Sheep's Clothing vs. Angel in Disguise

Public patience about higher education's lack of engagement appears to be wearing thin. Too many well-conceived and visible proposals to change curriculum or teaching practices—often suggested by faculty themselves as a result of assessment—have been shot down in faculty senates or been too-quickly abandoned in recent budget cuts. To public officials at the state-level, this signals the flaw they always feared in a decentralized assessment approach: a process to detect deficiencies—in the absence of more basic incentives—entails no guarantee that they will be addressed. More decisive, centralized, and intrusive enactments may be the consequence, if only to get our attention (Ewell, 1991, p. 17).

The political winds are blowing toward more assessment, not less, and there are ample data to verify that some of the following evaluation processes will be assuming increasingly significant roles in the conduct of our institutional and program affairs.

Minimum Competency Testing

Statewide assessment mandates play expanding and significant roles in shaping the evaluation processes of postsecondary education. Florida was one of the earliest states to mandate minimum competency skills testing, beginning at the high school level and, in 1984, extending into college. Currently, all sections of the CLAST must be completed successfully by any student wishing to receive an associate's degree or enroll in upper-division classes at a four-year institution in the state (Rogers and Steinhoff, 1991).

Strangely, a most basic question about these mandates persists without, apparently, generating any common response: "Is their primary intent to prompt instructional change within the academy or to inform the wider public about results?" (Ewell, 1991, p. 12). For example, the law which mandates the Texas Academic Skills Program and its mandatory placement examination for incoming college freshmen includes an evaluation component (as one of the five major provisions of the program), and it is not surprising that the details of compliance were hotly debated during the planning phase of the program (Hanson and Kerker, 1991). The evaluation component requires institutions to report effectiveness data annually to the Texas Higher Education Coordinating Board. These data relate both to the remedial program and to the advising program; the bulk of data collected consist of student unit record data that are supplied by the colleges. In addition, evaluation data regarding each college's advising program will soon include a narrative section that allows, among other things, respondents to explain unusual features of the institution's circumstances, such as economic or geographic factors, which are believed to impact their remedial programs. Moreover, a second provision mandates the reporting of effectiveness data back to secondary schools, placing the accountability for underpreparedness exactly where many postsecondary educators believe it belongs—in local high schools.

With the increasing interest in dropout prevention at the elementary and secondary levels, there have been renewed concerns, expressed by students' advocacy organizations and others, about the effects of minimum competency testing (MCT) legislation on students and curriculum. In an investigation of available evidence of links between MCT and dropping out, researchers discovered that these ongoing expressions of concern may be well-founded (Kreitzer, Madaus, and Haney, 1989). Acknowledging at the outset that evidence linking the effects of MCT on dropping out is sparse, at best, the researchers proposed to compare the nature of the testing programs in states with extremely high dropout rates with those in states with extremely low rates, to discuss the apparent effects of failing MCT on self-esteem, and to study the impact of competency tests on retention rates and curricular content.

Their findings and observations of the effects of minimum competency testing on K–12 students have some implications for postsecondary education.

- The high dropout and low dropout states differed, particularly in representation of minority and poor students, and in their test requirements and uses. The picture of MCT-drop connections could not be clearly painted; however, the pattern in the data provoked thoughts about possible connections. Data provoked suspicions that while high dropout rates may be symptoms of the educational system's failures that initially encouraged the legislation, MCT may be contributing, rather than offering solutions, to the dropout problem.

- Students who fail MCT are more likely to be from poor and minority groups. Data from MCT administrations confirm its adverse effects on students who are already having academic difficulties, who are poor and minority, and who are enrolled in vocational and special education programs. One state study that looked at the effects of failing the MCT on the attitudes and personality of low-achieving students discovered that the failure increased their feelings of alienation and anxiety and lowered their self-esteem. The relationships between alienation, low self-esteem, and dropping out are well-documented, and "unfortunately, there is evidence that MCT can harm these at-risk groups in ways that might increase their likelihood of dropping out" (Kreitzer, Madaus, and Haney, 1989, p. 138).

- The impact of MCT on dropout rates appears to depend most heavily on the degree to which standards are rigidly enforced. "When promotion decisions or instituional benefits are based strictly on test results...MCT can, it seems, increase the likelihood of a student dropping out" (p. 142).

- Concerns about the impact of MCT on curriculum are broad, and many are well-founded. While in theory MCT does not have to affect curriculum in a "pernicious manner, it seems that it often does...The worst case is that MCT atomizes the curriculum into components that closely match the form and content of the competency tests...In short, MCT does not at all drive the curriculum in the direction presumed best for students at risk. What ought to drive the curriculum...is their need for engaging in pertinent instruction—not the content of minimum competency tests" (p. 145).

- MCT does not appear to aid remediation efforts. "Too often, remediation equals test preparation" (p. 146). For example, when the Florida State Task Force on Educational Assessment studied the Florida Functional Literacy Test, it discovered practices of "spot remediation" in all cases it investigated. Moreover, the National Institute of Education's MTC Clarification Hearings documented that the practices discovered in Florida were not isolated incidents. In addition, results of a 1984 national survey conducted by The Children's Defense Fund determined that of the 31 states mandating retention standards, only 12 allocated significant levels of funding to support the remediation.

These researchers concluded that while a lack of solid evidence about MCT programs makes investigating the effects of competency testing on dropout rates difficult, they did agree that nothing they discovered would indicate that MCT decreased the likelihood of dropping out. "We did, however, uncover several indications that MCT may give students at risk of dropping out an extra push out the school door" (p. 146). The key is how the program is implemented, and there are clear contrasts between the ideal implementation—caring teachers in small classrooms with engaging learning processes—and the more realistic implementation—practice for the test. They urge more study about the consequences of MCT, about its effects on students and curricula, that will go beyond merely reporting student passing rates. Furthermore, they view with some alarm the rising national interest in nationwide systems of such tests.

Peter Ewell, Senior Associate at the National Center for Higher Education Management Systems, reports on the aforementioned national interest in assessment. He observes that for a time it appeared that bringing about instructional change and informing the public were compatible ends, and that, for the most part, states allowed institutions to design their own plans for assessing student learning. However, there is mounting evidence that this agreement is dissolving; there are increasing numbers of new state proposals for common outcomes testing, and moreover, a "*national* assessment effort has unfolded with astonishing consensus, force, and speed" (1991, p. 12).

What is happening at the federal level? Two national initiatives, in addition to the assessment of collegiate progress, emerged independently in 1990: "Ability to Benefit" legislation—"a single national performance standard for admission into postsecondary study"; "Student Right to Know"—requiring postsecondary institutions to disclose persistence and graduation rates (Ewell, 1991, p. 16). Why are these calls for tighter controls of the assessment process increasing? Ewell responds that accountability is back, that states and institutions feel they cannot afford assessment as a stand-alone activity, and that federal government intervention into the assessment arena will increase the costs and require institutions to endure, again, the history of state assesment initiatives (p. 12). Many state officials do not like what they hear when they ask for an accounting of institution-specific assessments, some are impatient with the combination of time lags and lack of tangible results, and some recognize that nothing is happening on many campuses. He addresses three specific difficulties in state assessment policy: the problem of closure—institutional inability to document effectiveness and improvement; uneven institutional response; and the inability of leaders at each level to see each other's problems (pp. 14–15). State leaders and institutional leaders often operate on different levels and with different objectives to the problem. For example, Tennessee state leaders were puzzled that institutional leaders did not want to retain the ACT-COMP, for by so doing they would strengthen their credibility with the legislature and promote higher education in tight economic times; however, institutional leaders were frustrated by what appeared to be the state's willingness to accept a test that institutional leaders believed and thought they had proven to be flawed.

Ewell reports that recent responses to state proposals have been varied: in South Carolina and other states, proposals for common postsecondary outcomes testing have been defeated, though narrowly; Missouri mandated a "College-Base" examination beginning in 1992; in 1991 Tennessee debated discontinuing the use of ACT-COMP examination as a key element of the state's performance-funding mechanism, with arguments based particularly on the inappropriateness of the exam; Texas and Minnesota legislators eye a "results-based" funding component in proposed budgeting approaches; Virginia institutions were warned by state authorities against reducing or eliminating their assessment programs in the face of tightened budgets; and New Jersey discontinued its General Intellectual Skills (GIS) assessment just as a national advisory panel recommended such a "performance-based" examination by which to assess collegiate progress (a logical outgrowth of the President's National Education Goals) and graduating college seniors' abilities to "think critically, communicate effectively, and solve problems" (p. 12).

What have state experiences taught us? According to Ewell, while the federal assessment initiatives appear to have been drawn without knowledge of state experiences, they would do well to note the following:

- Effective assessment requires *clear purposes*, as well as reasons why the goals ought to be *assessed* and the uses to which the information will be put.
- Meaningful assessment is dependent upon *long-term commitment* and requires *unusually long timelines* for development.
- Sustained assessment requires a *constituency*, and "information" alone provides an insufficient basis for sustaining it (1991, pp. 16–17).

Outcomes Assessment

At the legislative and policy-making level, there is an increasing demand for accountability to ensure that resources are being used wisely and producing a good return. Student outcomes information can be used outside the college to respond to questions from regulatory agencies, communities, and funding entitites regarding quality issues and justification for support (Kinnick, 1985). At the institutional level, college administrators are more frequently having to fund necessary improvements by reallocating existing resources, and they, too, have questions that must be answered in regard to educational gains (Ewell, 1985). Outcomes information can be used to promote the institution politically from a marketing standpoint and to justify internal decisions (Kinnick, 1985).

Kinnick (1985) identifies several obstacles to effective use of outcomes data: the combination of complexity and relative imprecision of the data; and institutional factors such as organizational structure, responsibility for performing the data collection, and the orientation of key administrators toward use of the data. Access can be impeded by restricting the knowledge that the data exist, by limiting access to the information, or by making it available in such a way that it is very difficult to access or use. Reports of results can be written with too much elaboration or detail, obscuring the actual findings; with data of doubtful validity or reliability; with data that are not *perceived* as accurate or that lack face validity; with information that is not timely; and with data that cannot easily be interpreted due to lack of reference points, such as historical benchmarks or comparisons with similar programs.

To overcome these obstacles, Kinnick suggests organizing data projects around problems, issues, or decisions, and avoiding such efforts as research projects that are "data-driven" and produce information that is of limited usefulness (1985, p. 97). Using outcomes data to solve problems involves successfully linking outcomes information with solutions to retention problems, organizing linkages among the people and the components that will be affected, and eliciting assurance from top administration that the proposed solution(s) will be implemented. Using outcomes data in program review for program improvement makes the data more palatable and the effort more likely to reoccur than if data are used for instituting cost-cutting measures. Some presentation strategies that have proven helpful in increasing the use of outcomes data include: disaggregating the unit of analysis; using comparative formats and graphics; disseminating the data in short, issue-specific reports; and integrating outcomes data with other information (Kinnick, 1985).

Performance-Based Funding. Several states are moving toward performance-based funding for a portion of their institutional support. In 1981 Tennessee became the first state to apply academic performance crtieria to funding decisions for state colleges and universities, considering the supplement a viable alternative to the existing enrollment-driven funding formula (Banta, 1985). The first year of its implementation, the potential value of the award was established at as much as 2 percent of each institution's budget and was increased to 5 percent in 1983. Institutions were eligible for the award based on their ability to demonstrate the quality of their academic programs, according to five standards of academic quality, in an annual report submitted to the Tennessee Higher Education Commission:

> ...the percentage of programs eligible for accreditation that are accredited; the percentage of programs that have undergone peer review, that have administered a comprehensive exam to majors within a five-year period, or both...; value added by the general education component of the curriculum, as measured by the American College Testing (ACT) College Outcome Measures Project (COMP) exam...; opinion concerning the quality of academic programs and services, as measured by surveys of students, alumni, employers, or community members; and implementation of a campuswide plan for instructional improvement based on findings derived from the procedures just described as well as from other sources (Banta, 1985, pp. 19–20).

In Texas, "results-based" components for funding allocations are currently being discussed for preparation for the 1993 state legislative session, using scores on the TASP test and student outcomes for measuring program effectiveness. Funds (5 percent for 1992–95, 10 percent thereafter) would be allocated to institutions in accordance with their achievement of 11 goals: nine teaching and two research. Three of the proposed outcomes for the performance-based system are related to evaluation of developmental programs, in which minority students are overrepresented:

- Remediation
  Goal: Increase the success rate of poorly prepared students
  Measure: The number of students who initially failed one or more portions of the TASP examination and subsequently passed all sections of that exam
- Minority Students
  Goal: Increase the number of minority students enrolled in Texas institutions of higher education
  Measure: The number of Hispanic, African American, and Native American U.S. citizens enrolled
- Minority Graduates
  Goal: Increase the succesful participation rates of minority students
  Measure: The number of Hispanic, African American, and Native American U.S. citizens graduated (Texas Higher Education Coordinating Board, April 1992, p. 4).

The plan calls for separate "funding pools" to be designated for each goal, allowing institutions to focus their efforts on as many or as varied an array of goals as seems appropriate; the funds in each pool would be prorated among all institutions competing for them, with each institution receiving equal amounts for one unit of performance (i.e., for graduating one minority student). The goals are broadly mixed, and it is anticipated that institutions with different missions would gain from performance in different areas (Texas Higher Education Coordinating Board, April 1992).

All evidence indicates that assessment is here to stay, and higher education must be involved in shaping it. Otherwise, postsecondary education not only risks being on the outside looking in at important national efforts to mold education, but also is in danger of what it fears the most—intrusive scrutiny and goal setting by entities outside its control.

Using Exit Criteria

Grades and credits may be useful in indicating student performance levels in programs and courses, but they do not reflect the competencies that students have actually acquired (Justiz, 1985). Competency is a cause of, not a synonym for, effective performance; defining and identifying appropriate competencies are critical to the process of describing exit criteria for a college degree (Klemp, 1979). Robert McCabe, president of Miami-Dade Community College, which may have the most diverse student population in America, argues that open-door colleges achieve excellence, among other things, by maintaining adequate exit standards. This implies a rethinking of the institutional role, shifting the emphasis from maintaining educational standards (by insisting on entrance requirements) to clearly defining exit requirements (McCabe, 1982). Moreover, it requires a shifting from the "opportunity model"—that is, shifting away from merely providing the student the opportunity to enroll and take his or her chances—and toward the "success model"— that is, meeting the student with a careful plan that will move him or her toward academic success (Levin and Unruh, 1990).

Individual program exit standards are becoming more common-place evaluation criteria. "The national movement toward specific exit standards for developmental courses, which suggests ways of document-ing such standards (competency testing using a variety of testing for-mats), is a healthy first step toward countering the relativity of evaluation in the last decade" (Barshis and Guskey, 1983, p. 96). The Southern Regional Education Board's survey of remedial studies in its regional colleges documented

- "Completion of course/program sequence" was used by over 77 percent of all institutions in writing and mathematics, and 63 percent in reading
- Less than half of all responding institutions required "the pass-ing of exit tests" as criteria for exiting remedial reading (46 per-cent), writing (49 percent), and mathematics (47 percent)
- In those institutions where students must pass exit tests in writing and math, over 62 percent used tests that differed from the test used for placement (Abraham, 1992, p. 20)

The National Center for Education Statistics's 1989 survey re-ported that approximately 80 percent of the responding institutions based remedial course exit skills on regular academic-course entry skills in math, 81 percent in remedial writing, and 70 percent in remedial reading (1991a, p. 8)

Evaluation: A Most Unwelcome Guest

Originally used to denote the testing of pupils, and still retaining some of that usage, the term *evaluation* has come to be associated with judgments of program quality. According to Popham (1988), Ralph W. Tyler's Eight-Year Study, conducted in the 1930s at Ohio State Uni-versity, was instrumental in changing the view of evaluation to a judg-ment of program quality rather than an appraisal of student learning. In conducting the evaluation, Tyler attempted to "determine the degree to which the objectives of an educational program had been attained" (Popham, 1988, p. 2), thereby devising the "objective-based" or "goal-based" concept of evaluation. Popham traces the popularity of educational evaluation to the era of the Elementary and Secondary Education Act of 1965, the most significant of a number of initiatives that channeled federal funds to local schools; at that time, he notes, there was a growing realization among legislators that "this consider-able financial investment in the nation's educationl system might be less effective than some were claiming" (p. 3). One result was the mandatory systematic evaluation of all federal grants to local agencies, throwing many educators into the evaluation business and henceforth injecting politics into educational decisions.

Early on, evaluators were advised to take a broader view, to avoid concentrating solely on influencing specific decision makers, and instead to "illuminate the thinking of a more widespread political com-munity" (credited to Cronbach by Popham, 1988, p. 6). By the 1970s some proponents of the new field adjusted their expectations to reflect the political reality that perceptions—that is, what the individuals believed about programs and outcomes—and funding—that is, what individuals were willing to contribute toward those programs in light of their successes and failures—were inseparable companions: "If, as a consequence of an evaluator's efforts, an enterprise can be improved in effectiveness even a few percentage points, those modest and hard-won percentages represent *benefits that otherwise would have been withheld from learners*" [emphasis added] (Popham, 1988, p. 6).

However, in a general sense, evaluation has never been particularly welcome as a guest at the educational table. Evaluation of regular educa-tional programs has spawned criticisms of narrowness, irrelevance, and unfairness (Weiss, 1983). Moreover, evaluation has been accused of creating anxiety, immobilizing faculty and staff, and developing useless, vague guidelines for implementation (Guba, 1969). When one consid-ers the diversity and magnitude of the criticisms and accusations di-rected at the processes of evaluating *regular* programs, the evaluation of at-risk programs appears particularly daunting. Programs for at-risk stu-dents have generated some unique concerns about the evaluation process, spawned by the extraordinary diversity of their students, their curricula, and the impact that they have on social-political entities and thinking. For example, McGrath and Spear charge that the current mix of "hard" outcomes of remediation with the "soft" outcomes of develop-ment make evaluating "the hybrid 'medial/developmental' [sic] pro-grams notoriously difficult" (1991, p. 52). They observe:

> The fact that few students ever successfully made the transition from the special precollege programs into the regular curriculum was not taken to show those programs to be failures; instead, such programs could be defended as encouraging and facilitating the full mental, moral, and emotional growth of students whose lives might be enriched by their coming to know, to appreciate, and ultimately to express themselves fully as members of society and as members of their social and racial group (p. 52).

In addition, Sever and Inbar report: "Decisions concerning the evaluation of such programs are not taken merely on a methodological basis; they are rooted in socio-political considerations, reflect contradicting value-judgments, and touch upon theoretical ambiguity" (Sever and Inbar, 1990, p. 288). The result is a dilemma of such proportions that many policy makers "are often inclined to foster a 'don't know' evaluation policy: i.e., keeping evaluation criteria obscure enough so as not to be able to tell whether a second-chance program is successful or not" (p. 288).

As many critics and researchers have discovered, "[f]ew people want their programs evaluated, but everyone wants to know what works" (Hanson and Kerker, 1991, p. 211). Moreover, as Adelman correctly observes, "When there is money on the table [federal, state, and local funding], no one will admit to either flaws or ambiguity in institutional performance" (1992b, p. 26). The negative issues that have traditionally swarmed around evaluation have not allowed it, as an educational phenomenon, to settle comfortably into program and institutional designs; implementation typically follows harsh words and accusations of disservice to particular groups, inappropriateness of instruments, and so on. Consequently, the issues have clouded what could have been clearer-headed thinking, and institutions of higher education have been at the mercy of informal and often inappropriate methods of evaluation, with the result that individual impressions, apocryphal stories, and other "word-of-mouth" evaluative procedures have significantly influenced their fates (Doucette and Hughes, 1990).

Currently, initiatives from inside and outside of higher education have put us, as Kay McClenney, vice president of the Education Commission of the States, observes, at "the fork in the road." "Down one path, increasing frustration with higher education can lead public policy makers toward greater prescription and intrusion; down the other, decentralized management and positive incentives are taken as the key to lasting improvement" (Ewell, 1991, p. 17). Which path will prevail remains to be seen.

Asking the Right Questions

A little girl was asked by her teacher to name the king whose daughter's marriage made possible the unification of Denmark and Norway in 1380. The student said, 'Wow, that's the kind of question that makes your temples throb. It makes your ears ring and your hair stand on end. It makes your eyes water and your cheeks burn, your mouth turn dry and teeth ache. A question like that can destroy your whole head.'

When we think of the magnitude of the educational task, just asking the difficult questions of our time can destroy our whole head. So the problem for us is making sure that we ask ourselves the *right questions* [our emphasis] (Owens, 1991, p. 58).

Even a brief history of findings from research efforts will attest to the difficulty of choosing the questions that then become useful criteria for evaluation. For example, on the surface, Robinson's simple, straightforward, strong proclamation, made more than four decades ago, appeared to lend itself to a simple evaluative process: "Academic performance is clearly the *sine qua non* for the validation of remedial courses" and that "[i]n the final analysis, remedial instruction must necessarily stand or fall on the basis of this single criterion" (Robinson, 1950, p. 83). But this process—using such quantifiable indices of grades, test scores, and performance in next-level courses as validating criteria—did not produce a tidy package of information that provided everything we needed to know (Cross, 1976, p. 37). In fact, a variety of researchers documented tremendous inconsistencies in using GPAs as criteria for evaluating remedial courses (Santeusanio, 1974); and others identified students with equally low scores, some of whom had taken remedial courses and some of whom had not, who made essentially the same scores in the next-level course, underscoring the unreliability of grades as indicators of success (Sharon, 1972). Moreover, others discovered that most colleges could not report on the numbers of students who had completed the required remedial work and/or the numbers of low-achieving students who persisted from remedial programs into regular college courses and with what success (Roueche and Snow, 1977). Others evaluating a specific program admitted that even with course grades and completion data, the answer to the question "Are developmental courses effective [at this college]?" could be answered only with "It depends [on many factors]" (Roueche and Baker, 1987, p. 72). The conclusion was that "the examination concerning the effectiveness of developmental instruction...has developed as many questions as it has answered" (Garcia and Romanik, 1984, p. 64).

As McCabe once remarked about the effectiveness of developmental courses at Miami-Dade, it is evident that the college believes "many students remain in the system and are successful because they took the developmental courses and simply would not be there at the end if they had not taken them" (Roueche and Baker, 1987, p. 74). Simply stated: It is difficult to know when you have arrived if you have never been certain where you are going. And, the evaluation field is rich with designs for helping one recognize "arrival." Second-chance programs cannot be evaluated with any single criterion or single evaluation method; their diversity demands an eclectic approach. Fortunately, this demand can be met. Evaluation designs are not hard-and-fast tools assigned for use in specific analyses of programs, or strategies, or performances. In fact, as Popham observed: "…a detailed dissection of many evaluation models would reveal, as was true with Dr. Frankenstein's monster, that they were built from the remains of others" (1988, p. 23).

Our intent here is not to design new models or endorse particular working models; rather, it is to present frameworks, in concert with and in addition to those described by the award-winning programs, that might be useful for adaptation or for creating unique situation-specific designs. There are many about which we know and many not yet discovered, but we offer three frameworks that we believe raise some important issues relevant to creating viable and unique evaluation designs for programs with goals, objectives, and populations similar to those featured in this study.

The first of these frameworks, from *Assessing Institutional Effectiveness in Community Colleges* (Doucette and Hughes, 1990), is designed to measure the following outcomes of an institution's basic skills and developmental education mission:
- Achieving educational outcomes
- Meeting student needs
- Meeting community expectations (p. 25)

The following key questions and data sources may serve as useful assessment tools (see Doucette and Hughes, 1990, pp. 25–26).

A Guide to Assessing Basic Skills and Developmental Education

QUESTIONS	DATA SOURCES
Achieving Educational Outcomes	
1. Are students attaining the skills identified as course and program objectives?	1. Pre- and post-competency testing, including assessments of nonacademic skills; follow-up surveys, interviews, or focus groups with teachers and employers; grades in courses; case studies.
2. Are students completing courses and progressing through programs at reasonable rates?	2. Student enrollment records; grades in courses; follow-up surveys and interviews with students; records of time on task.
3. Are students progressing to and succeeding at the next level	3. Student enrollment records; grades in courses; follow-up sur-

of education? In postsecondary education programs?

veys and interviews; results of studies comparing the performance of students who have completed developmental programs with those who enrolled directly in postsecondary programs.

Comment: Because underprepared students often follow intermittent enrollment patterns, longitudinal follow-up studies will require a database and research design that extend at least five years from initial enrollment. Long-term longitudinal follow-up is particularly important for underprepared students because their initial goals might not include enrollment in the next level of education, or they may not enroll in a postsecondary program immediately upon attaining basic skills competencies.

4. Are students from different subgroups succeeding at comparable rates? Are student success rates comparable among the various college programs for underprepared students?

4. Student enrollment records; indicators of student success by program.

Meeting Student Needs

5. Are students' career and personal development needs being met?

5. Pre- and post-tests using affective instruments; educational planning documents; follow-up surveys, interviews, and focus groups with students; case studies.

Comment: Implementing college processes that assist students to identify and regularly update their career and personal goals is a key step in assessing goal attainment. This must be done especially carefully with underprepared students, for many begin programs with vague or unrealistic goals.

6. Are students satisfied with course and program content, teaching methodologies, and support services?

6. Surveys, interviews, and focus groups with students.

7. Are assessment tests placing students in courses appropriate for their skills?

7. Course grades; teacher assessment of appropriate placements; test scores; high school grades; results of studies correlating

placement recommendations and course success.

8. Are developmental students being successfully integrated into college life?

8. Surveys, interviews, and focus groups with students; records of student participation in extra- or co-curricular activities.

Meeting Community Expectations

9. Are a reasonable number of high school dropouts, illiterate adults, and ESL students enrolling in appropriate college programs?

9. Student enrollment records; comparisons with national, state, and community census data and estimates of target populations; other secondary sources of data, including social service agencies, churches, etc.

10. Does the college cooperate effectively with other service providers in the community?

10. Inventory of other educational programs and related services in the community; evidence of cooperation, including client referrals, resource sharing, etc.; interviews with community leaders.

11. Do college programs for underprepared students assist in reducing related social and economic problems?

11. Agency studies; state and community socioeconomic data; crime data; interviews with community leaders.

Comment: Establishing a causal link between college programs for underprepared students and reduction in poverty or crime rates may be beyond the scope of college efforts. However, more direct relationships, such as those between college programs and increased community literacy levels, should be documented if feasible.

John Quinley
Central Piedmont Community College
from *Assessing Institutional Effectiveness in Community Colleges,*
Doucette and Hughes, 1990

A second conceptual framework is that proposed by Sever and Inbar (1990), who have researched second-chance programs and the impact they have had on institutions and participants for the last decade. They use as their frame of reference second-chance programs offered to high school dropouts who are seeking an opportunity to eventually enter a program of study in higher education. They approach evaluation on three levels—individual, program, and policy making.

To determine if a second-chance program is actually a *genuine* second chance, detailed questions should be asked about student makeup, admissions policy, staff, facilities, content, methodology, accreditation, and graduates.

At the *individual level,* the question is whether an individual has been given a *genuine* or an *artificial* second chance—that is, whether he or she will be able to take advantage of the second chance opportunity and/or the degree to which the opportunity will produce acceptable outcomes.

At the *system level,* the question is whether program enrollment includes higher percentages of individuals who are recipients of *artificial* second chances or higher percentages of individuals who are receiving *genuine* second chances. Factors that move the system toward a genuine or an artificial second chance are accessibility, adjusted educational technology, productivity, accreditation, and acknowledgment.

- The dilemma of access lies in the reality of the open-admissions policy: it will yield a higher percentage of "genuine second chances," but it also may attract a high proportion of those without requisite ability, for whom the program is only an illusory second chance; this is likely to result in a high dropout rate from the program. On the other hand, highly selective admissions criteria will result in a group of high-ability individuals, those who do not truly need the program and for whom it is only a redundant second chance.
- Adjusted educational technology refers to using different methods and materials in the second-chance program than were used in the previous situation of failure—that is, not "more of the same." The expectation is that adjusted technology contributes to the likelihood that greater numbers of students will be getting a *genuine* second chance.
- Productivity refers to the extent to which appropriate skills, as well as adequate numbers of skills, are taught.
- Accreditation refers to the program's certification that the participants have acquired the skills needed for full participation in the next desired opportunity.
- Acknowledgment is the larger system's agreement that the acquired credential is the proof needed; without this, no one in the program is receiving a genuine second chance. Acknowledgment of credentials by the larger system would *seem* to depend on the quality of the program—its productivity.

At this juncture Sever and Inbar suggest asking a number of questions:

△ The *students:* Who are they? How many of them do not actually need a second chance? How many of them are unable to achieve the promised end product (i.e., a certificate)?

△ The program's *admission policy:* How selective is it? What selection devices does it apply, if any?

△ The *staff:* What are their attitudes toward the program's target population? Do they believe their students are capable of achieving the end product? How well are they trained for dealing with this target population?

△ The *facilities:* Are physical prerequisites, such as room, laboratories, etc., met?

△ The *content:* Is the material taught appropriate for achieving the end product?

△ The *methodology:* Are the instructional methods adjusted to the program's aims and to the students' needs? Is the educational climate in the program appropriate? Are achievements evaluated and accredited?

△ The *accreditation:* Is it acknowledged by the wider educational system? Is it worth having for the job market?

△ The *graduates:* How many of them acquire accreditation? How many of those who *do not* acquire it belong to the illusionary type (individual lacks potential ability to succeed)? How many of those who *do* acquire it are in the redundant group (individual has not made a wrong choice or experienced an educational failure to the point of having important future options closed before him; *he does not really need a second chance*)? How many of the program's graduates actually continue on to higher education and/or get better positions in the job market? (Sever and Inbar, 1990, p. 291 and pp. 295–296)

At the *policy-making level,* answering two questions is critical to creating a clearer picture of the forces that influence the relative position of a second-chance program in an educational/social hierarchy. The first question is about accessibility. Maintaining an open-admissions policy and enrolling a high proportion of disadvantaged students typically are praised by policy makers who encourage the development of second-chance programs for their accessibility, even without any inquiry about the use of adjusted technology (no repeat of processes and materials that were ineffective before) or whether the productivity is high (material is relevant to further success).

The second question is about acknowledgment. The researchers note that a naive evaluator might assume that if the program has used proper technology and successfully trained its students, its credentials will be acknowledged by the larger system, and students will be allowed by the "gate keepers" to climb the social ladder. The ultimate success, however, turns on what happens at this final evaluation stage, and the researchers raise the following specter of a continuing debate:

As long as the target groups for second chance are relatively small in numbers and discernibly unique in character, the policy makers may be expected to welcome and acknowledge second-chance programs as providing a solution for the few....

But as soon as second-chance programs begin to cater for more visible proportions of the population, the policy-makers' attitude towards these programs is prone to change. There are at least two reasons for this expected change: one, because broad second-chance mechanisms are often conceived as contradicting the orientation towards excellence in the upper tiers of education; two, because second-chance programs which successfully reopen future options for considerable numbers of students may become a threat to the regular, mainstream educational system...if a considerable proportion of these students successfully acquire in these programs both the relevant resources and the accreditation to prove it, then the mainstream's selection procedures, as well as its educational inputs and instructional processes, are challenged....

Thus, the evaluator may judge two second-chance programs as not achieving the aim of giving their students a full second chance, but for very different reasons: one program because it mainly 'keeps the students in a framework' without actually supplying them with skills or knowledge relevant for further advancement; and the other because it fails to get its accreditation to be acknowledged as fully equivalent to the mainstream's accreditation, despite (or perhaps because of) the fact that quite a number of the students graduate from it with fair achievements and accreditation (Sever and Inbar, 1990, pp. 297–298).

Sever and Inbar's concerns are reminiscent of Zwerling's suspicions— expressed almost 20 years ago—of efforts (by four-year institutions) to curtail or limit educational opportunities "as new students are for the first time entering colleges and universities in significant numbers" (1976, p. 253), and of more current concerns that tightening budgets may provide additional incentives for action on the part of "elitists on the [community college] faculty and conservatives in the legislature, who already think that there are too many people in college who do not belong there anyway. It would be a shame if the result of fiscal belt-tightening is smaller and more efficient, but also more socially irrelevant community colleges—leaner and literally meaner institutions" (McClenney and Mingle, 1992).

Three of the award-winning programs featured in this study reported that the transfer function was their principal objective; therefore, we include this third and final framework, also from *Assessing Institutional Effectiveness in Community Colleges* (Doucette and Hughes, 1990), as one potential guide for assessing the institution's transfer mission. It is designed to measure the following outcomes:

- Achieving educational outcomes
- Accomplishing transfer
- Succeeding as a transfer student
- Articulating courses and programs (p. 10)

The following key questions and data sources may serve as useful assessement tools (pp. 11–12).

A Guide to Assessing Transfer

QUESTIONS   DATA SOURCES

Achieving Educational Outcomes

1. To what extent do students who transfer understand the content in the general education core?

1. Pre-and post-tests; exit exams or essays; "capstone" courses; grade reports from senior institutions.

2. To what extent do students master content in their areas of specialization?

2. Pre- and post-tests; exit exams or essays; grade reports from senior institutions; interviews with faculty from the transfer institution.

3. To what extent do transfer students exhibit growth and maturity in the noncognitive/affective domain?

3. Standardized assessments of personality development, moral or ethical values, and interpersonal relations; surveys of former students.

4. Are individuals satisfied with the overall instruction, delivery, and content of courses, programs, and services—including alternative delivery methodologies?

4. Surveys/interviews of current and former students.

Accomplishing Transfer

5. What is the college's transfer rate—reasonably measured?

5. Enrollment reports and student profile data; transcripts; stu-

dent surveys; reports from transfer institutions.

Comment: Determining how to calculate the transfer rate has far-reaching implications for assessing the effectiveness of a college's transfer mission. A number of groups and researchers have proposed various methods; as of this writing, some of these are under consideration for adoption as a national standard.

The key elements in determining a fairly measured transfer rate are 1) the definition of the population of students to be used as the base number of potential transfers—first-time students, full-time students, total credit hours earned at the college; 2) the definition of students considered to have transferred—credit hours completed at a four-year institution within a specified time. For instance, The Center for the Study of Community Colleges at the University of California, Los Angeles, has suggested the following definition for transfer rate: the percent of first-time college students who, within five years of enrolling in a community college, complete at least 12 credit hours there, and subsequently enroll in at least one course at a four-year institution.

6. To which recipient four-year colleges and universities do students transfer?

6. Transcripts; reports from transfer institutions; student surveys.

Succeeding as a Transfer Student

7. At what rates do transfer students make progress (in terms of credit hours earned) toward their bachelor's degrees, and how do these rates compare with "native" university students?

7. Transcripts; transfer institution records; follow-up surveys of transfer students.

8. What grades do transfer students earn, and how do these grades compare with those earned by native university students?

8. Transcripts; transfer institution records; follow-up surveys of transfer students.

9. What percentage of transfer students successfully complete their bachelor's degrees? How long does it take? In what majors? And how do their degree achievement rates compare to native university students'?

9. Transcripts; transfer institution records; follow-up surveys of transfer students.

Comment: Studies of the comparative academic progress, performance, and degree achievement of community college transfer students and their native university counterparts require complicated analyses conducted in close cooperation with transfer universities. Most published studies have selected comparable cohorts of transfer and native students and followed them for the equivalent of five years from initial college enrollment. This can be done retrospectively using existing historical student records, or studies can follow the progress of current student cohorts. In either case, extreme care must be taken in the complicated task of selecting comparable community college transfer and native university cohorts given their different enrollment patterns.

Articulating Courses

10. What percentage of students' total credit hours are accepted by the transfer institution?

10. Transcripts; transfer institution records; follow-up surveys of transfer students; state reports.

11. Are there barriers to articulation, and, if so, what are they?

11. Articulation agreements; interviews with students, advisers, and articulation officers.

12. Do students who complete "two plus two" programs at the community college transfer as juniors to the university?

12. Transcripts; transfer institution records; follow-up surveys of program completers.

13. Are credit hours earned in dual-credit high school and community college programs accepted by the transfer university?

13. Transcripts; transfer institution records; follow-up surveys of students exercising the dual-credit option.

Susan Carroll
Kirkwood Community College
from *Assessing Institutional Effectiveness in Community Colleges,*
Doucette and Hughes, 1990

Secondary Data Analysis: A Potential Evaluation Nightmare

Adelman accused the "most notable and persistent of the critics" of community colleges of "hocus-pocus analyses of secondary sources." He disparaged a common practice by which they identify and then support their common criticisms: "They take other scholars' studies, state system studies, institutional studies, and census data—all with different samples, different populations, different years (boom or bust), different definitions of variables—utter an incantation, and pretend that it all makes sense" (1992b, p. 26). His accusations raise the concern that, because of limited funds or time or opportunities to conduct new research, institution and program personnel oftentimes will analyze data from previous studies in order to answer present questions.

Secondary data analysis creates significant obstacles to quality evaluation: when there is a "mismatch of primary and secondary research objectives" (Kiecolt and Nathan, 1985 pp. 12–13), as, for example, when the primary research objectives could be met only by gathering aggregate data, and the secondary research objectives could be met only by having gathered data about individuals; when there is incomplete documentation of data—details that were not important during primary analysis were not documented and now may be the very items that the secondary data user needs; when there is difficulty in detecting errors in the data—typographical errors and sampling errors once data have been processed; and when data may be invalid—"survey items are imprecise measures of the concepts a secondary analyst has in mind, or...the variables have been poorly operationalized" (p.14).

An example of such an evaluation dilemma is a college's retrospective comparison of success rates and withdrawal rates of developmental students over three consecutive years, using registration files as a data source. Data indicated that, while statistically significant differences were found in success and withdrawal rates for only one subject—mathematics—for two of the years compared, there were also significant differences in withdrawal rates from developmental studies courses and arts and sciences courses, which had been eliminated by analytic procedures.

Confounding the analysis was the familiar dilemma: data-gathering procedures may be carefully planned for their original purpose, carefully carried out, and results accurately recorded, yet, the truth may be elusive. A "progress" grade, which was recorded for those students who were in the class at the end of the semester but had not yet successfully completed the course requirements, was not included as either a success or a withdrawal in the study, although it accounted for between 2.4 percent and 29.7 percent of the grades in those courses. Thus, while it was a sound method for dealing with differential learning rates among students, the progress grade option prevented a firm conclusion based on these data. On the plus side, however, undertaken as a descriptive study of what happened during the three academic years, with no specific hypothesis to test, this evaluation effort was successful descriptively, as well as in providing another perspective on recording grades or course status. Furthermore, the discovery was important because while the flexibility of multiple grade options appears to contribute to the success of developmental programs, it may affect future assessment/evaluation decisions—e.g., decisions to compare present with past outcomes, to compare institutional data with those of other institutions, or to compare institutional data with research data in the literature. The discovery also provided important information for the design of record-keeping systems with future evaluation needs in mind.

Some of What We Know About Evaluation of Programs for At-Risk Students

A history of the evaluation of remediation in higher education appears to have three distinct periods (see Cross, 1976, pp. 31-36). Before 1960 criteria for program success were unclear, research designs were naive, and the interpretation of data for program development and improvement was weak; there was a lack of adequate control groups; and, in universities, where most of the research was being conducted, there was little enthusiasm for research about programs from which so little was expected. During the 1960s evaluation had a more emotional orientation—e.g., do ethnic minorities have the potential for successfully completing academic work?—and less a research orientation—e.g., are the courses effective? Evaluations, and the lack thereof, mirrored the emotional times—fears were that poor results would reflect badly on the ability of both community colleges to perform the "second-chance" charge and ethnic minorities to succeed in higher education.

In *Salvage, Redirection, or Custody?*, Roueche (1968) decried the current state of evaluation in programs to remediate basic skills. Complicating the issue of evaluation were the continuing debates, such as whether remediation was to be a means to enable students to continue on to college-level work or whether it was an "end," providing a time for students to be "cooled out"—to get the message that college, or their chosen field of study, was not for them; whether remediation was indeed a function of community colleges; and whether the provision of a second chance for at-risk students was a legitimate program goal.

Given this widespread uncertainty and the relative newness of the field of evaluation, it is hardly surprising that in the early years evaluations of programs for at-risk students were filled with rare and haphazard phenomena. Overall, the early goals and objectives of developmental programs were characterized as "nebulous and ill defined because no one is absolutely convinced that it is even possible to remediate" (Roueche, 1968, p. 25). The recommendations of the study called for a "total program approach," which would be "characterized by carefully defined objectives and study of student outcomes" (p. 27). The five colleges featured in this first study were chosen because they had defined their goals and had "actually written up their programs and, to some degree, evaluated them" (p. 27). Noting that colleges had largely based their programs on "unproved assumptions," Roueche (1968) concluded with a call for further research into the provision of effective basic skills programs.

Several schools of thought prevalent in the 1960s led observers to various conclusions regarding the apparently ineffectual remedial programs: some declared the problem unsolvable and abandoned their efforts; others characterized the process as spending "good money on bad students"; others further clouded the issue by asserting that some races were innately less capable of learning academic curricula. Many educators took comfort in the "open-access" model, feeling that justice had been done when all had access to higher education. A popular view was that the college's duty to the nontraditional student was discharged at the point of access and that it then became the student's responsibility to make the best of the opportunity (Roueche and Snow, 1977). Such a philosophy left little need for evaluation.

Yet, during the late 1960s and 1970s, literally hundreds of reports of developmental programs appeared in the Educational Resources Information Center (ERIC) system. Some reports were of programs that had received national acclaim, and others appeared to have been written in response to some institutional or regional question. It was generally believed that these documents were little more than attempts to justify existence and that many authors were claiming successes that they could not verify or validate in any meaningful way. In the early 1980s one study determined that 504 such documents were listed in the ERIC system, but the researchers discovered that only 60 programs could be considered comprehensive enough to warrant further investigation (Kulik, Kulik, and Schwalb, 1982).

By the 1970s, as the fears of the previous decade had subsided somewhat, the evaluation process turned to questions of "how" all at-risk students could best be served. While the picture of evaluation for these programs was not yet focused, some identifiable benchmarks suggested a gradual improvement in methods and commitment.

In *Overcoming Learning Problems*, Roueche and Snow observed that very little, if anything, was done to measure the impact of programs for at-risk students. At that time, these programs were primarily remedial, and the continued demand for such instruction seemed to be justification enough. But, in those rare programs where evaluative data were available, the attrition rate was discovered to be as high as 90 percent, an especially disturbing figure in light of the fact that it came from an evaluation of programs designed to facilitate academic success (Roueche and Snow, 1977).

In the mid-1980s a nationwide survey of higher education institutions identified some common interests for program evaluation:

- The extent to which students were learning
- The retention of students (within the program)
- The satisfaction of students
- Follow-up retention information (of students in curriculum programs) (Roueche, Baker, and Roueche, 1984, p. 55)

In the final report these interests were listed in order of declining frequency, as above—that is, more institutions responded that identifying and measuring "the extent to which students were learning" were of more interest to them than was "the retention of students (within the program)," and so on. In basic skills reading, for example, 65 percent of these programs evaluated student learning; 61 percent examined student retention; 58 percent evaluated student satisfaction; and 43 percent evaluated students through a follow-up method. Percentages reported for writing and mathematics varied only by one or two percentage points in each case from those listed for reading, with community colleges overall appearing to conduct evaluation just slightly more frequently than did the average institution responding to the survey. In general, community colleges reported evaluating these four program aspects more often than did liberal arts colleges and less frequently than did four-year institutions. Only one-third of all responding institutions reported examining basic skills programs to determine their cost-effectiveness, while more than one-half of the major research universities gathered these data for basic mathematics and writing courses (Roueche, Baker, and Roueche, 1984).

More recently, a highly detailed profile of the strategies used in evaluating remedial programs was provided by a national survey of two- and four-year colleges, conducted by the National Center for Education Statistics (1991a). In the academic year 1989-90, 97 percent of responding institutions reported conducting at least one type of evaluation of remedial programs (i.e., student evaluation of courses, instructor evaluation, tracking of course completion rates, follow-up studies of grades at the next level). Ninety-two percent reported using at least two different methods to track program achievements, and more than 50 percent used four or more strategies to evaluate their programs.

The type of evaluation most commonly conducted was "student evaluation of courses"; however, "course/program completion rate" was considered to be the most important type of evaluation by the greatest number (30 percent) of respondents, followed closely by "student evaluations," which was considered most important by 25 percent of the respondents, and "instructor evaluations," which was considered most significant by 23 percent. Ranking a weak fourth in assigned importance were "follow-up studies of grades," which is somewhat puzzling, since approximately 80 percent of institutions reported that skill levels for exiting remedial courses were based on entry-level skills for subsequent academic courses. If this is so, following up the academic performance of remedial students would seem to be of prime importance for checking congruence between skills taught in remedial courses and skills needed in subsequent academic courses. Following up is clearly the most difficult of the evaluation methods rated in the study, possibly contributing to its relatively low ranking; nonetheless, 65 percent of institutions reported conducting evaluation by this method.

Seventeen percent of institutions surveyed were unable to provide percentage figures for enrollment of freshmen in remedial courses; this figure rises to 21 percent when only public institutions are considered. Of those with such available information, 30 percent were unable to break down enrollment by ethnic group. Similarly, about 25 percent of responding institutions were unable to provide passing rates of freshmen in remedial courses, and about half of the institutions surveyed could not break down passing rates for freshmen remedial students by ethnicity.

"One goal of the study was to compare retention rates to the second year for students enrolled in remedial courses with those for all freshmen. Too few institutions maintain these records, however, to provide valid national estimates" (National Center for Education Statistics, 1991a, p. 12). The survey question that asked for the percentage of full-time entering freshmen from the previous year who continued at an institution the second year was answered by only 73 percent of the respondents. A similar survey item regarding persistence of freshmen enrolled in remedial courses received responses from only about half, and questions regarding ethnic breakdowns went unanswered by as many as two-thirds of respondents. The survey results indicate that 81 percent of institutions nationwide do not maintain graduation data for freshmen who have enrolled in at least one remedial course, thus missing an opportunity to evaluate the contribution of remedial programs to the success of the college as a whole (National Center for Education Statistics, 1991a).

A 1991 national study conducted by Boylan, et al., investigated the effects of developmental programs on cumulative GPA, long-term retention, and subsequent student performance in regular college courses; and, more broadly, the efficacy of developmental education. The researchers surveyed 150 institutions representative of all institutional types, consistent with their representation in American higher education. Usable data were provided by 108 of these institutions. Student transcripts for a five-and-one-half-year period in four-year institutions and for a three-and-one-half-year period in two-year institutions were analyzed to determine persistence rates, individual term and cumulative

GPA in relation to participation in developmental courses, and grades in regular college courses. Preliminary data provide information previously unavailable for a national sample of developmental students. For purposes of this study, developmental students were defined as those judged by local institutional criteria to be unprepared for college work (typically, scores from standardized achievement or placement tests were used to assign students to developmental programs).

Boylan's study determined that persistence and graduation rates of community and technical college developmental students compared favorably with the national average; the percentage of developmental students graduating or still enrolled after four years was 24 percent at community colleges and 33.7 percent at technical colleges. In 1983 the U.S. Office of Education documented that about 45 percent of all students entering four-year institutions would eventually complete a baccalaureate degree; this study discovered that at research universities and private four-year institutions those who had participated in developmental programs persisted and graduated at rates of 48.3 percent and 40.2 percent respectively, comparing favorably with the national rate of 45 percent of four-year institutions. Boylan noted that one measure of the success of a developmental program is the extent to which it prepares students to succeed in regular college courses.

Data indicated that 77.2 percent of the students enrolled in developmental math passed the regular college math course, 91.1 percent of the students completing developmental English passed the college English course, and 83 percent of students completing the developmental reading course went on to pass their college social science course (because there were no regular curriculum college course equivalents to developmental reading, the comparison was made between the developmental reading and introductory social science courses). Data indicated that students who participated in developmental programs were as likely to persist and graduate as students who were apparently better prepared for college, but researchers advised that developmental students were targeted for special intervention and the intervention may have increased their likelihood of success. Boylan also noted that, while increasing retention is not the primary purpose of developmental education, participation in the developmental programs appeared to be associated with retention and graduation and reflected the most frequently cited purpose for these programs—to prepare students for success in later college courses. In effect, if the major criterion for judging the effectiveness of developmental programs is preparing students for success in later college courses, then they are most certainly successful. "The basic message from this portion of the study is that, on the whole, developmental education programs do seem to work" (Boylan and Bonham, 1992).

What the Award-Winners Say About Evaluation Criteria and Assessment

We asked our award-winning programs to respond to two questions regarding program assessment: "What evaluation criteria are used to assess program success (e.g., retention figures, student feedback)?" "What do you consider to be the program's most successful features?"

De Anza College's A STARTING POINT Minority Transfer Program evaluates its success based on student retention rates, transfer rates, internship involvements, and scholarships or special awards earned. Past evaluations of the program's effectiveness included a study by the college's Office of Institutional Research, which compared retention rates for participants and nonparticipants (matched by ethnicity, educational objective, age, gender, time of entry, and completion of a college orientation course.) While the total Transfer Project group and the control group differed in gender and ethnicity, they did not differ in age. In the continuously enrolled student comparisons, the ethnicity of the students did not differ significantly between the two groups. Findings were that program participants maintained a retention rate twice as high as that for nonparticipants (80 percent vs. 40 percent); program participants accumulated more units and achieved higher GPAs (2.54 vs. 2.16) than did the control group. Also, while not significantly different, a lower percentage of Transfer Project students were placed on academic probation than were the control group students in three of the four ethnic groups. The study was conducted over a period of four consecutive quarters during the pilot phase of the program.

As transfer is a central purpose of A STARTING POINT, the tracking of program participants who have been accepted for transfer is an important aspect of program evaluation; data indicate that the largest increases have been seen in the numbers of Hispanics transferring to the University of California and California State University systems. Student feedback and information from the college's computer network are combined with data on the progress of transferred students to measure the program's effectiveness.

Because internship involvement is a program objective, this activity is monitored and evaluated regularly. To date, 24 students have been accepted to various internships and experiential, educational, or service programs such as NASA's Scientific Technical Internship at Ames Research Center, Minority Leaders Fellowship Program in Washington, D.C., and Operation Raleigh in Japan. Participation in quality programs and the "fit" between the students' objectives and those of the program are critical to evaluation of this element.

At **William Rainey Harper College**, the athletic academic coordinator establishes goals for the Athletic Academic Advising program before each academic year, and at the end of the year, they are evaluated and revised. The comparison figures for the Academic Monitoring System are also useful in comparing how many students brought unsatisfactory grades to a satisfactory level by the 10-week reporting date. These results are examined after intervention by the athletic academic coordinator to help students find the support service most appropriate for them. Final grades are evaluated to determine if the early warning system has helped the students who had unsatisfactory grades. The numbers of students who make the conference all-academic and NJCAA academic all-American teams are used for evaluation as well. End-of-year reports are written and presented to the dean of physical education, athletics, and recreation.

Highland Community College relies on semester-to-semester and year-to-year retention figures, GPAs achieved, transfer rates, graduation/completion rates,as well as student and faculty feedback data to assess Student Support Services success. The program exceeded its primary objective, achieving an 85 percent graduation and/or transfer rate after two years of operation, with a rate of 86 percent.

At **Illinois Central College**, the major evaluation criterion of the QUEST program is its retention rate. Student enrollment in the program has grown at both the freshman and sophomore levels in each of the program's five years; enrollment was originally intended for 200 students; currently 400 students are involved. Total enrollment increased by 66.4 percent during 1987–91. Most significant was the rate of increase of sophomore enrollment of 115.5 percent during that same period and a 54.7 percent increase between 1990–91. In the second, third, and fourth years of the program, the rate of retention of sophomores from the freshman class of the previous year was in the 60 percent range. In 1991 that retention rate rose dramatically to 90.5 percent—evidence of the growing "holding power" of the program and the climate of student support the program has generated.

There is an ongoing effort to broaden the course offerings within the QUEST schedule and to monitor and evaluate the transferability of classes. Many of the four-year institutions are increasing their general education requirements and/or raising their standards, and QUEST attempts to keep up with the myriad of changes, and to describe each course in regards to where, if, and how it will transfer.

Staff evaluates QUEST quality by analyzing student performance. The computer center designed a program to randomly select a group of entering freshmen for both 1989 and 1990. The request included the following parameters: same age (traditional), full-time (12 or more hours), and enrolled in a transfer program. QUEST students were compared to the control group of ICC transfer students in two outcome measures: average number of credits earned per semester and the grade point for that semester. Two cohorts were used: students who entered fall 1989 and students who entered fall 1990.

In the 1989 class the incoming QUEST students had a higher ACT composite (20) than the control group (19); in 1990 the two groups had the same ACT composite (20). In both cohorts the performance of QUEST students was superior to that of the random group for each of their first four semesters at ICC. In each semester, the QUEST students earned an average of more than 12 credits per student, *a level that the random group failed to reach in any semester.* The grade point average of QUEST students was higher than that of their counterparts in the random group during each semester, with a difference of GPAs in the groups ranging from 0.043 in spring 1992 to 0.484 in spring 1991 for the first cohort. Average GPA for the 1989 QUEST class (for four semesters from fall 1989 to spring 1991) ranged between 2.646 and 2.874; for the random group, the average ranged from 2.386 to 2.499. For the 1990 class, average GPA for the QUEST class (for four semesters) ranged from 2.582 to 2.783; ranges for the random class was 2.429 to 2.740. Eighty percent of the QUESTers had earned a 2.00 GPA or better by the end of the fourth semester, as compared to 71 percent of the random group. Average credits earned by QUEST classes and random classes averaged between one and two credits over the eight semesters subject to analysis. Retention rates for four continuous semesters for the two groups were as follows: The 1989 QUEST class had a 73.2 percent retention rate and the random class a 55.2. The 1990 classes were almost identical: 73.4 percent for QUEST and 55 percent for random. Not counted as retained are those students who transferred early without a degree, as well as those who dropped out.

Graduation rates are critical QUEST evaluation data. Of 157 entering QUEST students, 72 graduated (46 percent) after six semesters (some of the students graduated after four semesters, some after five). Of the 123 entering in the random group, 34 graduated (28 percent after six semesters). Final statistics for QUEST and random groups reflect a national trend away from the two-year/four-semester traditional manner in which a junior college student obtains a degree.

To reinforce the academic purpose of the QUEST program, the staff publishes an "honors" list as a supplement to the weekly newsletter. A new category has been added, "Honorable Mention," to recognize students with a 3.00 to 3.249 GPA. Staff send congratulatory postcards to students completing the semester with 12 credits or more and a GPA of 2.00 or better. The dean sends a letter congratulating all students with a 2.00 GPA and above, applauding their hard work and urging them to continue their academic journey.

Faculty questionnaires request responses regarding differences between QUEST and non-QUEST students. In one survey (with a 90 percent response rate), faculty reported on their own QUEST classes: they maintained an 89 percent attendance rate; class participation was at 96 percent; 96 percent were in active modes of teaching; 89 percent had outside classroom contact with QUEST students; 88 percent reported relating their subject matter to other subjects taught at the college. Significant differences were reported between the QUEST students and the random groups: QUEST students were more willing to participate in class or were more responsive; they attended class more regularly; their attitude and behavior were more positive (and there were frequent faculty references to higher levels of student motivation). According to student questionnaires about classes, students thought there was more opportunity for in-class discussion in QUEST classes, more opportunity for input in class decisions, and more activities and group projects.

Future evaluation needs include systematizing records of QUEST students for follow-up procedures and for tracking individual students. Another need is to annually select a random control group against which to compare QUESTers' performance.

Surveys of QUEST students after transfer have provided program staff with the following important information for program improvement: QUEST courses need increased academic expectations, both qualitative and quantitative; there needs to be more reading assigned in addition to the course textbook; more exams need to be essay-oriented and not multiple-choice; final exams need to be comprehensive in content as well as requiring connections between broad concepts and principles. Staff learned from former QUESTers that they struggle with the sheer volume of work assigned at four-year institutions. Among many significant conclusions from an evaluative study of QUEST over its five-year history is this: "Briefly put, QUEST classes need to educate the student with the bachelor's degree as the goal, not the associate degree."

Miami-Dade Community College's Black Student Opportunity Program has retention as its primary focus for evaluation efforts; persistence rates are compared to national standards as well as to local dropout rates, both of which indicate that program efforts are highly successful. Subsequent college enrollment of BSOP participants is also monitored, and systems are being developed to track students longitudinally through the college years. Eventual achievement of the associate and/or baccalaureate degrees is considered an important student outcome of the program, although it has thus far proven difficult to follow over a period of several years.

The college district provides several additional programs that support the special needs of at-risk students, and these programs are evaluated on their achievement of the specific program outcomes desired: i.e., the number of high school participants who enroll at M-DCC following their senior year, the proportion of at-risk students who are retained in college from year to year, and grade-point averages earned by program participants (see Successful Program Features). External consultants are also employed to assist faculty or administrative planning groups in assessing ongoing efforts and in using outcomes information to improve the design of new programs.

Middlesex Community College regularly evaluates its Course Clusters option and Freshman Seminar based on student retention and evaluation responses from students and faculty.

From the time the Course Cluster program was developed, the anticipated outcomes have been improved student retention; better connections among students; more contact and support between students and faculty; and a stronger perceived identity between the students and the college community. These outcomes have provided the framework for the college's evaluation process.

Evaluation efforts often begin with the most objective criterion, retention—also viewed as most critical to the overall success of the college. Although the Course Clusters were limited to 25 students per group, which precludes matched sample comparisons because of the small sample size, some flavor of comparison was provided by comparing Cluster students to nonparticipant-entering students in the same academic program. Cluster students showed a much higher retention rate than nonparticipants. Most significantly, no students in the liberal studies Cluster (comprised of all developmental courses) left the college after the first semester (fall 1989). The retention rate for this potentially high-risk group, from fall 1989 to spring 1990, was 100 percent. By comparison, non-Cluster participants in traditionally scheduled liberal studies courses showed an attrition rate of 34 percent after one semester. For students in the business Clusters, an attrition rate of 15 percent was reported for the period from fall 1989 to spring 1990, a considerably better rate than that reported for non-Cluster business students (33 percent). In the liberal arts Cluster, the attrition rate was about the same: 33 percent for the Cluster students and 34 percent for non-Cluster participants. Attrition rates for these and subsequent Cluster groups are being monitored.

When students and faculty evaluated the Course Clusters through qualitative techniques such as interviews and open-ended questionnaires, the responses were overwhelmingly favorable. The students reported that they were able to meet others easily and could call

Cluster students when they needed support. Many Cluster students formed study groups and support networks outside class. Typical of the student responses were such comments as, "The best thing about the Cluster is you know everyone in your classes, which makes you feel more comfortable," and "I felt I got some real personal help from my professors. The Cluster also took a lot of pressure out of meeting new students."

Faculty reported that students participated more easily in class discussions and supported one another throughout the semester. One faculty member in the liberal studies/developmental Cluster told of a student who was having a particularly difficult time both emotionally and financially. The other Cluster students gave her a food basket and provided the emotional support that she needed to get through the semester. Faculty members characterized the support of these students toward one another as truly overwhelming. Among the faculty comments included in the evaluation: "This is a fabulous idea for the at-risk students. I was certainly amazed at how some 'hard cases' mellowed and helped each other."

Although there are many Freshman Seminar courses throughout the country, the program at Middlesex involves team teaching between faculty, student services staff, and administrators—one of the key features of its success. Two instructors, usually a faculty member and a student services staff member or administrator, teach a class of 25 students. The objective of team teaching is to allow students to be exposed to different teaching styles and different personalities and to provide the opportunity for the class to break into small discussion groups led by each instructor. Both instructors attend every class.

An enormous benefit of this team approach is that team members plan and collaborate on classroom teaching in a subject area that is equally new to both. By the end of the course, the paired instructors have "weathered" the class together and have developed an understanding of one another's teaching style and job responsibilities. Freshman Seminar has allowed group support to develop across all levels of the college community, resulting in a new-found appreciation and understanding among colleagues who might not have otherwise had a chance to work together.

Retention again provided the focus for the Freshman Seminar's earliest evaluation efforts. Results were initially measured for two years, 1988 and 1989, when the course had been approved as a pilot study. Sample groups from Freshman Seminar and a selected control group were matched based on six variables: entering reading level; full-/part-time status; gender; race; program; campus location. For the 1988 group the retention rate was significantly higher (.05 significance level) for Freshman Seminar students than for the control group. This remained true (.05 significance level) for three subsequent semesters. The greatest difference occurred during the fall 1989 semester. All students in the Freshman Seminar sample actually completed the semester, while only 85.8 percent of the matched sample completed. Freshman Seminar obviously had a strong impact on the students while they were enrolled in the course.

Grade point average for Freshman Seminar students was slightly higher than for nonparticipants, but not at a statistically significant level. Evaluations from faculty, staff, and students were collected over a three-year period and were extremely positive. Faculty reported that students appeared to gain more self-confidence and developed a stronger commitment to education, while students reported that they learned more about college resources and developed better connections with other students and faculty.

North Lake College's Advantage Center monitors the number and frequency of student contacts by semester as a baseline for its evaluation activities. Also recorded are the areas of concern most often addressed by mentors, such as study skills, academic advising, time management, and class scheduling. Because a significant function of mentoring is providing referrals to other student services, these interactions are also tracked by semester.

Students are identified for the program through traditional methods of counselor or faculty referral, self referral, and scholastic suspension, and the response rate of students to each type of referral is separately recorded. Additional students are identified by computer as exhibiting two or more of eight high-risk characteristics: frequent withdrawal/failure rates; late registration; low GPA; low assessment scores; probation/suspension; under the age of 25 and first-generation college student; working 21 hours or more and enrolled in four or more courses.

Because participation is voluntary for most of these students, the number of students who are actually persuaded to use the service is highly significant, and this information is carefully tabulated. Of 411 students identified using the computer database and contacted by program staff, 97, or 24 percent, actually interacted with a mentor or peer adviser, information that is useful in evaluating the program's recruitment strategies. Those referred to Advantage Center by counselors on the basis of low GPA also participated at a rate of 24 percent; faculty referrals, however, were acted upon by students at a somewhat higher rate of 40 percent.

Critical to evaluating the overall success of the program are data on grade point averages and on persistence before and after participation in the program. These data have been carefully recorded and exhaustively analyzed, with the result that the program's accomplishments are well documented: GPA and persistence rate comparisons of mentored students since the inception of the Advantage Program continue to prove its effectiveness.

Evaluation of the Advantage Program does not rely solely on quantitative data; qualitative data collected from faculty and students add life to the outcomes and effectiveness measures. For the spring 1991 semester, survey forms were developed and distributed to all full-time and part-time faculty, student participants from all referral sources, faculty/staff members who were hired to serve as mentors, and students who were hired to serve as peer advisers. Faculty comments were positive, although they expressed a need for better marketing of the program. Students responded that the Advantage Program was tangible evidence that the college really cared about their success, that the program was a way to connect with the college, and that it provided confidence as well as needed information. Peer advisers cited personal gains in study habits as well as great satisfaction in helping fellow students. The effectiveness of the Advantage Program has produced a steady increase in the number of students mentored since the program's inception.

At **Richland College,** the evaluation criteria used to assess program success include an annual review of student completion rates in all courses and programs. Students are invited to evaluate courses, programs, and faculty annually and to share their experiences and suggestions for improvement of instruction. Students' suggestions are reviewed, and some are implemented in the program. Faculty representatives serve on district curriculum committees where they design evaluation procedures and identify evaluation criteria based on innovations in the field.

Santa Barbara City College's Transfer Achievement Program is evaluated according to several different factors:
- Number of students participating in the program
- Course completion and college persistence rates of TAP students vs. non-TAP minority students with a goal of transfer
- Math course completion rates of TAP students who participate in the math study groups and course completion rates in English classes for TAP students who participate in the Multicultural English Transfer program (courses in the precollege English sequence and college-level English)
- The number of TAP students who apply for, are admitted to, and actually attend a four-year university

Research studies conducted by the college have documented that TAP students are performing well on each of these criterion measures.

A study compared the rates of college persistence and units completed (with a passing grade) for TAP students with the rates and units for non-TAP minority students planning to transfer to a four-year college or university. Because the majority of students who join TAP do so one or more semesters after their first term at SBCC, the resulting differences in their pre-TAP college experiences make it very difficult to evaluate TAP's effect on its participants in terms of persistence and course completion rates.

To create comparable groups of TAP and non-TAP students, the decision was made to include only those students who joined TAP in their first semester at SBCC. The comparison group consisted solely of newly entering SBCC minority students whose educational goal was to transfer. Although the sample sizes were very small, comparisons of persistence and course completion rates were made among the following groups of first-time students who entered the college in the fall semester of each year from 1988 through 1990:

- All matriculation transfer-oriented students
- TAP students
- Non-TAP/Non-Educational Opportunity Program (EOP) transfer-oriented students
- TAP/EOP students

Comparisons of the college persistence rates and course completion rates of students in each of the target groups revealed that:

- The first-to-second, first-to-third, and first-to-fourth semester persistence rates of TAP students were substantially higher than those of non-TAP minority transfer-oriented students and all matriculated students with a goal of transfer. Although the sample of TAP students was small, these results held true for students entering the college in each of the three years examined (fall 1988, fall 1989, and fall 1990).
- Although lower than TAP students, the persistence rate of non-TAP EOP students was higher than non-TAP/non-EOP minority transfer-oriented students.
- For most of the terms examined, the percentage of units completed with a passing grade was higher for TAP students than for non-TAP minority transfer-oriented students.

An invaluable aid to evaluation efforts is the computer-supported database, which stores all student demographic data as well as the Transfer Task Inventory (TTI). The latter is each student's record of progress toward the transfer goal, allowing TAP advisers to track each student's level of involvement.

It is likely that students who join TAP are more highly motivated to succeed than transfer-oriented minority students who did not join. Nevertheless, the course completion and college persistence rates of

TAP participants was impressive and substantially greater than those of students in the comparison groups (matriculated students with a goal of transfer and non-TAP minority students with a goal of transfer). These findings suggest that the TAP program is having a positive effect on the academic performance of students who enter the program in their first semester at the college. These positive findings will be used to recruit prospective TAP students in their first semester.

The finding that nearly twice as many TAP than non-TAP minority transfer-oriented students returned to the college for a second year suggests the need to recruit more students into the program in their first semester at the college.

The finding that students enrolled in either TAP or EOP had higher persistence rates than transfer-oriented students not in a special program suggests the value of expanding these structured programs and/or of creating new ones such as the Career Advancement Program for students pursuing vocational education objectives.

Santa Fe Community College's Student Success Model is a global concept that permeates every component and all functions of the college's operation, and, as is true of all higher-order goals, it is difficult to measure specifically. However, one very clear indicator of program success program is that, during the first three weeks of class, SFCC experiences only a 4 percent dropout rate, as compared to the national rate of 17 to 26 percent for the same period. Specific programs and their contributions are more easily monitored, as can be seen in the following summaries.

Retention Program: Intrusive Counseling Supports Student Success. The college's Early Alert System allows faculty and staff to respond to student behavior by expeditiously reporting such warning signs as excessive absences from class, sleeping in class, decline in class performance and grades, deteriorating physical appearance, disruptive behavior, tardiness, and neglecting homework assignments. When early alert referrals are made, a counselor contacts the student involved to discuss the situation and to offer assistance. Every effort is made to meet with even the most reluctant student, and the outcomes of the contact are carefully documented for evaluative and planning purposes. Typical student outcomes are a statement of intention to return to class, a change of class section, a change of status from credit to audit, referral to other departments or agencies for assistance, dropping the class, withdrawing from school, and referral to tutoring or counseling. During the most recent reporting period, 241 early alert referrals were recorded through the system; concerns included absence from class and personal problems.

Challenge Program: Mentoring for Student Success. Much information is gathered throughout the semester as mentors meet on a monthly basis with students and keep a record of all contacts. Data gathered after a recent mid-term exam period indicated that 82 percent of the Challenge Program's first group of participants were in good standing. The mentors typically review and discuss mid-term grades with the students, sending follow-up letters to those whose GPAs fall below a 2.0 average. Mid-term and final grades are used for evaluation, as are records of monthly meetings with mentors.

Developmental Studies Program. Evaluation of the effectiveness of developmental preparation in mathematics and English is based on the assumption that, because the Developmental Studies Division prepares students who are deficient in mathematics or English for college-level work in those subjects, students who successfully complete the developmental courses should be able to compete with students in subsequent college-level math and English courses. This assumption is tested regularly.

One study compared the success rates in college-level mathematics and English courses for two groups of students: students who began in developmental studies classes in math or English and then went on to classes in the Arts and Sciences Division; and students who took English or math only in the Arts and Sciences Division. It was expected that the results of this study would indicate that students who first took developmental classes would later have a success rate at least as high as the students whose first math/English class was at the college level; and, indeed, it was found that the developmental studies students experienced a 92 percent success rate, in contrast to the nondevelopmental studies students' 72 percent success rate, in Math 130, the first course in the college credit mathematics sequence. The difference between these success rates was statistically significant. A similar comparison for English students indicated that those who had taken developmental English experienced an 81 percent success rate, as compared to a 73 percent success rate in English 111 for those students who had not taken developmental English. The difference was not statistically significant.

Regularly scheduled studies indicate that the success rates of those students who complete developmental studies courses are statistically equivalent to or higher than success rates of those who go directly into college-level courses. This answers the original question, "Are SFCC's developmental math and English courses effectively preparing students for college-level work in those subject areas?" with a resounding *yes.*

The success of programs for at-risk students is measured both by the numbers of students who complete their coursework and the numbers who progress to the next level of college work. Students recently evaluated the developmental program using the 1991 ACT Student Opinion Survey, and the following percentages of students rated themselves satisfied or very satisfied with the services:

- 84 percent were positive about personal counseling they had received
- 71 percent indicated that vocational guidance and career counseling had been helpful
- 87 percent of the respondents rated job placement positively

The same program components were also evaluated in 1991 by the New Mexico Department of Education, which rated the areas of counseling, career advisement, and job placement in full compliance with no recommendations or action required.

Learning Support Lab. Student attendance and completion records are used for evaluation, as is feedback from faculty regarding the effectiveness of the academic support provided by the laboratory.

Suffolk Community College continuously evaluates its retention program. Because the highest percentage of students drop out after one semester, a longitudinal study of almost four years (eight semesters) charted the number of students remaining after one semester of work. Data indicated that persistence rates rose from an average of 72.6 percent for the first year to an average of 88.9 percent for the fourth year of program operation. (A high of 97.1 percent was reached during the seventh semester of the study.)

At the **University of Toledo Community and Technical College (ComTech)**, both quantitative and qualitative data are routinely collected to evaluate the Developmental Education program. For evaluating curricular improvement, course grade distributions indicate the frequency of student success in the program itself, while an analysis of success in subsequent courses provides a measure of whether developmental courses are preparing students to compete in college-level classes. Because sociology is a paired co-requisite with reading, the distribution of grades earned in sociology by students in the reading class, as compared with grades of those who waived the class, provides a measure of the effectiveness of the developmental reading program. Individual students' reading gains are measured by a commercial instrument in order to monitor individual progress; when aggregated, the scores can also be used for program evaluation. Hard data, such as retention figures, are amplified by such qualitative data as videotaped interviews; the latter are collected to ascertain which academic strategies are most useful to students short- and long-term.

The evaluation plan for the Learning Assistance Center includes collecting summative data for the number of times a student has attended Supplemental Instruction (SI) or a traditional tutoring session and grade distributions for those students who attend SI three or more times, compared to those who attend fewer times. Grade distributions and retention rates are collected and compared for those who attend SI and those who choose not to use the service.

Students' degrees of satisfaction with tutoring services are determined via questionnaires, which are mailed each quarter to a random sample of participants. Such evaluations indicate positive perceptions of the tutorial services provided, with fewer than 10 percent of the respondents indicating that any aspect of the operation needed improvement. A computerized tracking system identifies student demographic data for grant-reporting purposes and other uses. GPA and retention data are collected especially for athletes who participate in the Providing Athletic Study Strategies program.

Each quarter, students have the opportunity to evaluate advisers. Feedback is used to improve services; in advisement, more so than in curricular areas, the students' perceptions of the learning and assistance gained from advisers are clear indicators of success.

An analysis of graduating students' transcripts indicates that during the four quarters of academic year 1990–91, developmental students represented between 35 and 53 percent of the total ComTech graduating class. Analyses are also performed to determine the proportion of developmental education students from each degree program: proportions range from 67 percent in general studies to 29 percent in technical science and mathematics. These measures are significant indicators of developmental education's contribution to the success of the overall college program.

What the Award-Winners Say About Their Programs' Most Successful Features

The director of **De Anza College**'s A STARTING POINT Minority Transfer Program expressed strong feelings when asked about the program's most successful features:

> Because this question taps into my heart and soul, it is perhaps the most difficult item to respond to. Overall, I would point to the top-down support of the program's broadened philosophical base, which is strongly tied to the politics of being an ethnic minority in America. While number crunching is a bottom-line necessity, such support has allowed for the realization of a mission statement which goes beyond quantity of participants to address the need for quality graduates. It is also this very support which has allowed the program to evolve dynamically and to be highly responsive to student input and unexpected and sudden opportunities.

The specific features of A STARTING POINT the director considered most successful included:

- The extent to which students networked with each other and the affiliations they formed with the college
- The extent of student participation in internships and the amount of scholarship and achievement awards
- The program's recruitment method, which results in the involvement of 95 percent of its target group
- The program's orientation experience
- The comprehensive database that has been developed and maintained by the program, which provides staff members with the capability of instantly identifying students by GPA, major, ethnicity, gender, or transfer school of choice, and assists in timely advisement and student support.

William Rainey Harper College's student-athlete program's most important feature is staff commitment to a proactive and comprehensive approach to student success. This includes: diagnostic testing and use of other assessment instruments to identify needs and problems; monitoring of academic progress during the semester; proactive support services; personal contact with students to recognize achievement and encourage progress; and comprehensive academic advising and personal counseling.

Another feature of the program is that, while it continues through the student-athlete's entire college experience, even those student-athletes who decide to no longer participate in athletics still have program services available to them. Among these services are the Tutoring Center, the Math Lab, the Writing Lab, a Learning Assistance Center, and Disabled Student Services.

Computer support has been available to facilitate the compilation of student data essential in assisting students and implementing the academic monitoring system (addresses and phone numbers, past coursework, present course schedule transfer credit, ACT scores, high school GPA, and so on).

Faculty commitment to student success is evidenced by the high response rate generated by the academic progress report cards. The college's administration also places great value on the Athletic Academic Advising program and provides important assistance to the coordinator.

Highland Community College's Student Support Services program is described as "truly mission-driven," with support from both internal and external faculty and staff. The adoption of a Total Quality Management philosophy has been so successful that the director has been asked to advise the college administrative council in its efforts to implement TQM on a collegewide basis, which has in turn given student support service issues a high profile in strategic planning efforts. Another successful feature has been the resulting integration of at-risk student services in the college's overall academic planning.

The success of **Illinois Central College**'s QUEST program is most apparent from the number of students choosing to be involved; the program has doubled in size since its inception. Bonding occurs between QUEST students and staff; they keep in touch by writing, visiting, and calling. Many QUEST students go on to room together or live near another QUESTer after transfer. A third indication of success is the impact on the regular college transfer program—the establishment of a Transfer Center, a similar program for returning adults (the Adult Re-Entry Program), and a collegewide orientation program for all incoming freshmen.

One of the original visions of the QUEST program was that it would generate new transfer classes that would be piloted as QUEST classes. The courses would then be evaluated, refined or revised, and finally offered as non-QUEST classes to all students in a liberal arts and sciences transfer program. This exportability of courses has occurred recently for two classes, chemistry and psychology (the latter has been revised and titled "Strategies for Success"). Two courses originally developed for QUEST in English have now been assimilated into the regular English program. The QUEST program also enabled the math department to pilot placement tests. After two years of requiring all incoming QUEST students to take a math "pilot" placement exam, *all incoming freshmen* are now required to do so.

Another QUEST activity, a day-long orientation session, has been expanded to include all new students to the college. QUEST data indicated that students who attend the QUEST orientation are more active in QUEST and in the college as a whole. Thus, there are now two three-hour formalized orientations for all students the week before college classes begin. A collegewide orientation committee, of which the QUEST director is a member, continues to expand orientation activities and fine-tune the two orientation sessions.

QUEST staff and students were the first to attend the Campus of Difference training session. This weekend exposure to the celebration of "differences" has now become a regular event open to all faculty and students. In addition to Campus of Difference, there is another session in the early fall dedicated to leadership training. Again, QUEST students were the first participants, and now all officers of clubs and organizations on campus are invited. These weekend activities develop a strong group of student leaders who are bonded together and who very quickly network their activities.

Finally, because so many students must work part-time to continue their education, many on-campus jobs are filled by QUESTers. Many form close working and mentoring relationships with their college supervisors.

Based on their collaboration in developing and implementing QUEST courses, groups of faculty have organized to develop interdisciplinary courses, thereby achieving more integration in the curriculum in general. Even experiments that have been tried in QUEST and failed—such as the attempt to measure student achievement through pre- and post-competency testing—have been useful lessons to the college and now are conducted in a limited way. Through QUEST, a number of bridges with four-year institutions have been built.

Conceived as a "total program" or a "mini-college," QUEST has achieved many of its goals of addressing the academic, social, and personal well-being of its students. There has been a definite shift from a social orientation to an emphasis on academics and transfer to a four-year institution. The concept of collegiality has replaced the social club *feel* of the program. Holistic growth is discussed, and there is increasing interaction among QUESTers and the entire college community. The QUEST aim has been to involve the student and the parents in the transfer process.

Much effort has been made in recruiting students from various rural, urban, and suburban backgrounds. They are socioeconomically and experientially diverse, and their worldviews are quite different. This mixture creates a more exciting student population for staff and students alike.

Staff of **Miami-Dade Community College**'s Black Student Opportunity Program designate as its most successful features the mentoring relationships the program fosters, the "earnings" formula that allows participants to earn credit toward tuition costs by completing college preparatory courses in high school, and the special attention and recognition afforded to students via the program's social, cultural, personal, and academic experiences.

Other programs are noteworthy as spin-offs and have been evaluated as similarly successful programs:
- College Reach-Out Program (recruitment)—to provide minority and disadvantaged high school and junior high school students with information about postsecondary education and to lower barriers that frequently decrease minority participation; four-year participants in the program receive college scholarships.
- Comprehensive Opportunity to Pursue Excellence (retention)— facilitators meet with students identified as high-risk to decrease the numbers dropping out of classes prior to semester's end; the

national average retention rate at two-year public institutions is 52 percent, while the retention rate of high-risk students in the COPE program is 82 percent.

- Challenge Center (retention)—an integrated academic and student support network for newly enrolled, full-time Black students whose assessment test results show marginal basic skill levels and who would benefit by additional support as they enter the regular academic mainstream; average GPA after one year of academic work for these high-risk students is 2.50, and 75 percent of the participants re-enroll from one academic year to the next.
- Urban Community College Transfer Opportunity Program (facilitating minority transfer)—utilizes data from a three-year project on barriers to minority student success to improve the assistance Miami-Dade provides minority students who plan to transfer to upper-division institutions; includes retention strategies, "survival skills," and strengthened articulation with the college's principal feeder universities.

The team teaching arrangement of **Middlesex Community College**'s Freshman Seminar has created a number of benefits, described earlier in this chapter. In addition to benefitting the student participants, Freshman Seminar benefits the student services staff, faculty, and administrators who are brought together to collaborate on classroom teaching. The Course Cluster model has built camaraderie among teaching groups and students alike: students enrolled in Cluster courses report that they are able to meet one another easily and that they can call fellow Cluster students when support is needed; likewise, faculty and student services staff who teach in the Cluster groups meet periodically to identify high-risk students and to share teaching strategies. This collaboration has been a critical element in the success of both the Freshman Seminar and the Course Clusters.

The staff of **North Lake College**'s Advantage Program designates its mentoring component as the most critical of the program's innovations and as the best indication of the college's commitment. From the program's inception, its focus has been the needs of at-risk students, and the aim of the mentoring component—to establish more effective communication among students, faculty, and staff—has been supported consistently by the college (although some downsizing may occur among peer advisers as a result of current funding concerns, and these responsibilities will be given to the full-time staff).

The most successful features of **Richland College**'s developmental studies program are methods of student assessment and placement;

prepared and dedicated faculty; instructional support services that include both individual and laboratory tutoring; and administrative support. Several instructional delivery techniques are being implemented, and the developmental math program permits students to attend any lab class that is in session for additional instructional assistance. Similar flexibility is evidenced by an attendance policy that enables students to change to a nontraditional attendance option if they find they are unable to attend a class in which they initially enrolled. All aspects of the program focus on student success.

Santa Barbara City College's Transfer Achievement Program identifies several overarching features of its success:
- Aggressive outreach—active recruiting at the high school and junior high school levels; on-campus recruiting, including early identification of students enrolled in basic skills courses and various college student organizations
- Joining and belonging—in direct contrast to the "smorgasbord" approach taken by some other colleges; coordinated efforts to build positive connections with member of the college community, particularly outside the classroom
- Structure and involvement—demystifying the transfer process by using the Transfer Task Inventory, a four-stage developmental map or checklist of essential transfer-related activities to be completed by the student: assessment and orientation; transfer exploration; academic planning and progress; and transfer transition
- Tracking and feedback—providing Transfer Task progress reports to students, which are checks against work to be completed and encouragements to continue or begin new tasks

According to program staff, assigning each student to a TAP adviser is central to the program's success; the adviser is responsible for assisting the student in staying on track with the activities needed to accomplish the goal of transfer, as well as discussing needs, resources, and strategies for examining available transfer options.

A key element contributing to TAP's success is the creation of the math support group, which offers cooperative learning, sharing of experiences, and swapping strategies. The math study groups are not remedial in orientation, but rather are designed to expose students to challenging and aggressive exercises and assignments that will complement the course curriculum. Another key element is the MET program, a multidisciplinary English program; the English Division at SBCC has initiated a transfer program designed specifically to assist underrepresented students in making the transition to a four-year institution. The program offers students a multicultural classroom environment and a multicultural and multidisciplinary curriculum that allows them to see their own cultures reflected in what they study.

Finally, agreements with 11 (to date) universities provide Guaranteed Admissions Contracts for SBCC students. These agreements serve as an incentive for student persistence and completion of the required classes for transfer.

Santa Fe Community College's Student Success Model is highly personalized, giving both students and college employees a satisfying sense of dealing with people, not with faceless numbers. This is consistent with the role of "service-oriented," "student-oriented," and "success-oriented" faculty and staff that are "central to the SFCC model." Employees are selected according to these criteria, and they are encouraged to hold high expectations for the students, participating actively in all phases of the Student Success Model. Other important reminders of the central importance of students are quality controls for classroom instruction and frequent opportunities for in-service training. Instructors are observed and critiqued in the classroom by a peer at least once each semester, for the purpose of strengthening teaching skills.

Characterized as an "integrated approach" to student success, the program provides services for those individuals who appear to be at risk without "pulling them out" of the general student population. An example is the "Successful Student Series" of workshops, conducted throughout the semester on topics that promote student success, such as time management and conquering test anxiety. While these topics are critical for individuals who are at risk, they are relevant and available to all students.

Retention Program: Intrusive Counseling Supports Student Success. A highly successful feature of the Intrusive Counseling Program is two series of "safety checks," the first of which is conducted during the first three weeks after registration, to make certain that students are following through with their plans. Among these safety checks are "no-show calls" to students who applied for admission but did not enroll during the regular registration period. These students are invited to take advantage of late registration; if other problems are indicated, support is offered. When classes are canceled, students are contacted by telephone with suggestions of other related courses they might take.

Early alert calls are made when students miss class during the first three weeks, and an adviser assists in seeking solutions for conflicts or problems. The timeliness of this contact usually allows for intervention before a situation has gone irretrievably wrong and the student has lost a semester.

Another important feature of the Intrusive Counseling Program is that faculty and staff make a special effort to be sensitive to student classroom and work habit behaviors that portend future academic difficulties. When a counselor receives an early alert form, he or she contacts the student to discuss the situation and to offer assistance.

A second series of "safety checks" sees the students safely through the semester; these checks include advisement, counseling, and academic progress reviews by an assigned adviser who tracks their progress. The adviser follows up with students who received a grade of D or F at mid-term and encourages them to begin academic counseling.

Even with all this support, a student may not complete the semester, but the college's philosophy allows for that: withdrawing from a class may sometimes be the best decision, but only if it is an *informed* decision. Before dropping a class, the student must meet with an adviser to discuss whatever difficulties have arisen and to explore alternatives. Finally, quality advisement and nonpunitive academic regulations set the stage for the student's eventual return to SFCC.

The major benefits of Intrusive Counseling to the students are appropriate advisement, continual monitoring of their progress, a support system that helps them achieve their educational goals, and professional intervention to address impediments to educational progress. Students also express the feeling that the frequent and timely contacts indicate a caring attitude on the part of faculty and staff.

Challenge Program: Mentoring for Student Success. The guiding principle of the program is its framework of characteristics of successful college students: full-time status, broad involvement with the college, mentoring by a caring individual, and receiving a scholarship. By fostering these attributes in students who exhibit both potential academic and financial need, the Challenge Program encourages students to obtain the maximum benefit from their time at SFCC.

Developmental Studies Program. The strongest feature of this program component is that it offers a wide range of courses and services aimed at enhancing basic academic skills and developing human potential, both in credit and noncredit formats. The centerpiece of the credit program is the Course Placement Evaluation, which assesses students' reading, writing, and math skills in order to determine appropriate courses and services.

Suffolk Community College, Eastern Campus, identifies portability—its potential for adaptation by other institutions—as a major success of its retention program. In addition, the college's support of program expenses belies its serious interest in making retention a priority. Training sessions and workshops, orientation, academic advisement, the developmental program, the College Skills Center and tutoring, Early Warning and Notification, and the honors programs—all of which are included in the annual budget—have become standard practices and services at the college.

University of Toledo Community and Technical College's **(ComTech)** developmental studies program has become an integral part of the college's services to students, and several components of the program contribute to its success.

- The program's faculty and staff are characterized as dedicated and professional. They choose to teach developmental courses while still teaching the subsequent courses in the curriculum, allowing for a global view of how developmental courses fit into the overall curriculum. They are committed to curricular improvement; curriculum and services are continually evaluated and revised in order to offer a better product to students and to other faculty and businesses that receive the college's students. Such work requires a high degree of collaboration on curriculum projects, and faculty who teach developmental courses are known throughout the college for their cooperation and leadership.
- Departmental leadership encourages faculty and staff to attend professional development conferences.
- The college administration recognizes that an excellent developmental education program is the foundation of an exemplary college, and, to that end, leaders have given the program monetary as well as other support. The Developmental Studies Education Advisory Committee (DSEAC) actively assists the director in establishing priorities for developmental education.
- Developmental education has addressed four areas—placement, advising, curriculum, and learning assistance, all of which are continually being assessed. Several results of this ongoing evaluation have been the hiring of a full-time learning assistance center manager; the hiring of a full-time developmental adviser; and the initiation of the ASSET placement system.
- All personnel involved in developmental education express the desire to continually improve student services. Data collection and research efforts have expanded exponentially since the program's early days, when there were few data to support the efforts of faculty and staff; the result is ample information to confirm positive programming and to point out areas in need of improvement. Recent improvement efforts in developmental mathematics have led to the initiation of a national developmental mathematics curriculum reform endeavor.

Conclusion

The diversity of age, work and educational background, socioeconomic status, and ethnic or national origin represented among at-risk students increases the challenge of creating an evaluation system for programs that serve them. Practitioners must press on with designing and implementing evaluation designs that can produce useful data, even though the early designs admittedly may be imperfect; we do not have the luxury of waiting until every problem has been resolved before establishing some indices of where we are and how we are doing.

If developmental educators are to be held accountable for the outcomes of their programs, against which standards should they be evaluated—student retention within the programs, grade-level gains, improved grade-point averages, successful negotiation of college-level work? Roueche (1984) warns about pronouncing developmental courses successful simply because their enrollment remains consistently high; Inbar and Sever (1986) warn against using secondary criteria—as in counting the numbers of disadvantaged students engaged in the program—since they are little more than "tranquilizing" social devices and public relations information (p. 288); Cross (1976) cautions against using pre- and post-testing to determine grade-level improvement and to demonstrate cause-effect relationships between developmental work and grade gain; Sharon (1972) advises against using GPA at program's end as an adequate measure of success when grades have been proven to be such unreliable predictors of future success; and Boylan and Bonham (1992) observe that successful negotiation of college-level work, in the final analysis, was the most critical criterion for judging effectiveness of developmental programs.

Clearly, evaluation of at-risk programs cannot be limited to any single measure. If service to students is the central mission of the college, then the central question for evaluation may well be: "Is this program effective in promoting student success?" Yet, ask that one question and expect a flurry of excitement around demands for more specific questions that will identify *success*, measure the effects of specific program activities on the problems of academic underpreparation, determine who should be involved in the assessment, address the relative dearth of students transferring to four-year institutions, and so on. To provide some structure for coming to terms with evaluation demands, Popham recommends:

- Defining the program so clearly that it can be *replicated*, and ensuring that what is being evaluated is, indeed, the program *rather than the enthusiasm and ability of a few superior teachers*
- Formally appraising the quality, the worth, of the educational phenomena
- Attaching relative values to observations in order to provide an information base for educational decisions (1988)

Moreover, Cross offers both an admonition and a warning: "Whether a remedial program is judged 'successful' or not depends on the criteria used" (1976, p. 36). This is the double-edged sword of evaluation. If the questions are neither broad nor deep, the criteria drawn from them may reflect only superficial indices of success: for example, if the criterion for success in a developmental course is successful completion of that course, then what is to be said about its success when students cannot negotiate the work in the follow-on course? However, if the questions develop criteria for success that include success in appropriate follow-on courses and eventual success in the institution, the evaluation design becomes significantly more complex, but also a more realistic appraisal of program success. Asking and answering only the easy questions creates a false sense of success, and a program so created will collapse eventually under the weight of its own shortsightedness.

Page Smith, in *Killing the Spirit*, a history of American higher education, observed a widespread commitment to ignoring evaluation of long-standing beliefs. However, while he disparages "high-status institutions" for their ineffectiveness, he maintains some certainty that "low-status institutions"—specifically, community colleges—should not be painted with the same brush.

> It seems reasonable to say that, although the prestige conferred on graduates of high- and low-status institutions varies widely, the human beings who pass through them are astonishingly similar by the almost three hundred indices that an ingenious surveyer dreamed up. We have, of course, relatively few data on 'what comes out the other end'—that is to say, how the entering freshmen, so similar in talent, background, and expectations at their entrance, compare as seniors or alumni. It is the major thesis of this work that the great majority of them, whatever their capability, are short-changed by the system. The principal exceptions would, of course, be those who attend small, private, once-denominational colleges and community colleges, where there is a strong tradition of placing the needs of students rather than the ambitions of professors at the center of the institutions (1990, p. 221).

Curiously, his assertion that "placing the needs of students...at the center of the institutions" will guarantee that they are not "short-changed by the system" is an expression of yet another "long-held habit." We can only *hope* that we understand their needs and meet these needs to everyone's advantage, but we shall know if that is true only when serious attempts are made to prove Smith's assertion and to evaluate whether we are indeed using what we have learned to improve "the system."

Through the Looking Glass:

Toward a Vision of Student Success

I am increasingly impatient with people who ask whether a student is 'college material.' We are not building a college with the student. The question we ought to ask is whether the college is... student material. It is the student we are building, and it is the function of the college to facilitate that process. We have him as he is, rather than as we wish he were...we are still calling for much more change in the student than we are in the faculty...Can we come up with... the professional attitudes... [necessary to] put us into the business of tapping pools of human talent not yet touched?

The greatest challenge facing the community college is to make good on the promise of the open door.
—Edmund J. Gleazer, Jr.
1970

We have penned *Between a Rock and a Hard Place* from a perspective of more than 25 years of direct experiences in working with the at-risk student, primarily those enrolled in community colleges across North America. As we began this 1992 study, it brought home a most sobering and unsettling reality—very little has changed since the first noticeable and persistent rumblings of a crisis in education began in the mid-1960s. At that time, those of us who were involved with teaching and conducting research about at-risk students believed that the literacy problem would be short-lived. After all, was this reformation of education, with specific attention to populations previously unserved, not one of the major goals of LBJ's Great Society? Had a U.S. Commissioner of Education not given national literacy his highest priority?

We can still remember early conversations with developmental studies colleagues regarding their apprehensions as to what would happen when and if the problem were resolved— that is, when all of the students who were not able to read and write and figure well enough to be in college were fully prepared and able to negotiate college work. Some of the major topics of conversation might well have been labeled At-Risk Jobs with At-Risk Students. These professionals could not help but worry about where they would find jobs. We also clearly remember hosting the first national conference on developmental education in 1974, in Dallas, Texas. This conference was the first to focus all of its attention on the problems of the at-risk student and college strategies for addressing these problems. Almost no one in attendance would admit to an involvement with at-risk students as a full-time or a long-term effort; in fact, most did not want to disassociate themselves from their departments of English, mathematics, and so on, to be associated fully with developmental programs and students.

What has happened in the intervening years? Students are leaving high school no better prepared than they were in the mid-1960s. In fact, evidence indicates that despite higher grade point averages, these students' skills and competencies are at the lowest levels in American history. Moreover, we are not talking only about literacy, or unprepared or underprepared students as viewed from their mastery or their attainment of cognitive skills; we are looking at a new generation of adult learners characterized by economic, social, personal, and academic insecurities. They are older adults, with family and other financial responsibilities that require part-time, or often full-time, jobs in addition to coursework requirements; they are first-generation learners with unclear notions of their college roles and their goals; they are members of minority and foreign-born groups; they have poor self-images and doubt their abilities to be successful; and they have limited world experiences that further narrow the perspectives they can bring to options in their lives.

The Problem Will Not Go Away

It was a sobering reality to be sitting in an audience at the 1991 Leadership 2000 Conference and hear former Secretary of Education Terrel Bell, the architect of national education reforms, proclaim the national reform initiatives total failures. We are not disparaging state and national efforts to improve public schools, but rather pointing to the data that are available with respect to the impact of those reforms. For the first time in our history, we are seeing generations of youth less educated than those preceding them. Community colleges cannot expect more literate entering freshmen in the foreseeable future. Johnny still cannot read, write, and figure well enough to begin a job, much less pursue a college education.

At the beginning of this book, we identified some of these sobering achievement data as we set the context for our 1992 study. Results of the National Assessment of Educational Progress in 1990 documented that the mathematics, reading, and writing skills of American students were at the same alarming levels in the 1980s as they were in the 1970s. Specifically, more than one-third of all students tested in mathematics performed at levels *below the lowest identified level;* more than 80 percent of students appeared to be functioning below their appropriate grade level. Skills tests conducted by the Educational Testing Service in 1990 indicated a significant disparity between Anglo and minority students; and Kozol and the National Center on Education and the Economy, among others, further identify a high correlation between poverty, undereducation, and minority status.

As a backdrop for these data, we described the "mission blur" that public education is experiencing—commissioned with being all things to all people. We described classroom climates that were radically affected by inner-city decline, single parents working long hours and having little time to devote to their children, and poverty. We described the prevailing public misconceptions that there are plenty of jobs for those who are motivated to work and that those with jobs do not need retraining. We described workplace casualties—individuals who cannot read, figure, or think well enough to negotiate job demands; companies that are forced to "de-skill" their assembly lines and/or mount major educational initiatives to develop operational and problem-solving skills in their workers. We described the staggering implications of the social, educational, and economic impacts created by spiraling numbers of public school dropouts—the condemning of generations of children to undereducation, to menial or no employment, to poverty; and the condemning of America to higher levels of crime and lower levels of productivity. Finally, we warned that these issues may only appear to be traveling parallel paths, that they will collide—no doubt already have collided—on many fronts with such magnitude that viable repair cannot occur for decades.

Implications and Recommendations

This 1992 attempt to take some measure of contemporary responses to at-risk students has been bittersweet. On the bitter side, there is dramatic evidence that the problems that at-risk students present for all of education, but especially for community colleges, remain the stuff of academic nightmares. Moreover, from a national perspective, we have not resolved a significant number of the issues that were alive and well more than 25 years ago. On the sweeter side, from more focused perspectives, there is evidence that many individual colleges are mounting initiatives, within situationally reasonable parameters, to tackle the problems that they admit will not go away. Furthermore, there are indications that research and practice are taking measured, but nonetheless more active, steps toward some collaborative efforts. From our study of some of these initiatives, and from a review of selected contemporary research and criticism, we are able to identify some major implications that in turn have generated several recommendations for improving college performance toward making good on the promise of educational opportunity for all.

Over-Arching Recommendation: *Colleges must increase support and structure for at-risk students.*

Colleges must have policies and procedures that reflect deeply held organizational values with respect to student success as a basic college goal. It is clear from our current and previous studies that at-risk students need more structure and more support than any other group of learners in American higher education. Yet, there is a reluctance on the parts of many college administrators and faculty to implement academic standards that would improve student persistence and achievement. We believe that there are two major causes for this reticence or hesitance. The first inhibiting factor is a deeply held belief that open-door colleges should have no impediments to entry, access, or opportunity—students should be allowed to choose relatively freely among the curriculum offerings, and the establishment of any structural requirements and/or curriculum prerequisites is definitely at odds with this traditional view of the meaning of the open door. The second inhibiting factor that keeps colleges from building more structure and academic standards into institutional requirements is the fear that enrollment will go down if colleges dare require anything more of entering students than has been required in the past. For faculty, the fear is even more personal—namely, what will happen to me if my classes do not "make"?

Data to date indicate that the establishment and implementation of rigorous academic policies and procedures (academic structure) dramatically improve student success and quickly build college enrollments. Most of these policies and procedures are not new; most have been the subject of discussion over many a committee table. However, they continue to offer the best hope for grappling with the problem that will not go away—the problem that without doubt will become more severe if it is only timidly combatted.

Institutional Policies for Increased Structure

• *Pre-enrollment activities should be proactive.* Pre-enrollment activities should begin long before a student expresses an active interest in the college by way of a phone call, a letter, or an appointment for advisement. Colleges should actively encourage younger and younger student groups to consider including the college in their plans for the future. **Miami-Dade Community College**'s Black Student Opportunity Program reaches into the early high school years, as deeply as the ninth grade; **Illinois Central College**'s QUEST program annually recruits actively at each high school in the district; **De Anza College**'s A STARTING POINT staff involve local junior and senior high students in on-campus cultural events and encourage minority enrollment in the Summer College for Kids; and **Santa Barbara City College**'s TAP provides aggressive outreach to local high schools and recruits through the junior and senior high schools' Math, Engineering, and Science Achievement programs.

Santa Fe Community College currently is implementing several aggressive, long-term programs for tapping ever-younger populations and involving them in the life of the college. Among these programs is Magic of Education, created to complement and reinforce public school efforts to convince local children that they should remain in school. Solving the dropout problem begins when children are encouraged early to develop positive self-images and to set long-term goals; the Magic of Education, with the theme of "Catch the Magic," is the first part of a six-year joint program with SFCC and the Santa Fe school system. Program staff plan to meet with the same students every other year to reaffirm the importance of education and available opportunities, beginning in the sixth grade. Sixth-grade students visit the college and receive a "Magic" pin, as well as observe various demonstrations provided by several disciplines taught on campus. One demonstration by the computer lab uses a "paint" program to illustrate the diversity that computers bring to the classroom. In the nursing laboratory, children work with mannequin patients, make black marshmallows with a few simple chemicals, and go live over the airways to identify SFCC's own radio station. In addition, SFCC students meet with the children to talk about staying in school, and the children receive "Class of 1997" buttons and informational brochures to take home to their parents or guardians. More than encouraging students to stay in school, the brochure identifies junior and senior high school courses to help students in preparing for college and career training. A checklist is included to help parents help their children "meet the challenges of the future." Eighth grade students complete a four-year plan for high school and participate in a tour of the college and a Career Fair. Tenth grade students attend a day-long Educational and Employment Options Fair on campus. Twelfth-grade students attend SFCC's annual College Night, which boasts representatives from approximately 100 colleges and universities across the nation. Students have opportunities to obtain first-hand information regarding admissions, scholarships, and other financial aid. They are encouraged to use SFCC's college planning services, whether or not SFCC is their college of choice. SFCC's recruitment brochure lists the advantages of choosing SFCC, includes a "people you know" section (one-third of Santa Fe area high school graduates attend SFCC), and discusses the convenience and lower cost of living at home and attending a beautiful campus that soon will include child care, physical education, and fine arts centers. Local school and college officials have high hopes that future program evaluations will prove that there is magic in educating school children early to think about their education.

Once a potential student has indicated an interest in a college, active pre-enrollment activities should include letters and calls from college personnel. At Jefferson Community College (JCC) (Kentucky), students who write or call the college about admission are notified promptly about their acceptance status. They receive a letter of welcome from the division chairperson of the student's intended major (if declared) and the student's academic department. JCC's classified staff holds staff development sessions focusing on providing accurate and proper information for students when they call, directing troubled or confused students to the appropriate college personnel, and providing personalized referral services (Roueche, 1991). The key is to personalize the college for the student by addressing primary concerns early on—namely, what do I have to do to enroll in college?

• *Orientation should be required and should initiate the building of student support structures.* Most selective American universities seriously orchestrate more structure into the early days of their entering freshmen's college careers than do open-access colleges. Almost all major universities require orientation to provide new students with information that will answer the questions that they bring and the questions that have not yet occurred to them. Moreover, most do not abandon the structure after the initial period of orientation but provide formal orientation courses throughout the freshman year to further socialize the students to the academic environment. The content of these ongoing courses may include such topics as time and stress management, team building, and study skill strategies.

As Beal and Noel (1980) discovered, freshmen retention can be improved by more than 20 percent if orientation programs also pair students with faculty mentors who have similar specialization interests and/or students who have some history with the college, preferably a second-year student who can provide some collegial guidance and be available for answering those questions that a student may feel more comfortable asking another. **De Anza College**'s A STARTING POINT includes an "Introduction to College" course that focuses exclusively on transfer-related and college survival information; furthermore, students are required to meet with their counselors regularly. **Illinois Central College**'s QUEST holds a special full-day orientation for its students so that they can meet staff and college officials, as well as former QUESTers who share their own experiences. **Middlesex Community**

College's Freshman Seminar aims to build students' communications skills, assist in their career planning, and expose them to various teaching styles. **Santa Fe Community College**'s Challenge Program students receive both the standard orientation to the college and a special orientation to the Challenge Program, where, among other activities, they meet other new students, tour the campus, and register.

• *Late registration should be abolished.* The tradition of allowing late registrants to enter classes that have begun and are well into their activities constitutes a disservice to the teacher, the class, and the student who is entering late. Faculty know that the first days of a course, perhaps even the first few hours, are among the most important learning experiences that a student will have; they set the tone for the course and may turn a delicate balance toward the positive decision to "stay the course." Colleges, including Moraine Valley Community College (Illinois), that have collected data regarding the casualties of late registration and then conducted studies of the effects of ending late registration, report that retention and student performance significantly improve once the policy is abolished. While none of our award-winning programs addressed this issue directly, many of their practices—particularly the practices of early selection and mandatory orientation—support the notion that late registration is not an acceptable admissions policy.

A late registration policy indicates to the student that beginning class late is of no consequence, that they will miss little or nothing by being absent when the class begins. Most colleges have discovered, sadly, that those students who register as late as a week or two will drop out or fail. If the student is accepted as a later registrant, then the instuctor should be willing to contract to provide the time to bring the student up to speed, and the student should be required to fulfill her part of that commitment. Simply put, if late registration is policy, then *the last day of late registration should be that day before classes begin.*

• *Basic skills assessment and placement in appropriate courses should be mandatory.* In our 1984 study (Roueche, Baker, and Roueche), the majority of institutions of higher education were firmly in support of mandatory assessment; however, only in recent years has mandatory placement been more widely supported. It is in this arena that many colleges are most compelled to suggest that they could be mistaken, that perhaps the tests did not provide unrefutable evidence that the student needed additional work prior to beginning college-level courses. However, while most general tests of basic skills do not provide targeted indications of specific deficiencies, they do indicate problems. As Cross (1976) has indicated, they remain our best indicators of a need for additional instruction and development. Institutions practicing serious assessment and placement policies report dramatic evidence that students are better served by these policies than by those that provide students with access to all courses irrespective of their ability to be successful in them.

In our own college and university experiences, we were tested and assigned to courses based on initial assessments. It never occurred to us that this practice was unfair; in fact, the author whose freshman assessment essay contained a fragment sentence that immediately identified her as a "remedial" student (assigned to English 101 rather than English 101A) was fortunate to have a professor her first semester who so excited her about English that she changed her declared major, began to consider teaching as a profession, and developed her love of English as an academic discipline and as a personal pleasure for all times. Universities today do not hesitate to require students to register for appropriate courses; community colleges should not even consider doing otherwise.

Illinois Central College's QUEST students must agree to complete any remedial work that assessment scores indicate is necessary for success prior to enrolling in related college-level courses. **Middlesex Community College** requires mandatory placement in reading, writing, and mathematics courses; and co- and prerequisites are established for all college courses based on reading, writing, and mathematical skills. **Santa Fe Community College** has a mandatory assessment and placement policy in its developmental studies courses; **Suffolk Community College** established Universal Testing in 1987 and simultaneously mandated placement in developmental courses for students failing to achieve designated cut-off scores; and **the University of Toledo Community and Technical College**'s award-winning developmental education program has both mandatory testing and placement.

• *Eliminate dual/simultaneous enrollment in skill and regular academic courses.* National surveys indicate that institutions of higher education are more likely to allow dual enrollment in skill development courses and regular academic courses than not; however, overwhelmingly, dual enrollment is allowed *with some restrictions.* For example, regular academic courses that require heavy reading assignments would not be available, under restricted policies and guidelines, to students whose test scores indicated their reading skills were weak. These students would be required to successfully complete a developmental reading course prior to enrollment in regular courses. **Illinois Central College**, **Santa Fe Community College**, and **ComTech** mandate successful completion of any prescribed developmental courses as basic prerequisites for all subsequent college-level programs; at ComTech all science courses carry a reading prerequisite, and many science courses carry both a reading and a math prerequisite. While some colleges maintain that a student's interest in pursuing an academic goal will be weakened by the college's requirement that he take preparatory courses prior to embarking on his "major" interest, the injustice for both student and instructor is obvious when neither can cope with insufficient skill levels for course completion.

• *Working students should be strongly encouraged to take reduced hours.* The responsibilities of maintaining households and families impose significant constraints upon students' time and energy for completing course assignments. As increasing numbers of full-time students are working more and more hours at jobs, colleges should permit them limited numbers of credit hours per semester—recommendations include no more than six academic hours in any semester in which the student is working 30 hours a week or more, nine credit hours per 20 working hours, and so forth. Data indicate that students at all levels of higher education are working more hours and taking more semesters to complete degrees; a five- or six-year effort to earn a "four-year" degree is not uncommon. Moreover, two-year colleges are so in name only; "two-year graduates" of community colleges are rare. Today's average associate degree graduate is a three- to four-year matriculant. It is imperative that colleges help students make realistic choices about appropriate levels of additional responsibilities. What brought these students to the community college in the first place—namely, an interest in pursuing an academic goal within the parameters of incredible outside responsibilities—should not become the impediment that keeps them from pursuing their goal.

Institutional Strategies for Increased Support

• *Provide more comprehensive financial aid programs.* There has been limited focus on the impact that financial aid programs have on recruitment, enrollment, and retention in higher education. Yet, there is ample evidence to support the contention that financial aid recipients have higher retention rates than do students who have similar financial needs with limited or no support (Lenning and Beal, 1980; Jackson, 1988). Astin (1985) and Cope (1978) document in their studies that financial difficulties are among the three most frequently reported reasons for dropping out of college. As the cost of an education increases, students more seriously question the idea of encumbering themselves or their family with excessive debt levels.

Students should be provided information as early as possible about financial awards, preferably before admission to the college. In addition, not only entering students, but continuing students should be advised about financial aid packages. There should be more work-study programs connected to course and workload decisions; data indicate that students who work at the college are more involved with the institution, more integrated within the institution's social and academic structures, and, thereby, are more inclined to persist (Tinto, 1987). There should be provisions for budget counseling and emergency loan services. Moroever, financial arrangements with external sources can provide important support for students needing part-time work (Gillett-Karam, Roueche, and Roueche, 1991). In sum, traditional student loan programs must be rethought in the context of today's social and economic realities. As Astin and Cross (1979) suggest, perhaps the long-forgotten concepts, such as a national student loan bank and repayment based on appropriate percentage of income, should be reconsidered as a basis for student financial aid.

The responsibility of identifying financial aid packages and opportunities should not be placed directly on the shoulders of financial aid officers and counselors. Rather, individual faculty members should seek out information for themselves and share it with their students as a group, bringing bulletins and other sources of information to the classroom or taking students to the financial aid office and researching potential sources for aid. Lloyd Willis, a biology professor at Piedmont Virginia Community College, keeps a scholarship file in his office and updates it regularly; he seeks out the scholarships advertised in the local newspapers; he regularly queries students and collects information sought by scholarship sources, advises these students when they have qualified to seek funding from particular agencies, and directs their application activities; and he leads them in proactive searches for scholarship monies from colleges where they plan to transfer (Willis, 1991). We have discovered at our own institution, The University of Texas at Austin, that sources of thousands of dollars go untapped as a result of an unwillingness to research sources, a pervasive belief that "if the funds were there, someone would tell us about them," or a more contemporary concern that additional money will be difficult to find in tough economic times.

Miami-Dade Community College's BSOP participants can earn scholarship dollars for their education as early as the tenth grade, assuring that money for their college tuition and fees will be there when they need it. Future recommendations include additional funds for supporting activities include the students' parents—documentably a critical support group. **De Anza College**'s A STARTING POINT staff regularly provides information on available scholarships, financial aid, and internships to their students. **Santa Fe Community College** pays the tuition and required fees for all students participating in its Challenge Program. And, **Illinois Central College**'s QUEST students are employed on campus in part-time jobs, and these students often form close working and mentoring relationships with their college supervisors. With what we know about the economic difficulties with which most at-risk students enter college, we believe that some creativity and resourcefulness on the part of the institution to identify sources of aid and to craft sources of their own will serve to improve retention figures and potential academic performance.

• *Establish critical safety nets with faculty mentors and peer support.* Many community college students are first-generation attenders, and they are particularly in need of faculty mentors and peer supporters. They are in alien territory, and role models, survival information, and special academic support are vital. In our own department, upon his or her acceptance, every graduate student is assigned a faculty mentor whose expertise in his/her chosen field and whose willingness to act as an available listening ear combine to provide invaluable ongoing support. A community college should assume no less responsibility for its students, although many colleges would offer the excuse that commuting students have no time for extracurricular meetings and, therefore, such strategies would be ineffective.

Claire Weinstein, whose learning-to-learn seminars at The University of Texas instruct hundreds of university students about basic learning strategies, urges faculty to create "study-buddy" systems, to urge students to pair up for regularly scheduled study sessions in which each can play the roles of teacher and student. She observes that when students commit to each other, meet agreed-upon schedules for study, and seek to identify the most effective strategies by which the course material can be learned and applied, they develop important shared responsibilities for academic success.

Courses and programs that build student networking features in their designs provide students with important opportunities to share learning experiences, to talk about "student" issues, and thus to make critical connections with the college. **De Anza College**'s A STARTING POINT considers the development of a student network one of its most successful program features; **Illinois Central College**'s QUESTers' group activities develop a strong collegial relationship among participants and with the college; **Middlesex Community College**'s Cluster Courses build student "communities" within large academic programs and foster camaraderie among teaching groups and students; **North Lake College**'s Advantage Program's mentoring component is identified as its most innovative and critical feature for student success; and **Santa Barbara City College**'s TAP's math support groups encourage cooperative learning and strategy-swapping experiences.

• *Require increased problem-solving and literacy activities in all courses.* In our University of Texas 1981 study of literacy development in the community college for the National Institute of Education, we discovered that reading, writing, and math skills were taught and practiced regularly in developmental courses; however, they were infrequently required in regular academic college-level courses. That is, more reading, writing, and figuring occurred in developmental courses than in the majority of regular academic, college-level courses! The criticisms that colleges require insufficient reading and writing in all of their courses have grown louder over the last decade. A sad commentary, indeed. Objective tests are still the overwhelming design of choice in most college classrooms. Only through required writing—which requires thinking, analyzing, and problem solving—can students achieve the goals to which we pay lip service. Literacy is developed only in the performance of literacy tasks.

Over the past decade, new college, state, and national initiatives have been put in place—and others are finding their ways into legislative halls—requiring that all courses and academic programs direct more serious attention to skill development; many of these initiatives mandate developmental education, seek proof that skills are practiced in college courses and that students are becoming more literate as a result of their college experiences. In fact, results of "writing across the curriculum" initiatives, for example, provide clear evidence of qualitative improvement of student success—as measured by improved retention and outcome measures; we refer specifically to the results of the CLAST in Florida community colleges. Finally, we expect that within the next several years we shall witness a proliferation of initiatives from a variety of sources external to our colleges that will ask us to answer some serious questions about our responses to literacy issues.

• *Increase the impact of classroom instruction and provide critical time for skill practice and development with supplemental instruction and tutoring.* All of the award-winning programs described in the previous chapters incorporated tutoring components; many provided scheduled supplemental instruction by way of small study groups, and some included expanding tutorial services and study group options in their future plans. They described learning assistance centers and other academic support services that increased the time and attention that is understandably limited by the parameters of regularly scheduled courses and teacher-student ratios.

The concepts of collaborative learning and teamwork figure prominently in designs for both in- and out-of-class activities. Programs that require evidence of additional instruction—that is, require attendance at tutoring and supplemental instruction sessions—document that student resistance to these out-of-class requirements quickly dissipates when grades improve and when they experience the enthusiasm that team learning can generate. According to program staff, many of the students returning to "tell their story" to incoming program participants recounted that additional time expended in these collaborative efforts not only provided special support at critical steps along the way, but also helped them develop study strategies that are effective in negotiating content and activities in subsequent courses.

• *Recruit, hire, and develop the best faculty available.* The heart, the key to student success resides in the faculty selected to implement programs and teach students. The at-risk student requires a particularly special breed, accepting of the students, accepting of the changes that these students may need the teachers to make in teaching philosophy and methodology, and accepting of the increased commitments of time and energy that these students require, as well. We need faculty who care as much about their students as they do about their disciplines.

Recruit and hire the best. Over the next decade, the average community college will be required to replace more than 40 to 60 percent of its faculty, support staff, and administrative leadership team (Roueche, 1991). Colleges must replace these retiring or otherwise departing faculty with others who are even better prepared to tackle contemporary challenges. They must do so in the face of tightening budgets—that too frequently affect professional development activities severely—and in the face of declining numbers of graduate schools offering programs for careers in college teaching.

However, there are community colleges today that are filling their vacancies with an eye to identifying faculty and staff who believe in the open-door mission and who are more representative of the student body they serve. **Miami-Dade Community College**, St. Petersburg Junior College (Florida), and the Los Angeles Community College District (California) have each charted future courses of action that will provide for the recruitment and hiring of professionals meeting these two critical requirements. In the hiring process, colleges must be more attuned to two realities: the academic credentials of potential faculty do not guarantee that students will be motivated or inspired to learn in the classroom; and no matter what they say about their own teaching performance, faculty who cannot keep students involved and excited for several hours in the classroom should not be there. We recommend that any candidate considered for classroom teaching be required *to display* accomplished literacy skills by writing about what he or she expects to accomplish in his or her teaching, and *to demonstrate* those teaching skills by teaching a class of potential colleagues and students for at least the equivalent time of one regularly scheduled class period.

Actively provide and support professional development. Once hired, faculty should be oriented to the norms and values of the institution.

Beyond the orientation period, faculty should be required to engage in professional development activities that both the college and the individual have deemed purposeful and valuable to improved teaching and learning. At **Miami-Dade Community College**, all new faculty and staff must complete as a condition of employment two graduate courses offered for credit by the University of Miami. The university teaches these courses in conjunction with Miami-Dade and has designed the curriculum collaboratively with faculty and staff at the college.

Recognize excellent teaching. Among the most successful features that the award-winning programs identified in our survey was the quality of their faculty. After the initial two years, the faculty in **Highland Community College**'s Academic Information Monitoring System chose to remain with the program, although they were offered opportunities to return to their original teaching duties and volunteers were waiting to take their places. **Middlesex Community College** faculty volunteer to teach the Freshman Seminar (the first faculty group volunteered in addition to their full contractual workload for no additional compensation) and actively engage in team teaching and other collaborative activities, including serving on curriculum design committees that seek to provide critical linkages between developmental and regular courses in their discipline areas. **ComTech**'s developmental faculty frequently choose to teach multiple sections every quarter.

Faculty in the award-winning programs are characterized as excellent teachers. They choose to teach at-risk students and program courses, they are quick to adapt to and practice new teaching techniques (e.g., team teaching and other collaborative activities), and they are willing to accept the responsibilities of increased time and energy of extracurricular activities and other instructional out-of-class activities to make the students and the programs successful. Their enthusiasm for innovation appears to be contagious!

△ The teachers make classrooms "fun" places to be. They characterize the essence of Page Smith's observation:

> I came away from my years of teaching on the college and university level with a conviction that enactment, performance, dramatization are the most successful forms of teaching. Students must be incorporated, made, so far as possible, an integral part of the learning process. The notion that learning should have in it an element of inspired play would seem to the greater part of the academic establishment merely frivolous, but that is nonetheless the case. Of Ezekiel Cheever, the most famous schoolmaster of the Massachusetts Bay Colony, his one-time student Cotton Mather wrote that he so planned his lessons that his pupils 'came to work as though they came to play,' and

Alfred North Whitehead, almost three hundred years later, noted that a teacher should make his/her students 'glad that they were there' (1990, p. 210).

△ The teachers get personally involved; they enjoy in- and out-of-class contact with their students. "There is no decent, adequate, respectable education, in the proper sense of that much-abused word, without personal involvement by a teacher with the needs and concerns, academic and personal, of his/her students. All the rest is 'instruction' or 'information transferral'…but *it is not teaching* and the student is not truly learning" (Smith, 1990, p. 7).

Years after graduating from a small community college in a small North Carolina town, John Roueche was asked to give the college's commencement address. In that address, he recalled that his classmates were invited to socials and discussions outside of class on a regular basis. Every Sunday night, faculty and students would gather at the president's home to discuss current events and topics; a full range of ideas were regularly a part of those open discussions. In so doing, the teachers and administrators communicated a genuine interest in students as human beings and established an expectation for each. It also created for all of these students a very special image of undergraduate education. Granted, it is easier for a residential college to address the problems of at-risk students because they are on campus and the college can better influence their activities and behaviors more hours of the day. However, community colleges must be more creative, more imaginative, more proactive in engaging these students in more community-building activities. We know that students learn best by doing, and the more involved they are in the life of the college and their courses, the more successful they will be.

The award-winning programs identified a wide assortment of activities in which students, faculty, and staff engaged on a regular schedule. In particular, we recall **Illinois Central College**'s QUEST program, in which students and faculty are frequently engaged in field trips and cultural events, equal partners in the learning experiences. The QUEST director described well what Alfred North Whitehead's wife, Evelyn, also described about her husband's love of teaching:

When we first came to Harvard, Altie's [Whitehead's] colleagues in the department said, '*Don't let the students interfere with your work!* Ten or fifteen minutes is long enough for any conference with them.' Instead of following his colleagues' advice, Whitehead, who lectured three times a week, would give students a whole afternoon or a whole evening…The traffic was two-way, for Whitehead felt that he needed contact with young minds to

keep his own springs flowing. 'It is all nonsense,' he said, 'to sup-
pose that the old cannot learn from the young' (Smith, 1990, p.
217).

△ These teachers avoid over-specialization and embrace innovative practices. Many of the award-winning programs build bridges
between and among the various disciplines of the college. The faculty
choose to teach and design curriculum collaboratively with faculty from
other areas of specialization. Their choices are reflected in the questions that Ernest Boyer posed at the 1992 Leadership 2000 Conference
to an audience of community college presidents and their administrative teams:

> Would it be possible in the twenty-first century to stop organizing
> the curriculum around these dreary and outdated academic sub-
> jects, which scholars themselves no longer find very useful? Can
> we begin instead to organize learning around the human com-
> monalities so that students would not study the subjects, they'd
> study themselves, and they would use the academic subjects to
> illuminate larger, more consequential ends?...In so doing, the
> academic subjects would be put toward larger ends. We would
> make education applicable to the student...(1992, p. 5).

• *Evaluate student and program outcomes regularly, and disseminate the
findings.* Evaluation remains one, if not the single most, critical issue not
yet resolved in college responses to at-risk students. Most colleges have
not yet defined carefully enough *what* they want to achieve, and, therefore, cannot describe viable outcomes well enough to design viable, useful mechanisms for evaluating whether they have been achieved.

Most of the award-winning programs describe some carefully crafted
evaluation policies and procedures. This study has provided them with
another forum for disseminating the processes and the results of these
evaluation efforts. We encourage those colleges that regularly and
effectively evaluate program and student outcomes to disseminate the
results, not only within their institutions, but beyond. Because evaluation is commonly recognized as the weakest piece of the program puz-
zle, it is imperative that colleges become serious about describing so
well what they intend to accomplish with at-risk students that they can
recognize their accomplishments, as well as expeditiously determine
when they are falling short of meeting progam goals.

• *Become more humane organizational structures.* In 1969 Lamar
Johnson wrote that the community college was capable of managing a
"changeable environment":

The junior college seems to me to offer the best chance to stimulate genuinely fresh investigations, and then to do something
about the answers. Free of the rigid traditions which tie most
schools and colleges to their administration and instructional
arrangements, junior colleges can tinker with all sorts of new
ideas and put them to work in their classrooms (p. 34).

Yet, interests in streamlining the organization have moved to mitigate
against the building of humane organizational structures.
Organizations build fiefdoms; they become at odds with themselves
over concerns with enrollments and budgets. Smith observed, "When
an organizational structure of an institution of higher education is
indistinguishable from that of a major corporation, the spirit dies"
(1990, p. 298).

We need to promote for the at-risk student—indeed for all students—the establishment of entire institutions responding to the needs
and requirements of their students. Many exemplary programs have
done a great job of identifying targeted populations or groups, and by
many measures they have done a good job of addressing the needs of
those so identified. However, this is simply not enough. What we need
is for institutions to so identify the *larger population*. Very few colleges
have responded holistically to the needs of hundreds of thousands of
community college students who cannot be successful in any academic
arena.

Conclusion

William Wenrich, chancellor of the Dallas County Community
College District, tells the following story in his "State of the District"
speech; he says it is a true story, but he urged us not to attribute it solely
to him as he had heard it before and did not know the author.
However, it was as appropriate for the "state of the district" then as it is
now for the "state of the community college at-risk student movement."

Georgine Johnson, a middle-aged woman living in Cleveland,
was beginning to feel paunchy and out-of-shape, so she began a
regimen of jogging. Little by little, with discipline and encouragement from friends, she bought the running paraphernalia,
maintained a regular exercise schedule, and increased her
distances.

After a time, these same friends encouraged Georgine to enter a
race. She selected the 10K (roughly six miles), registered, and
appeared one bright, early Sunday morning to compete in the

race. She warmed up, heard the call to the starting line, and was off and running, feeling good, knowing in her heart she would finish the race.

As you may know, about halfway through a race, it is typical to double back, retracing steps, completing the race where you began. So, several miles in, when no turnback was in sight, she queried a sideline official about when the turn would come. 'Not for another 10 miles,' was his astounding reply. Confronting her expression of dismay, he further clarified that she, Georgine Johnson, was running the Cleveland marathon (26 miles)!

Well, she wasn't exactly happy about what she learned. But even as she continued to run, she had a decision to make. In spite of the odds, she decided to try to finish the race. And she did!

The press discovered what had happened, and they interviewed her at her home the next day. When they asked her why she decided to try to finish the race, this is what she said:

> 'It wasn't the race I wanted.
> 'It wasn't the race I trained for.
> 'It wasn't the race I thought I was in.
> 'But it was the race! If I were going to finish the race, it was the only one available.'

As did Wenrich in thinking about the future of his college district, we too frequently have wondered about the "race" we are in. However, as did Georgine Johnson and Bill Wenrich, we agreed that while more demanding than the race we believed we had begun more than 25 years ago, this one could bring a greater sense of accomplishment and indeed have a greater impact on all other races yet to be run. It is not a race for the timid and fainthearted!

We conclude with this poignant observation by Page Smith, a former university professor, university provost, and a noted historian, whose insights and searingly honest evaluations of the state of university and college teaching, as written in *Killing the Spirit*, were unparalleled in our readings. It is with the compliment he gives and the confidence and hope that it generates that we choose to close.

> Finally…there are community colleges, where thousands of able and intelligent men and women take their teaching opportunities with the greatest seriousness and give more than value received. These institutions, with close ties to their parent

communities, free for the most part of their snobbish pursuit of the latest academic fads that so warp their university counter-parts, and free also of the unremitting pressure to publish or perish, are, I believe, the hope of higher education in America. Unheralded and scorned or patronized by 'the big boys,' they carry out of their mission with spirit and élan. There are, I am sure, indifferent community colleges as well as good ones, but the ones I have visited have all charmed me, and I am pleased to have an opportunity to express my gratitude for the lively times and good spirit I have experienced in my visits (1990, pp. 19–20).

Letter of Invitation to Award-Winning College Programs

We are currently conducting a new national study of developmental education—students, policies, organization, strategies, and outcomes—and are inviting you and «college» to participate.

Increasing numbers of underprepared and at-risk students are bringing an overwhelming array of serious academic issues to the immediate attention of all in higher education. We propose, with this present study, to provide both a state-of-the-art report and an update on the array of institutional responses to the challenges these students create, by identifying and describing programs and strategies that have been recognized for their success.

«program» is well regarded in the field, and we do hope that you will join us in this effort to describe the issues and identify successful, working responses to the problems. Once we receive word of your willingness to contribute to this update, we will send along a survey designed to help us accurately describe your program and/or strategies in depth. We may wish to follow up on some of your responses with a telephone interview and will look forward to getting to know you better at that time.

We are excited about this new study and eagerly await word of your interest in participating. We expect the final report to be published by the Community College Press. With every good wish.

Sincerely,

John E. Roueche	Suanne D. Roueche
Professor and Director	Director, NISOD
Sid W. Richardson Regents Chair	Editor, *Innovation Abstracts*

JER/SDR:sf

Award-Winning Programs Selected for the 1992 Study

College	Program	Director
De Anza College (Cupertino, CA)	A STARTING POINT Minority Transfer Program	Donna Fung
William Rainey Harper College (Palatine, IL)	Athletic Academic Advising Program	Lisa Brady
Highland Community College (Highland, KS)	The Academic Information Monitoring System	Arves Jones
Illinois Central College (East Peoria, IL)	The Quality Undergraduate Education for Student Transfer (QUEST)	Susan Rogers Strand
Miami-Dade Community College (Miami, FL)	The Black/Hispanic Student Opportunity Program	Marzell Smith
Middlesex Community College (Bedford, MA)	The Freshman Seminar and Course Clusters Program	Evelyn Clements
North Lake College (Irving, TX)	Counseling and the Advantage Program	Lynda Edwards
Richland College (Dallas, TX)	Developmental Studies Program	Angie Runnels • *replaced by* Perry Carter
Santa Barbara City College (Santa Barbara, CA)	Transfer Achievement Program	Jack Friedlander
Santa Fe Community College (Santa Fe, NM)	Student Success Model	Paul Fornell
Suffolk Community College (Riverhead, NY)	The Eastern Campus Retention Program	Randolph Manning
University of Toledo Community and Technical College (Toledo, OH)	Developmental Skills Education Program	Charles Bohlen • *replaced by* Donna Adler

Abraham, Ansley, A. *College Remedial Studies: Institutional Practices in the SREB States.* Atlanta: Southern Regional Education Board, 1992.

Abraham, Ansley, A. *A Report on College-Level Remedial/Developmental Programs in SREB States.* Atlanta: Southern Regional Education Board, 1987.

Abraham, Ansley, A. "They Came to College?" A Remedial/Developmental Profile of First-Time Freshmen in SREB States (No. 25). Atlanta: Southern Regional Education Board, 1991.

"Access, Assessment, and Developmental Education in the Community College." *Community, Technical, and Junior College Journal,* June/July 1987, 38–41.

Adelman, Clifford. *Tourists in Our Own Land: Cultural Literacies and the College Curriculum.* Washington, D.C.: U.S. Department of Education, 1992a.

Adelman, Clifford. *The Way We Are: The Community College as American Thermometer.* Washington, D.C.: U.S. Department of Education, February 1992b.

American Association of Community Colleges. "Follow-up and Transfer of Two-Year College Students." Washington, D.C.: American Association of Community Colleges, 1979.

Anandam, Kamala. "Expanding Horizons for Learning and Technology." In O'Banion, Terry (Ed.), *Innovation in the Community College.* New York: ACE/Macmillan, 1989.

Armstrong, C. "Basic Writers' Problems Are Basic to Writing." Paper presented at the 39th annual meeting of the Conference on College Composition and Communication, St. Louis, Missouri, March 1988. (ED 298 152)

Aron, Helen. "A Community College Reading and Study Skills Program: What Is It, What Does It Do?" *Journal of Reading,* 1978, *22,* 231–235.

Astin, Alexander W. *Achieving Educational Excellence.* San Francisco: Jossey-Bass Publishers, 1985.

Astin, Alexander W. *Four Critical Years: Effects of College on Beliefs, Attitudes, and Knowledge.* San Franciso: Jossey-Bass, 1977.

Astin, Alexander W. *Minorities in American Higher Education.* San Francisco: Jossey-Bass, 1988.

Astin, Alexander W. *Minorities in American Higher Education: Recent Trends, Current Prospects and Recommendations.* San Francisco: Jossey-Bass, 1982.

Astin, Alexander W. "Strengthening Transfer Programs." In Vaughan, George B. (Ed.), *Issues for Community College Leaders in a New Era.* San Francisco: Jossey-Bass, 1983.

Astin, Alexander.W. and Cross, K. Patricia. *Student Financial Aid and Persistence in College.* Los Angeles: Higher Education Research Institute, 1979.

Atkinson, J.W. and Feather, N.T. *A Theory of Achievement Motivation.* New York: John Wiley and Sons, 1966.

Baird, Leonard L. "The Undergraduate Experience: Commonalities and Differences Among Colleges." *Research in Higher Education*, 1990, *31* (3), 271–278.

Banta, T.W. "Use of Outcomes Information at the University of Tennessee, Knoxville." In Ewell, Peter T. (Ed.), *Assessing Educational Outcomes.* San Francisco: Jossey-Bass, 1985, No. 47.

Barr, R. and Dreeban, R. "Instruction in Classrooms." In Shulman, Lee S. (Ed.), *Review of Research in Education 5, 1977.* Itasca, Ill.: F.E. Peacock Publishers, 1978.

Barshis, Donald E. "Comprehensive Block Program for Students Reading Below the Seventh Grade." *Center Notebook* (Center for the Improvement of Teaching and Learning, Chicago), 1982, *1* (7).

Barshis, Donald E. and Guskey, Thomas R. "Providing Remedial Education." In Vaughan, George B. (Ed.), *Issues for Community College Leaders in a New Era.* San Francisco: Jossey-Bass, 1983, 76–99.

Beal, P.E. and Noel, L. *What Works in Student Retention.* Iowa City, Iowa: American College Testing Program and National Center for Higher Education Management Systems, 1980. (ED 197 635)

Bell, Terrel. Keynote Address, Leadership 2000 Conference, Chicago, July 1991.

Bell, Terrel. "Technology in Education in the Nineties." *Leadership Abstracts*, 1991, *4* (7).

Bender, Louis W. "Applied Associate Degree Transfer Phenomenon: Proprietaries and Publics." *Community College Review*, Winter 1991, *19* (3), 22–28.

Bender, Louis W. "Transfer in the Spotlight." *Community, Technical, and Junior College Journal*, June/July 1990, *69* (6), 24–25.

Bloom, B.S. "Mastery Learning." In Block, J.H. (Ed.), *Mastery Learning: Theory and Practice.* New York: Holt, 1971.

Bloor, Earl G. "The Instructional Skills Workshop: A Mechanism for Instructional and Organizational Renewal." *Innovation Abstracts*, 1987, *IX* (10).

Bogue, Jesse Parker. *The Community College.* New York: McGraw-Hill, 1950.

Bonham, B.S. and Claxton, C. "Summary of Preliminary Findings: Research Project on Developmental Education." Boone, N.C.: Appalachian State University, National Center for Developmental Education, 1992.

Book, W.F. "How Well College Students Can Read." *School and Society*, August 1927, *26 (669)*, 242–248.

Bossone, Richard M. *Remedial English Instruction in California Public Junior Colleges: An Analysis and Evaluation of Current Practices.* Sacramento: California State Department of Education, September 1966.

Bourque, Mary Lyn and Garrison, Howard H. Volume I: *National and State Summaries of the LEVELS of Mathematics Achievement: Initial*

Performance Standards for the 1990 NAEP Mathematics Assessment. Washington, D.C.: National Assessment Governing Board, September 30, 1991.

Boyer, Ernest L. *College: The Undergraduate Experience in America.* New York: Harper and Row, 1987.

Boyer, Ernest L. "Curriculum, Culture, and Social Cohesion." *Celebrations,* October 1992, 4.

Boyett, J.H. and Conn, H. *Workplace 2000: The Revolution Reshaping American Business.* New York: Dutton, 1991.

Boylan, H.R. "The Historical Roots of Developmental Education." *Review of Research in Developmental Education,* 1988, *5* (3), 1–3.

Boylan, H.R. "Is Developmental Education Working: An Analysis of the Research." (Research Report 2. National Association of Remedial/ Developmental Studies in Postsecondary Education) Chicago: National Association of Remedial/Developmental Studies in Postsecondary Education, 1983.

Boylan, H.R., Bingham, E.L., and Cockman, D.C. "Organizational Patterns for Developmental Education Programs." *Review of Research in Developmental Education,* 1988, *5* (4), 1–4.

Boylan, H.R. and Bonham, B.S. "The Impact of Developmental Education Programs." *Research in Developmental Education,* 1992, *9* (5).

Boyle, M.R. "Projections of Changing Labor Force Skill Mix Through the Year 2000." *Economic Development Review,* Winter 1990, 7–9.

Brawer, Florence B. "Bad News/Good News: Collecting Transfer Data." *Community College Review,* Winter 1991, *19* (3), 48–53.

Breneman, D.W. and Nelson, S.C. *Financing Community Colleges: An Economic Perspective.* Washington, D.C.: The Brookings Institution, 1981.

Brier, Ellen. "Bridging the Academic Preparation Gap: An Historical View." *Journal of Developmental Education,* 1984, *8* (1), 2–5.

Brint, S. and Karabel, J. *The Diverted Dream: Community Colleges and the Promise of Educational Opportunity in America, 1900–1985.* New York: Oxford University Press, 1989.

Brophy, J. "Teacher Effects: Research and Quality." *Journal of Classroom Interaction,* 1987, *22* (1), 14–23.

Brown, C.R. "The Attitudes of Community College Faculty Toward Academically Disadvantaged Students." Unpublished doctoral dissertation. *Dissertation Abstracts,* 1978, *39,* 4614A.

Brubacher, John S. and Rudy, Willis. *Higher Education in Transition: A History of American Colleges and Universities. 1636–1956.* New York: Harper and Row, 1958.

Bushnell, D.S. and Zagaris, I. *Strategies for Change: A Report from Project Focus.* Washington, D.C.: American Association of Community Colleges, 1972.

Business-Higher Education Forum. *Three Realities: Minority Life in the United States.* Washington, D.C.: American Council on Education, 1990.

Buttenweiser, Peter L. *Achieving Fundamental Change Within in a Change-Resistant Environment: The Transfer Opportunities Program Experience in Community College of Philadelphia.* A report prepared for the Ford Foundation, August 1987.

Cage, Mary Crystal. "Fewer Students Get Bachelor's Degrees in 4 Years, Study Finds." *Chronicle of Higher Education,* July 15, 1992, A29–36.

Caminiti, S. "A Bigger Role for Parents." *Fortune,* Spring 1990, *121* (12), 25, 28, 30, 32.

Campbell, C.B. "A Supportive Services Program for Students with Predicted Low Academic Abilities: A Coordinated Approach." *Journal of College Student Personnel,* 1981, *22,* 453–454.

Canfield, Albert. "Two Years on the Road." Speech delivered to the National Conference on the Experimental Junior College, Fourth Session, University of California, Los Angeles, July 11, 1967.

Carnevale, A.P., Gainer, L.J., and Meltzer, A.S. *Workplace Basics Training Manual.* San Francisco: Jossey-Bass, 1990.

Carnegie Commission on Higher Education. *Quality and Equality: New Levels of Federal Responsibility for Higher Education.* New York: McGraw-Hill, 1968.

Carnegie Foundation for the Advancement of Teaching. In *Change Trendlines: Community Colleges—A Sector with a Clear Purpose. Change,* May/June 1990, *22,* 23–26.

Carroll, Lewis. *Alice in Wonderland.* U.S.A.: Grosset and Dunlap, 1980.

Centra, J.A. "Faculty Development Practices." In Centra, J.A. (Ed.), *Renewing and Evaluating Teaching: New Directions for Higher Education.* San Francisco: Jossey-Bass, 1977, *17,* 49–55.

Chall, J.S. *Stages of Reading Development.* New York: McGraw-Hill, 1983.

Charters, W.W. "Remedial Reading in College." *Journal of Higher Education,* March 1941, *12,* 117–121.

Chickering, A.W. *Commuting Versus Resident Students.* San Francisco: Jossey-Bass, 1974.

Clagett, Craig A. and Huntington, Robin B. "Assessing the Transfer Function: Data Exchanges and Transfer Rates." *Community College Review,* Spring 1992, *19* (4), 21–26.

Clark, B.R. "The 'Cooling-Out' Function in Higher Education." *American Journal of Sociology,* 1960, *65* (6), 569–576.

Clark, B.R. "The 'Cooling-Out' Function Revisited." In Vaughan, George B. (Ed.), *New Directions for Community Colleges: Questioning the Community College Role,* No. 32. San Francisco: Jossey-Bass, 1980.

Cohen, A.M. "Assessing College Students' Ability to Write Compositions." *Research in the Teaching of English,* 1973, *7* (3), 356–371.

Cohen, A.M. "Counting the Transfer Students." *Junior College Resource Review.* Los Angeles: ERIC Clearinghouse for Junior Colleges, 1979. (ED 172 864)

Cohen, A.M. *Dateline '79: Heretical Concepts for the Community College.* Beverly Hills, California: Glencoe Press, 1969.

Cohen, A.M. "Leading the Educational Program." In Vaughan, George B. (Ed.), *Issues for Community College Leaders in a New Era.* San Francisco: Jossey-Bass, 1983.

Cohen, A.M. "Toward a Professional Faculty." In Cohen, A. and Brawer, F. (Eds.), *New Directions in Community Colleges.* San Francisco: Jossey-Bass, 1973, *1,* 101–117.

Cohen, A.M. and Brawer, F.B. *The American Community College.* San Francisco: Jossey-Bass, 1982.

Collins, C. "2 Measures Provide Ammunition in U.S. Campaign Against Illiteracy." *Los Angeles Times,* August 26, 1990, D2.

Collins, Mary Beth and Stanley, Karen. "Bringing Worlds Together: Internationalizing the Curriculum Through Focused Interaction." *Innovation Abstracts,* 1991, *XIII* (1).

Commission on the Future of Community Colleges. *Building Communities: A Vision for a New Century.* Washington, D.C.: American Association of Community Colleges, 1988.

Committee on Testing. *A Generation of Failure: The Case for Testing and Remediation in Texas Higher Education.* Austin: Coordinating Board, Texas College and University System, July 17, 1986.

"Construction and Basic Skills." *Business Council for Effective Literacy,* April 1991, 1, 9.

Cope, R. "Why Students Stay, Why They Leave." In Noel, L. (Ed.), *New Directions for Student Services.* San Francisco, California: Jossey-Bass, 1978.

Cope, R. and Hannah, W. *Revolving College Doors.* New York: John Wiley and Sons, 1975.

Cross, K. Patricia. *Accent on Learning.* San Francisco: Jossey-Bass, 1976.

Cross, K. Patricia. *Beyond the Open Door.* San Francisco: Jossey-Bass, 1974.

Cross, K. Patricia. *The Junior College Student: A Research Description.* Princeton, New Jersey.: Educational Testing Service, 1968.

Cross, K. Patricia. "Leadership for Teaching and Learning." *Leadership Abstracts,* 1990, *3* (5).

Cross, K. Patricia. "On Old Practices and New Purposes in Education." Speech presented to the Conference on Remedial and Developmental Mathematics in College: Issues and Innovations, New York, April 9, 1981.

Cross, K. Patricia. "Societal Imperatives: Need for an Educated Democracy." Unpublished paper presented at the NISOD International Conference on Teaching Excellence, Austin, Texas, May 1984.

Cross, K. Patricia. "Teaching for Learning." Paper presented at the annual meeting of the American Association of Higher Education, Chicago, March 2, 1987.

Cross, K. Patricia. "Teaching to Improve Learning." Paper presented at the annual meeting of South Carolina Association of Colleges and Universities, Columbia, South Carolina, January 27, 1989.

Cross, K. Patricia and Angelo, Thomas A. *Classroom Assessment Techniques: A Handbook for Faculty.* Ann Arbor, Michigan: National Center for Research to Improve Postsecondary Teaching and Learning, 1988.

Cutrona, C.E. "Transition to College: Loneliness and the Process of Social Adjustment." In Peplau, L. and Perlman, D. (Eds.), *Loneliness: A Sourcebook of Current Research, Theory and Therapy.* New York: John Wiley and Sons, 1982.

D'Amico, Louise A. and Bokelman, Robert W. "Tuition and Fee Charges in Public Junior Colleges, 1961-1962." *Junior College Journal,* 1962, *33,* 36–39.

Davis, J.A. and others. *The Impact of Special Services Progams in Higher Education for Disadvantaged Students.* Princeton, New Jersey: Educational Testing Service, June 1975. (ED 112 790)

Deming, W.E. *Out of the Crisis.* Cambridge: Massachusetts Institute of Technology, Center for Advanced Engineering, 1992.

Dewey, John. *Art as Experience.* New York: Minton, Balch, and Company, 1934.

Donovan, R.A., Schaieer-Peleg, B., and Forer, B. *Transfer: Making It Work.* Washington, D.C.: American Association of Community Colleges, 1987.

Doucette, D. and Hughes, B. (Eds.). *Assessing Institutional Effectiveness in Community Colleges.* Laguna Hills, California: League for Innovation in the Community College, 1990.

Drew, Claudine Paula. "We Can No Longer Love 'Em and Leave 'Em: A Paper on Freshman Retention." *Community College Review,* Spring 1990, *17* (4), 54–60.

Dunphy, L. and Miller, T., et al. "Exemplary Retention Strategies for the Freshman Year." *New Directions for Student Services,* 1987, *60,* 39–60.

Eble, K.E. and McKeachie, W. *Improving Undergraduate Education Through Faculty Development.* San Francisco: Jossey-Bass, 1985.

Eells, William Crosby. *The Junior College.* Boston: Houghton Mifflin, 1931.

Eitelberg, Mark J. *Manpower for Military Occupations.* Alexandria, Va.: Human Resources Research Organization, April 1988.

Endo, J.J. and Harpel, R.L. "The Effect of Student-Faculty Interaction on Students' Educational Outcomes." *Research in Higher Education,* 1982, *16* (2), 115–138.

Entwisle, D.R. "Evaluations of Study-Skills Courses: A Review." *Journal of Educational Research,* March 1960, *53,* 243–251.

Ewell, Peter T. "Assessment and Public Accountability: Back to the Future." *Change,* November/December 1991, *23* (6), 12–17.

Ewell, Peter T. "Some Implications for Practice." In Ewell, Peter T. (Ed.), *Assessing Educational Outcomes.* San Francisco: Jossey-Bass, 1985, No. 47.

Feinberg, L. "Remedial Work Seen as Erosion of Education." *The Washington Post,* April 29, 1984, Al, A6, A7.

Feldman, K.A. "The Superior College Teacher from the Students' View." *Research in Higher Education,* 1976, *5,* 243–259.

Fields, Ralph R. *The Community College Movement*. New York: McGraw-Hill, 1962.

Flanigan, J. "Making Postwar America a Land Fit for Heroes." *Los Angeles Times,* January 20, 1991, D1, D3.

Ford, F.L. "Today's Undergraduates: Are They Human?" *Harvard Magazine*, March/April 1984, 29–32.

Forman, Sid. "Hunting for Orientation Ideas." *Innovation Abstracts*, 1990, *XII* (17).

Freire, P. *Pedagogy of the Oppressed*. New York: Herder and Herder, 1970.

Friedlander, Jack. "The Importance of Quality of Effort in Predictig Student Attainment." Unpublished doctoral dissertation. University of California at Los Angeles, 1980.

Friedlander, Jack. "Should Remediation Be Mandatory?" *Community College Review,* 1981–1982, *9*, 56–64.

Friedlander, Jack and MacDougall, Peter. "Achieving Student Success Through Student Involvement." *Community College Review*, Summer 1992, *20* (1), 20–28.

Futrell, M.H. "Toward Excellence." *National Forum*, 1984, *44*, 11–24.

Gaff, J.G. *General Education Today*. San Francisco: Jossey-Bass, 1983.

Gaff, J.G. *Toward Faculty Renewal: Advances in Faculty, Instructional and Organizational Development*. San Francisco: Jossey-Bass, 1975.

Gallagher, Paul. "The Next Leadership Challenge." *Celebrations,* May 21, 1990.

Garcia, R. and Romanik, D. (Eds.). "Volume II: Prescriptive Education." In Preston, J. (Ed.), *Miami-Dade Community College 1984 Institutional Self-Study*. Miami: Miami-Dade Community College, 1984.

Gardner, H. *The Mind's New Science: A History of the Cognitive Revolution*. New York: Basic Books, 1985.

Gardner, John. *Excellence: Can We Be Equal and Excellent Too?* New York: Harper and Row, 1961.

Gardner, John W. "Leadership and Power." *New Management*, Fall 1987, *5* (2), 8–14.

Gillett-Karam, Rosemary, Roueche, Suanne D., and Roueche, John E. *Underrepresentation and the Question of Diversity: Women and Minorities in the Community College*. Washington, D.C.: The Community College Press, 1991.

Gleazer, Edmund J. "American Community Colleges in 2000: The Past As Prologue." *Celebrations*, October 19, 1990.

Gleazer, Edmund J. "The Community College: Issues of the 1970s." *Educational Record*, 1970, *51*, 47–52.

Gleazer, Edmund J. (Ed.). *American Junior Colleges* (6th ed.). Washington, D.C.: American Council on Education, 1963.

Gold, B.K. *Performances on the Fall 1976 Los Angeles City College Guidance Examination: Research Study #77-7*. Los Angeles: Los Angeles City College, 1977. (ED 140 919)

Greene, Maxine. "Revision and Reinterpretation: Opening Spaces for Second Chance." In Inbar, Dan E. (Ed.), *Second Chance in Education: An Interdisciplinary and International Perspective*. London: The Falmer Press, 1990, 37–48.

Greening, John. "Learning Biology Through Writing." *Innovation Abstracts*, 1987, *IX* (9).

Griffith, W.S. "Harper's Legacy to the Public Junior College." *Community College Frontiers*, 1976, *4* (3), 14–20.

Guba, E.G. "The Failure of Educational Evaluation." *Educational Technology*, 1969, *9* (5), 29–38.

Halpin, R.L. "An Application of the Tinto Model to the Analysis of Freshman Persistence in a Community College." *Community College Review*, Spring 1990, *17, 4*.

Hanson, G.R. and Kerker, R.M. "Evaluating the Effectiveness of TASP." In Matthews, J.M., Swanson, R.G., and Kerker, Richard M. (Eds.), *From Politics to Policy: A Case Study in Educational Reform*. New York: Praeger, 1991.

Harman, D. *Illiteracy: A National Dilemma*. New York: Cambridge, 1987.

Henderson, Algo D. *Policies and Practices in Higher Education*. New York: Harper and Row, 1960.

Hillway, Tyrus. *The American Two-Year College*. New York: Harper and Row, 1958.

Hiroto, D.S. "Locus of Control and Learned Helplessness." *Journal of Experimental Psychology*, 1974, *102*, 187–193.

Hodgkinson, H.L. *All One System: Demographics of Education, Kindergarten Through Graduate School*. Washington, D.C.: Institute for Educational Leadership, 1985. (ED 261 101)

Hollinshead, B.S. "The Community College Program." *Junior College Journal*, 1936, *7*, 111–116.

Hollinshead, B.S. *Who Should Go to College*. New York: Columbia University Press, 1952.

Holt, J. *How Children Fail*. New York: Dell, 1970.

Hughes, Julie A. and Graham, Steven W. "Academic Performance and Background Characteristics Among Community College Transfer Students." *Community Junior College: Quarterly of Research and Practice*, January–March 1992, *16* (1), 35–46.

Immerwahr, J., Johnson, J., and Kernan-Schloss, A. *Cross Talk: The Public, the Experts, and Competitiveness*. Washington, D.C.: The Business-Higher Education Forum and the Public Agenda Foundation, February 1991.

Inbar, Dan E. "The Legitimation of a Second Chance." In Inbar, Dan E. (Ed.), *Second Chance in Education: An Interdisciplinary and International Perspective*. London: The Falmer Press, 1990.

Inbar, Dan E. and Sever, Rita. "The Transformation of a Goal Definition: The Story of a Second-Chance Evaluation Study." *Studies in Educational Evaluation*, 1986, *32* (2), 232–242.

Jackson, G.A. "Did College Choice Change During the 1970s?" *Economics of Education Review*, 1988, *7* (1), 15–17.

Jacobi, M. *The Transfer Student Experience: Findings from 7 Focus Groups.* University of California Los Angeles, Student Affairs Information and Research Office, 1988.

Jefferson, Thomas. Letter to Colonel Charles Yancey, January 6, 1816.

Jencks, C. "Social Stratification and Higher Education." *Harvard Educational Review*, 1968, *38*, 277–316.

Jennings, F.G. "The Two–Year Stretch." *Change*, 1970, *2*, 15–25.

Jenrette, M. "Staffing for a New Century: An Opportunity for Institutional Renewal." *Leadership Abstracts*, 1990, *3* (2).

Johnson, B. Lamar. "Encouraging Innovation in Teaching." *Junior College Journal*, March 1969, 39.

Johnson, H. "Why Johnny Still Can't Read." *The Washington Post*, January 12, 1990, A2.

Johnston, W. and Packer, A. *Workforce 2000: Work and Workers for the Twenty-First Century*. Indianapolis: Hudson Institute, 1987.

Justiz, Manuel J. "Fulfilling the Educational Promise of a Changing Nation." [Fifth Annual Harry S. Truman Lecture] *Community, Technical, and Junior College Journal*, April/May 1990, *60* (5), 19–24.

Justiz, Manuel J. "Involvement in Learning: The Three Keys." *Community and Junior College Journal*, April 1985, *55* (7), 23–28.

Karabel, Jerome. "Community Colleges and Social Stratification: Submerged Class Conflict in American Higher Education." *Harvard Educational Review*, 1972, *42*, 521–562.

Karabel, Jerome and Astin, Alexander W. "Social Class, Academic Ability, and College 'Quality.' " *Social Forces,* 1975, *53*, 381–398.

Kearns, D.T. and Flanigan, F., "Why I Got Involved." *Fortune*, Spring 1990, 46–47.

Keim, M.C. "Two Year College Faculty: A Research Update." *Community College Review*, 1989, *17*, 34–43.

Kiecolt, K.J. and Nathan, L.E. *Secondary Analysis of Survey Data*. Newbury Park, California: Sage, 1985.

Kinnick, M.K. "Increasing the Use of Student Outcomes Information." In Ewell, Peter T. (Ed.), *Assessing Educational Outcomes*. San Francisco: Jossey-Bass, 1985, No. 47.

Kipps, Carol. "Basic Arithmetic Offered in California Public Junior Colleges." Unpublished doctoral dissertation. Los Angeles: University of California, School of Education, 1966.

Klemp, G.O. "Identifying, Measuring, and Integrating Competence." *New Directions for Experiential Learning*, 1979, *3*.

Klemp, G.O. "Three Factors of Success." In Vermilye, D.W. (Ed.), *Current Issues in Higher Education*. San Francisco: Jossey-Bass, 1977.

Knoell, Dorothy M. and Medsker, Leland L. *From Junior to Senior College*. Washington, D.C.: American Council on Education, 1965.

Kozol, J. *Savage Inequalities: Children in America's Schools.* New York: Crown, 1991.

Kraetsch, G.A. "The Role of the Community College in the Basic Skills Movement." *Community College Review*, 1980, *8*, 18–23.

Kreitzer, Amelia, Madaus, George F., and Haney, Walt. "Competency Testing and Dropouts." In Weis, Lois, Farrar, Eleanor, and Petrie, Hugh G. (Eds.), *Dropouts from School: Issues, Dilemmas, and Solutions.* New York: State University of New York Press, 1989, 129–152.

Kulik, J., Kulik, C-L., and Schwalb, B. "College Programs for High Risk and Disadvantaged Students: A Meta-Analysis of Findings." *Review of Educational Research*, 1982, *53*, 397–414.

Labich, K. "What Our Kids Must Learn." *Fortune,* January 27, 1992, 64–66.

Lanham, Richard. "UCLA vs. the Literacy Crisis." *The UCLA Monthly*, April 1982.

League for Innovation in the Community College. *Serving Underprepared Students.* Laguna Hills, California: League for Innovation in the Community College, September 8, 1990.

Lederman, M.J., Ribaudo, M., and Ryzewic, S.R. "Basic Skills of Entering College Freshmen: A National Survey of Policies and Perceptions." *Journal of Developmental Education*, 1985, *9* (1), 10–13.

Lenning, O.T. and Beal, P. "Attrition and Retention." *Evidence for Action and Research.* Boulder, Colorado: National Center for Higher Education Management Systems, 1980.

Leonard, George B. *Education and Ecstasy.* New York: Delacorte Press, 1968.

Lesnick, M. "Reading and Study Behavior Problems of College Freshmen." *Reading World*, May 1972, *11*, 296–319.

Lester, Barbara. "The Partnership Exam." *Innovation Abstracts*, 1987, *IX* (12).

Levin, Benjamin and Unruh, Donald J. "Equality of Access and Equality of Condition: Second-Chance Programming for Success." In Inbar, Dan E. (Ed.), *Second Chance in Education: An Interdisciplinary and International Perspective.* London: The Falmer Press, 1990.

Levine, Arthur. *Handbook on Undergraduate Curriculum: A Report for the Carnegie Council on Policy Studies in Higher Education.* San Francisco: Jossey-Bass, 1978.

Lewis, L.S. *Scaling the Ivory Tower.* Baltimore: Johns Hopkins University Press, 1975.

Light, R. John. "Explorations with Students and Faculty about Teaching, Learning, and Student Life." *The Harvard Assessment Seminars.* Cambridge, Mass.: Harvard University Graduate School of Education and Kennedy School of Government, 1990.

Lindquist, J. *Designing Teaching Improvement Programs.* Battle Creek, Mich.: W.K. Kellogg Foundation, 1979.

Lombardi, J. "Developmental Education: A Rapidly Expanding Function." *Community College Review*, 1979, *7*, 65–72.

London, Howard. "In Between: The Community College Teacher." *Annals of the American Academy of Political and Social Science,* 1980, *448.*

Lynes, R. "How Good Are the Junior Colleges?" *Harper's Magazine,* 1966, *233,* 53–60.

Magnet, Myron. "How to Smarten Up the Schools." *Fortune,* February 1, 1988, 86–94.

Mauksch, H.O. "What Are the Obstacles to Improving Quality Teaching?" *Current Issues in Higher Education,* 1980, *1,* 49–57.

Maxwell, M. *Improving Student Learning Skills: A Comprehensive Guide to Successful Practices and Programs for Increasing the Performance of Underprepared Students.* San Francisco: Jossey-Bass, 1979.

McCabe, Robert H. "Excellence Is for Everyone: Quality and the Open Door Community College." Paper presented at the annual meeting of the American Association for Higher Education, Washington, D.C., March 1982.

McCabe, Robert H. "Viewpoint: America's Most Essential Institutions." *Community College Week,* 1992, *5* (2), 4.

McCabe, Robert H. and Skidmore, Suzanne B. "New Concepts for Community Colleges." In Vaughan, George B. (Ed.), *Issues for Community College Leaders in a New Era.* San Francisco: Jossey-Bass, 1983, 232–248.

McClenney, Kay and Mingle, James. "Higher Education Finance in the 1990s: Hard Choices for Community Colleges." *Leadership Abstracts,* September 1992, *5* (7).

McGrath, Dennis and Spear, Martin B. *The Academic Crisis of the Community College.* New York: State University of New York Press, 1991.

McKeachie, Wilbert J. *Teaching Tips: A Guidebook for the Beginning College Teacher* (7th ed.). Lexington, Mass.: D.C. Heath, 1978.

McNamara, R.S. *Essence of Security: Reflections in Office.* New York: Harper and Row, 1968.

Medsker, Leland L. *The Junior College: Progress and Prospect.* New York: McGraw-Hill, 1960.

Medsker, Leland L. and Tillery, Dale. *Breaking the Access Barriers: A Profile of Two-Year Colleges.* New York: McGraw-Hill, 1971.

Meisler, S. "Reading the Signs of a Crisis." *Los Angeles Times,* May 11, 1990, A1, A18, A19.

Mekis, Donna F. "A Review of the Barriers Underrepresented Minority Students Face in Transferring from California Community Colleges to Four-Year Institutions and an Evaluation of the De Anza College A STARTING POINT: Minority Transfer Program Which Has Been Developed to Overcome Those Barriers." Unpublished master's thesis. University of California at Santa Cruz, 1990.

Merson, Thomas B. "Let's Find the Answers." Speech delivered to the American Personnel and Guidance Association, March 28, 1961. [Mimeo.]

Miller, R.I. *Evaluating Faculty for Promotion and Tenure.* San Francisco: Jossey-Bass, 1987.

Minerbrook, S. "A Different Reality for Us." *U.S. News and World Report*, May 11, 1992, 36.

Molnar, M. "Save Our Schools: The California and Texas Systems Look to Big Business for Help." *Spirit*, April 1992, *39*, 61–66.

Moore, W., Jr. *Against the Odds*. San Francisco: Jossey-Bass, 1970.

Moore, W., Jr. *Blind Man on a Freeway*. San Francisco: Jossey-Bass, 1971.

Moore, W., Jr. and Carpenter, L.N. "Academically Underprepared Students." In Noel, L. (Ed.), *Increasing Student Retention*. San Francisco: Jossey-Bass, 1985, 95–115.

Muehl, S. and Muehl, L. "A College Level Compensatory Program for Educationally Disadvantaged Black Students." *Journal of Negro Education*, 1972, *41*, 65–81.

Naisbitt, J. *Megatrends*. New York: Warner Books, 1982.

Naisbitt, J. and Aburdene, P. *Megatrends 2000: Ten New Directions for the 1990s*. New York: William Morrow and Company, 1990.

"The Nation." *The Chronicle of Higher Education Almanac*. September 1989, 5.

National Center on Education and the Economy. *America's Choice: High Skills or Low Wages!* Rochester, New York: National Center on Education and the Economy, 1990.

National Center for Education Statistics. *College-Level Remedial Education in 1983–84*. Washington, D.C.: U.S. Department of Education, 1986.

National Center for Education Statistics. *College-Level Remedial Education in the Fall of 1989*. Washington, D.C.: U.S. Department of Education, 1991a.

National Center for Education Statistics. *Dropout Rates in the United States: 1990*. Washington, D.C.: U.S. Department of Education, 1991b.

National Center for Education Statistics. *Public Elementary and Secondary State Aggregate Data for School Year 1990–91 and Fiscal Year 1990*. Washington, D.C.: U.S. Department of Education, Office of Educational Research and Improvement, May 1992.

National Center for Education Statistics. *Trends in Academic Progress*. Washington, D.C.: U.S. Department of Education, Office of Educational Research and Improvement, 1991c.

National Commission on Excellence in Education. *A Nation at Risk: The Imperative for Educational Reform*. Washington, D.C.: U.S. Department of Education, April 1983.

National Institute of Education. *Involvement in Learning: Realizing the Potential of American Higher Education*. Washington, D.C.: U.S. Department of Education, 1984.

National Society for the Study of Education. *The Public Junior College*. The 55th Yearbook, Part I. Chicago: University of Chicago Press, 1956.

Noel, L., Levitz, R., and Kaufmann, J. "Campus Services for Academically Underprepared Students." In Noel, L. and Levitz, R. (Eds.), *How to Succeed with Academically Underprepared Students*. Iowa City, Iowa: The ACT National Center for the Advancement of Educational Practices, 1982.

Noel, L., Levitz, R., Saluri, D., and Associates. *Increasing Student Retention.* San Francisco: Jossey-Bass Publishers, 1986.

Northcutt, N. et al. *Adult Functional Competency: A Summary.* Austin: The University of Texas: Division of Extension, 1975.

O'Banion, Terry. *Community College Staff Development for the 80s.* New York: Associated Press, 1981.

O'Banion, Terry. "The Renaissance of Innovation." In O'Banion, Terry (Ed.), *Innovation in the Community College.* New York: ACE/Macmillan, 1989.

O'Banion, Terry. *Teachers for Tomorrow: Staff Development in the Community-Junior College.* Tucson: The University of Arizona Press, 1972.

Ortego, Sheila R. "Involving Administrators in the Teaching Process: A Team-Teaching Approach." *Innovation Abstracts,* 1991, *XIII* (23).

Owens, Jerry Sue. "Collaboration Within the College." In Angel, Dan and DeVault, Mike (Eds.), *Conceptualizing 2000: Proactive Planning.* Washington, D.C.: The Community College Press, 1991.

Pace, C. Robert. *The Undergraduates: A Report of Their Activities and Progress in College in the 1980s.* Los Angeles: Center for the Study of Evaluation, University of California, 1989.

Paoni, Frank. "I Know It When I See It: Great Teaching." *Innovation Abstracts,* 1990, *XII* (23).

Parnell, Dale. *Dateline 2000: The New Higher Education Agenda.* Washington, D.C.: The Community College Press, 1990.

Parnell, Dale. *The Neglected Majority.* Washington, D.C.: The Community College Press, 1985.

Pascarella, E.T. and Terenzini, P.T. *How College Affects Students.* San Francisco: Jossey-Bass, 1991.

Pascarella, E.T. and Terenzini, P.T. "Interaction Effects in Spady's and Tinto's Conceptual Model of College Dropout." *Sociology of Education,* 1979, *52,* 197–210.

Pascarella, E.T. and Terenzini, P.T. "Patterns of Student-Faculty Informal Interaction Beyond the Classroom and Voluntary Freshman Attrition." *Journal of Higher Education,* 1977, *55,* 540–52.

Pascarella, E.T., Terenzini, P.T., and Wolfle, L. "Orientation to College as Anticipatory Socialization: Indirect Effects of Freshman Year Persistence/Withdrawal Decisions." Paper presented at the annual meeting of the American Educational Research Association, Chicago, 1985.

Pascarella, E.T. and Wolfle, L.M. "Persistence in Higher Education: A Nine-Year Test of a Theoretical Model." Paper presented at the annual meeting of the American Educational Research Association, Chicago, 1985.

Perrow, C. "Disintegrating Social Sciences." *Phi Delta Kappa,* June 1982, *63* (10), 684–688.

Peters, T.J. and Waterman, R.H. *In Search of Excellence.* New York: Warner Books, 1982.

Phelps, Donald G. "What Must We Do to Strengthen and Keep Community Colleges Strong in Our Metropolitan Cities?" *Celebrations,* April 15, 1991.

Philbrick, Kathilyn Durnford. "The Use of Humor and Effective Leadership Styles." Unpublished dissertation. University of Florida, 1989. *Dissertation Abstracts,* 51-06A, 1861.

Pickett, V.R. "Focusing on the 'Right' Questions." In Brass, R.J. (Ed.), *Community Colleges, the Future, and SPOD.* Stillwater, OK: New Forums Press., 1984.

Pilenzo, R.C. "Why Literacy is Everybody's Business." *Modern Office Technology,* November 1990, 82, 84.

Pincus, F.L. and Archer, E. *Bridges to Opportunity: Are Community Colleges Meeting the Transfer Needs of Minority Students?* New York: Academy for Educational Development, 1989.

Pintozzi, Frank. "Developmental Education: Past and Present." Paper developed for Task Force on the Future, School of Education, Kennesaw College, 1987.

Pittman, J.A. "A Study of the Academic Achievement of 415 College Students in Relation to Remedial Courses Taken." *Journal of Negro Education,* 1960, 29, 426–437.

Popham, W.J. *Educational Evaluation* (2nd ed.). Englewood Cliffs, N.J.: Prentice Hall, 1988.

Powell, Hope M. *Implementing a Curriculum for Provisional Students.* California: Los Angeles City College, January 1966. [Mimeo.]

President's Commission on Higher Education. *Higher Education for American Democracy.* New York: Harper and Row, 1948.

Ramsberger, P.F. and Means, B. "Military Performance of Low-Aptitude Recruits: A Reexamination of Data from Project 100,000 and the ASVAB Misnorming Period (HumRRO FR-PRD-87-31). Alexandria, Va.: Human Resources Research Organization, September 1987.

Raspberry, W. "We Know What Works in School, Let's Do It." *The Washington Post,* January 12, 1990, A23.

Recktenwald, Rita and Schmidt, Carrie. "Writing to Learn Math: A Dialogue." *Innovation Abstracts,* 1992, *XIV* (13).

Reinhard, Bill. "Post-Transfer Prosperity." *Community College Times,* September 22, 1992, *IV* (18), 1,6.

Rendon, L.I. and Amaury, N. *Salvaging Transfer Students: Toward New Policies that Facilitate Baccalaureate Attainment.* New York: Carnegie Corporation of New York; Cambridge: Massachusetts Institute of Technology, 1988. (ED 305 098)

Reyes, F. "Operating Model for an Early Alert Academic Monitoring System." *Journal of College Student Personnel,* 1986, 27, 77–78.

Richardson, Richard C., Jr. and Bender, Louis. *Minority Access and Achievement in Higher Education.* San Francisco: Jossey-Bass, 1987.

Richardson, Richard C., Jr. and Martens, K.J. *A Report on Literacy Development in Community Colleges.* Washington, D.C.: National Institute of Education, 1982.

Richardson, Richard C., Jr. and Rhodes, William R. "Building Commitment to the Institution." In Vaughan, George B. (Ed.), *Issues for Community College Leaders in a New Era.* San Francisco: Jossey-Bass, 1983, 186–204.

Richardson, Russell. "The Associate Program: Teaching Improvement for Adjunct Faculty." *Community College Review*, Summer 1992, *20* (1), 29–34.

Robinson, H.A. "A Note on the Evaluation of College Remedial Reading Courses." *Journal of Educaitonal Psychology*, February 1950, *41*, 83–96.

Rockefeller Brothers Fund. *The Pursuit of Excellence* (Special Studies Report 5). New York: Doubleday, 1958.

Rodriquez, Roberto. "CA Universities to Redirect Freshmen to CC." *Community College Week*, September 28, 1992, 1, 5.

Rogers, C.R. *On Becoming a Person: A Therapist's View of Psychotherapy.* Boston: Houghton Mifflin, 1961.

Rogers, G.E. and Steinhoff, C.R. "Florida Community Colleges Meet the Challenge: Preparing Students for Minimum Competency Testing." *Community College Review*, Spring 1991, 33–38.

Romoser, R.C. *Results of the Second Assessment Study of Developmental Education Programs in Ohio.* Prepared for the Ohio Statewide Advisory Committee on Developmental Education, 1978. (ED 157 587)

Ross, E.D. *Democracy's College: The Land-Grant Movement in the Formative Stages.* Ames: Iowa State University Press, 1942.

Rossman, J.E. and others. *Open Admissions at the City University of New York: An Analysis of the First Year.* New York: Prentice-Hall, 1975.

Roth, Carolyn. "Tandem Testing." *Innovation Abstracts*, 1986, *VIII* (29).

Roth, M. "Immigrant Students in an Urban Commuter College: Persistors and Dropouts." Unpublished doctoral dissertation. Adelphi University, New Jersey, 1985.

Rotter, J. "Generalized Expectations for Internal Versus External Control of Reinforcement." *Psychological Monographs*, 1966, *80*, 1–28.

Roueche, John E. "Accommodating Individual Differences." *Community College Review*, July/August 1973, *1*, 24–29.

Roueche, John E. "Between a Rock and a Hard Place: Meeting Adult Literacy Needs." *Community and Junior College Journal*, April 1984, *54* (7), 21–24.

Roueche, John E. "The Challenge of the Underprepared Student." Address delivered to the ninth annual National Association of Developmental Education Conference, Chicago, April 1982.

Roueche, John E. "Insuring Excellence in Community College Teaching." *Leadership Abstracts*, 1990, *3* (10).

Roueche, John E. "Leadership for 2000." *Management Report, 1989–90/1.* California: Association of California Community College Administrators, 1991.

Roueche, John E. *Salvage, Redirection, or Custody?* Washington, D.C.: American Association of Community Colleges, 1968.

Roueche, John E. "Staff Development: Nipping at the Heels of the Master." *Community and Junior College Journal,* 1982, *56* (6), 28–31.

Roueche, John E. and Baker, George A. *Access and Excellence: The Open-Door College.* Washington, D.C.: The Community College Press, 1987.

Roueche, John E. and Baker, George A. *Profiling Excellence in America's Schools.* Arlington, Va.: American Association of School Administrators, 1986.

Roueche, John E., Baker, George A., and Rose, Robert. *Shared Vision: Transformational Leaders in American Community Colleges.* Washington, D.C.: The Community College Press, 1989.

Roueche, John E., Baker, George A., and Roueche, Suanne D. *College Responses to Low-Achieving Students: A National Study.* Orlando: HBJ Media Systems, 1984.

Roueche, John E. and Clarke, D.L. "Compensatory Education: Toward a Holistic Approach." *Community College Frontiers,* 1981, *9* (2), 35–41.

Roueche, John E. and Kirk, Wade. *Catching Up: Remedial Education.* San Francisco: Jossey-Bass, 1973.

Roueche, John E. and Mink, Oscar G. *Holistic Literacy in College Teaching.* New York: Harcourt Brace, 1980.

Roueche, John E. and Mink, Oscar G. "Overcoming Learned Helplessness in Community College Students." *Journal of Developmental and Remedial Education,* Spring 1982, *20,* 2–5.

Roueche, John E. and Pitman, John C. *A Modest Proposal: Students Can Learn.* San Francisco: Jossey-Bass, 1973.

Roueche, John E. and Roueche, Suanne D. *Developmental Education: A Primer for Program Development and Evaluation.* Atlanta: Southern Regional Education Board, 1977.

Roueche, John E. and Roueche, Suanne D. "Innovations in Teaching: The Past as Prologue." In O'Banion, Terry (Ed.), *Innovation in the Community College.* New York: ACE/Macmillan, 1989.

Roueche, John E. and Snow, Jerry J. *Overcoming Learning Problems.* San Francisco: Jossey-Bass, 1977.

Roueche, Suanne D. and Comstock, V.N. *A Report on Theory and Method for the Study of Literacy Development in Community Colleges.* Technical Report NIE-400-78-0600. Austin: Program in Community College Education, The University of Texas, 1981.

Rumelhart, D.E. "Schemata: The Building Blocks of Cognition." In Spiro, R.J., Bruce, B.C., and Brewer, W.F. (Eds.), *Theoretical Issues in Reading Comprehension.* Hillsdale, N.J.: Lawrence Erlbaum, 1980, 33–58.

Santeusanio, R.P. "Do College Reading Programs Serve Their Purpose?" *Reading World,* May 1974, *13,* 258–271.

Schenz, Robert F. "What is Done for Low Ability Students?" *Junior College Journal,* May 1964, *34,* 22–28.

Schuster, J.H. and Bowen, H.R. "The Faculty at Risk." *Change,* September 1985, 13–21.

Seidman, Earl. *In the Words of the Faculty.* San Francisco: Jossey-Bass, 1985.

Seligman, M.E.P. *Helplessness: On Depression, Development, and Death.* San Francisco: W.H. Freeman, 1975.

Sellman, Wayne S. "Response to Panel Discussion on Issues in the Implementation of a Job Performance Measurement Program." In Baker, H. and Laabs, G. (Eds.), *Proceedings of the Department of Defense/ Educational Testing Service Conference on Job Performance Measurement Technologies.* San Diego: Navy Personnel Research and Development Center, March 1987.

Sever, Rita and Inbar, Dan E. "Evaluating Second-Chance Programs: A Conceptual Framework." In Inbar, Dan E. (Ed.), *Second Chance in Education: An Interdisciplinary and International Perspective.* London: The Falmer Press, 1990.

Sharon, A.T. "Assessing the Effectiveness of Remedial College Courses." *Journal of Experimental Education,* Winter 1972, *41,* 60–62.

Shaw, Ruth. "Curriculum Change in the Community College: Pendulum Swing or Spiral Soar?" In O'Banion, Terry (Ed.), *Innovation in the Community College.* New York: ACE/Macmillan, 1989.

Shulman, L.S. "Paradigms and Research Programs in the Study of Teaching: A Contemporary Perspective." In Wittrock, M. (Ed.), *The Handbook of Research on Teaching* (3rd ed.). New York: Macmillan, 1985.

Sledge, Linda Ching. "The Community College Scholar." *Community College Humanities Review,* 1987, *8,* 61–66.

Smith, Page. *Killing the Spirit: Higher Education in America.* New York: Viking, 1990.

Sprout, A.L. "Do U.S. Schools Make the Grade?" *Fortune,* Spring 1990, 50–51.

Sticht, T. "Functional Context Education: Policy and Training Methods from the Military Experience." Background Paper No. 41. Washington, D.C.: Department of Labor, September 1989a. (ED 317 710)

Sticht, T. "Military Testing and Public Policy: Selected Studies of Lower Aptitude Personnel." National Commission on Testing and Public Policy. Berkeley: University of California, January 1989b.

Sticht, T., Armstrong, William B., Hickey, Daniel T., and Caylor, John S. *Cast-off Youth: Policy and Training Methods from the Military Experience.* New York: Praeger, 1987.

Sticht, T. and McDonald, B. *Making the Nation Smarter: The Intergenerational Transfer of Cognitive Ability.* San Diego: Applied Behavioral and Cognitive Sciences, Inc., January 1989. (ED 309 279)

Sticht, T. and McDonald, B. *Teach the Mother and Reach the Child: Literacy Across Generations.* Geneva, Switzerland: International Bureau of Education, 1990. (ED 321 063)

Sticht, T. and Zapf, D.W. *Reading and Readability Research in the Armed Forces: Final Report.* Alexandria, Va.: Human Resources Organization, September 1976. (ED 130 242)

Sticht, T. et al. "Teachers, Books, Computers and Peers: Integrated Communications Technologies for Adult Literacy Development." Monterey, Calif.: U.S. Naval Postgraduate School, 1986.

Tabb, C.E. "Community College Teacher Attitudes Regarding Academically At-Risk Community College Students." Doctoral dissertation, The Ohio State University. *Dissertation Abstracts,* 1991, *52,* 3810A.

Tagle, Tessa. "Building Conscience, Community, and Caring." *Celebrations,* May 21, 1991.

Terenzini, Patrick T. and Pascarella, Ernest T. "Toward the Validation of Tinto's Model of College Student Attrition: A Review of Recent Studies." *Research in Higher Education,* 1980, *12,* 271–282.

Texas Higher Education Coordinating Board. "Proposed Performance-Based Funding Process for Texas General Academic Institutions." Unpublished document. Austin: Coordinating Board, Texas College and University System, April 1992.

Theophilides, C. and Terenzini, P.T. "The Relation Between Nonclassroom Contact with Faculty and Students' Perceptions of Instructional Quality." *Research in Higher Education,* 1981, *15,* 255–269.

Thornton, James W., Jr. *The Community Junior College* (2nd ed.). New York: John Wiley and Sons, 1966.

Time. "Open Admissions: American Dream or Disaster?" October 19, 1970.

Tinto, Vincent. "Dropout from Higher Education: A Theoretical Synthesis of Recent Research." *Review of Educational Research,* 1975, *45,* 89–125.

Tinto, Vincent. *Leaving College: Rethinking the Causes and Cures of Student Attrition.* Chicago: The University of Chicago Press, 1987.

Towns, E. "Adult Illiteracy Is as Dangerous to the U.S. as Substance Abuse" [Letter to the editor]. *The New York Times,* February 16, 1990, A16.

Toy, Terrence J. "Increasing Faculty Involvement in Retention Efforts." In Noel, Lee, Levitz, Randi, Saluri, Diana, and Associates (Eds.), *Increasing Student Retention.* San Francisco: Jossey-Bass, 1985, 383–401.

Trent, J.W. and Medsker, L.L. *Beyond High School.* San Francisco: Jossey-Bass, 1968.

Triggs, F.O. "Remedial Reading Programs: Evidence of Their Development." *Journal of Educational Psychology,* December 1942, *33,* 678–685.

Trow, M.A. "Underprepared Students at Public Research Universities: Maintaining Access and Standards." *Current Issues in Higher Education,* 1983, *1,* 16–26.

Tuckman, H.P. "Who Is Part-Time in Academe?" *AAUP Bulletin,* December 1978, 305–315.

Turner, Caroline Sotello Viernes. "It Takes Two to Transfer: Relational Networks and Educational Outcomes." *Community College Review,* Spring 1992, *19* (4), 27–33.

Ullom, Jack. "Music Series Discs Are Popular in California." *Music Disc News,* 1989, *1* (2), 8–9, 19.

Valek, Millicent. "Faculty Mentors: New Roles, New Relationships." *Innovation Abstracts*, 1987, *IX* (14).

Vallejo, M. Personal interview (November 30, 1988). In Drew, Claudine Paula, "We Can No Longer Love 'Em and Leave 'Em: A Paper on Freshman Retention." *Community College Review,* Spring 1990, *17* (4), 54–60.

Vaughan, George B. and Associates. *Issues for Community College Leaders in a New Era.* San Francisco: Jossey-Bass, Inc., 1983.

Walleri, Dan R. "Book Review: Ernest Pascarella and Patrick Terenzini's *How College Affects Students.*" *Community College Review*, Winter 1991, *19* (3), 8–10.

Warnock, M. *Imagination.* Berkeley: University of California Press, 1978.

Wattenbarger, James L. and Godwin, Winfred L. (Eds.). *The Community College in the South: Progress and Prospects, 1962.* A report of the Southern States Work Conference, Committee on Education Beyond the High School.

Weber, John. "Thoughts and Actions on Student Retention." *Innovation Abstracts,* 1985, *VII* (30), 1–2.

Weddington, Doris. *Faculty Attitudes in Two Year Colleges.* Los Angeles: Center for the Study of Community Colleges, 1976.

Weidman, J. "Retention of Non-Traditional Students in Postsecondary Education." Paper presented at the annual meeting of the American Educational Research Association, Chicago, 1985.

Weidner, H.Z. "Back to the Future." Paper presented at the 41st annual meeting of the Conference on College Composition and Communication. Chicago, 1990. (ED 319 045)

Weiner, B.A. "Theory of Motivation for Some Classroom Experiences." *Journal of Educational Psychology*, 1979, *71*, 3–25.

Weinstein, Claire E. "Working Hard Is Not the Same Thing as Working Smart." *Innovation Abstracts*, 1992, *XIV* (5).

Weiss, H.C. "The Stakeholder Approach to Evaluation: Origins and Promise." In Bryk, A.S. (Ed.), *New Directions for Program Evaluation.* San Francisco: Jossey-Bass, 1983, No. 17, 3–14, 1983.

Wiggins, Grant. "10 'Radical' Suggestions for School Reform." *Education Week*, March 9, 1988, *VII*, (24), 28, 20.

Willett, L.H. "Are Two-Year College Students First Generation College Students?" *Community College Review,* Spring 1989, *17* (2), 48–52.

Willis, Lloyd L. "Encouraging Student Applications for Scholarships." *Innovation Abstracts*, 1991, *XII*, (6).

Wilson R.C., Gaff, J.G., et al. *College Professors and Their Impact on Students.* New York: Wiley, 1975.

Wilson, R.C., Wood, L. and Gaff, J.G. "Social-Psychological Accessibility and Faculty-Student Interaction Beyond the Classroom." *Sociology of Education*, Winter 1974, *47*, 74–92.

Wittrock, M. (Ed.). *The Handbook of Research on Teaching* (3rd ed.). New York: Macmillan, 1985.

Wlodkowski, R.J. *Enhancing Adult Motivation to Learn.* San Francisco: Jossey-Bass, 1985.

Wolfle, D. *America's Resources of Specialized Talent.* Report of the Commission on Human Resources and Advanced Training. New York: Harper and Row, 1954.

Wranosky, Vernon L. and Mitchell, Kenneth E. "Science and Art: A Cross Discipline Approach." *Innovation Abstracts,* 1987, *IX* (4).

Wyatt, Monica. "The Past, Present, and Future Need for College Reading Courses in the U.S." *Journal of Reading,* September 1992, *36* (1), 10–20.

Zwerling, L. Steven. "The Miami-Dade Story: Is It Really Number One?" *Change,* January/February 1988, 10–23.

Zwerling, L. Steven. "Reducing Attrition at Two-Year Colleges." *Community College Review,* 1980, *7,* 55–58.

Zwerling, L. Steven. *Second Best: The Crisis of the Community College.* New York: McGraw-Hill, 1976.

John E. Roueche is professor and director of the Community College Leadership Program at The University of Texas at Austin, where he holds the Sid W. Richardson Regents Chair in Community College Leadership. He has served as director of the program since 1971.

Roueche is the author of 28 books and more than 100 articles and monographs on educational leadership and teaching effectiveness. He is the recipient of numerous national awards for his research, teaching, service, and overall leadership, including the 1986 National Distinguished Leadership Award from the American Association of Community Colleges; the 1988 B. Lamar Johnson Leadership in Innovation Award from the League for Innovation in the Community College; and the 1986 Distinguished Research Publication Award from the National Association of Developmental Education. He received The University of Texas Teaching Excellence Award in 1982.

His award-winning books include *Access and Excellence: The Open-Door College* (with George A. Baker, 1987), *Overcoming Learning Problems* (1977), and *College Responses to Low-Achieving Students* (with George A. Baker and Suanne D. Roueche, 1984). He recently completed a term on the Board of Directors for the American Association of Community Colleges. With Terry O'Banion, he serves as co-director for the *Leadership 2000* project, funded by the W.K. Kellogg Foundation.

Suanne D. Roueche is the director of the National Institute for Staff and Organizational Development (NISOD); editor of *Innovation Abstracts*, NISOD's weekly teaching tips publication; and lecturer in the Department of Educational Administration, College of Education, The University of Texas at Austin.

Roueche received the 1990 Distinguished Graduate Award from the College of Education, University of Texas. Author or co-author of eight books and more than 20 articles and chapters, she was awarded the 1988 Distinguished Research and Writing Award from the National Council for Staff, Program, and Organizational Development. She received the 1984 Outstanding Research Publication Award from the Council of Colleges and Universities for *College Responses to Low-Achieving Students: A National Study*, which she co-authored. She has spoken to more than 100 colleges and professional conferences.

Roueche is the recipient of numerous state and national awards and recognition for her leadership and service. In 1989 she received the Distinguished Leadership Award and the "Great Seal of Florida" from the governor and legislature for outstanding contributions to Florida higher education. In 1988 she received The University of Texas at Austin's College of Education Distinguished Service Award.

Governor Bill Clinton named her an Arkansas Traveler in recognition of her service to Arkansas higher education; in 1983 she was named a Yellow Rose of Texas by Governor Mark White, designated for native Texas women providing meritorious service to the state; and in 1979 she was named Kentucky Colonel by Governor Julian B. Carroll and the Kentucky legislature for contributions to Kentucky higher education. She is listed in *Who's Who in Women* and in *Men and Women of Distinction*. Since 1986 she has served as a member of the editorial board for the *Journal of Staff, Program, and Organization Development.*

Her most recent publications include *Underrepresentation and the Question of Diversity: Women and Minorities in the Community College* (1991), co-authored with Rosemary Gillett-Karam and John E. Roueche.